MICHIGAN
STATE
UNIVERSITY

MICHIGAN STATE UNIVERSITY

The Rise of a Research University and the New Millennium, 1970–2005

Douglas A. Noverr

Michigan State University Press • *East Lansing*

This book was made possible by support from Michigan State University, the Office of the President, Michigan State University, and the Office of the Provost, Michigan State University.

∞ The paper used in this publication meets the minimum requirements of ANSI/NISO Z39.48-1992 (R 1997) (Permanence of Paper).

Michigan State University Press
East Lansing, Michigan 48823-5245

Printed and bound in the United States of America.

21 20 19 18 17 16 15 1 2 3 4 5 6 7 8 9 10

Library of Congress Control Number: 2015936768
ISBN: 978-0-87013-788-4 (cloth)
ISBN: 978-1-60917-490-3 (ebook: PDF)

Book and cover design by Charlie Sharp, Sharp Des!gns, Lansing, Michigan
Jacket art: A west looking view of the Shaw Lane corridor on the Michigan State University campus. Clockwise from lower left is the National Superconducting Cyclotron Laboratory, Biochemistry, Biomedical and Physical Sciences, Anthony Hall, Farrall Hall, Chemistry, Shaw Residence Hall, and Epply Center (lower right). At center is the Law College. Image courtesy of the Michigan State University Archives.

green press INITIATIVE Michigan State University Press is a member of the Green Press Initiative and is committed to developing and encouraging ecologically responsible publishing practices. For more information about the Green Press Initiative and the use of recycled paper in book publishing, please visit *www.greenpressinitiative.org.*

Visit Michigan State University Press at www.msupress.org

Contents

Preface

I came to the Department of American Thought and Language at Michigan State University as an instructor in the tenure track because I had not yet finished my dissertation at Miami University. By December of 1972 I had my PhD and became an assistant professor at MSU.

I personally had no direct connection with MSU, but in various ways members of my family had. My father, Joseph Noverr, had taken a short (very short) course from John Hannah on grading eggs. My paternal grandfather ran a hatchery west of Battle Creek, and my dad was expected to learn the business. He did not become a hatchery man, finding instead a liking for the world of newspapers and eventually politics, but he was always proud of the certificate he earned with Hannah's name written on it. My mother's sister, Aileen Brothers, lived in East Lansing in the 1950s and did contract work for the MSU Press. I would hitchhike up to East Lansing from Battle Creek to visit my cousin, Neil Brothers, and we would go to football games at Spartan Stadium. Aileen returned to East Lansing in the mid-1970s, and through dinners at her apartment, I met Lyle Blair and Jean Busfield of the MSU Press. My oldest brother, Jim Noverr, had also worked at the *State News* for a period of time, managing the layout and paste-up for the newspaper.

In all, I spent forty-two years at MSU until my official retirement on 15 May 2012, two days after my seventieth birthday. Other than the academic year 1976–77, when I was a Senior Fulbright Lecturer in American Literature at Maria Curie-Skłodowska University in Lublin, Poland, all of my time has been spent on this campus. My career at MSU coincides with the main time period covered in this text, 1970–2005. Some of the developments documented in this narrative had a direct impact on my life (as well as that of my colleagues) and turned my career in a certain way. In the serious budget cutting of early 1981, the four general education departments, including my home department, were under consideration for elimination but were partially reinstated with cuts to the budget and faculty positions. Reading the 3–4 April 1981 Minutes of the Board of Trustees and the actions taken made me realize how dire the financial situation was and how deeply University College was affected with over $400,000 in budget reductions and the loss of seventeen FTE (full-time equivalent) positions. Besides these cuts, the Board of Trustees endorsed a recommendation from the University Committee on Academic Policy (UCAP) that general education instruction should be shared by disciplinary and general education departments. As it turned out, the clock was ticking on University College—in 1980 Provost Lee Winder dissolved University College and divided the four departments (Humanities, Natural Science, Social Science, and American Thought and Language) into three disciplinary colleges. He did not explain the administrative philosophy behind the abolition of University College, stating only that it was finished and that its faculty were being redistributed. It was after I read the 20 September 2000 Sesquicentennial Oral History Project interview with Winder that I gained a sense of his perspective and motivation. As he indicated in that interview, he thought a "very flat kind of organization" was best for the university and believed that middle-level management in higher education was not cost-effective and did not further the "really important academic work [that] goes on at the level of the faculty."

I offer these two personal connections to university-level developments early in my career here at MSU to illustrate how the passing of time and how the research into existing historical documents can provide a more comprehensive, balanced, and nuanced view of developments that, at the time, could not be fully comprehended or viewed in their full context. To me, the value of what has been a four-year project in researching and writing this book is the gaining of an appreciation of the larger operations of MSU, the individuals and personalities involved, and the reasons certain distinctive successes have been realized. My large target goal in this volume is to trace and describe the forces and factors that have made MSU a nationally and internationally recognized research-intensive institution with strong advanced degree programs and innovative research facilities. As a land-grant institution, the university advanced and developed new dimensions and meanings in its agricultural identity. Its presidents from John A. Hannah to Lou Anna K. Simon have played the role of perpetuating the land-grant philosophy and its renewal and extended applications.

Besides detailing the growth of scientific research at the university from the later part of the twentieth century into the twenty-first, this volume focuses on a number of themes and developments, including the following:

- the university's development of a commitment to access, affirmative action, inclusion, and multiculturalism as resources of internal strength
- the role of the Board of Trustees in carrying out its mandate and developing a relationship with the presidents
- the various state financial crises and their impacts on the university and its budget
- major changes in undergraduate curriculum with the end of general education and the introduction of integrative studies
- the changing physical campus
- the personalities, challenges, and leadership of the succession of presidents
- intercollegiate sports as part of the university structure and operation
- the place and role of the humanities and the arts on a campus becoming increasingly scientific, technical, and technological

It is hoped that this text will prompt the future writing of more focused, specialized histories. In some ways this is already happening, as departments, programs, and centers are posting their histories and chronologies on their respective websites, including documentation of faculty members' work. References to relevant online sources can be found in the sources cited at the end of the book. As the reader will see, I have relied heavily on this information.

In every project like this debts are incurred and acknowledgements are imperative. I want to thank the University Archives and Historical Collections; Director Cynthia A. Ghering and Assistant

Director Portia L. Vescio provided generous assistance in locating and providing the majority of the photographs for this volume. But I owe them an even larger debt for having put all the MSU Board of Trustees Minutes online as well as the transcripts of the Sesquicentennial Oral History Project interviews, sources that I used extensively, and I hope, productively. Thank you also to Whitney A. Miller, processing archivist for the UAHC, for her careful review of the manuscript and to Sarah Roberts, acquisitions archivist for the UAHC, for her always timely response to my queries on photographs. I also want to thank Derrick L. Turner, multimedia specialist in Communications and Brand Strategy at MSU, who provided invaluable assistance in locating and securing photographs.

I want to thank Professor Jeff Charnley, a longtime colleague and friend, for his stellar and time-consuming work in conducting numerous interviews for the Sesquicentennial Oral History Project. Recognition and appreciation also go to Dr. Frederick Honhart, emeritus director of the University Archives and Historical Collections and longtime friend, who oversaw the Sesquicentennial Oral History Project, and to former university President M. Peter McPherson, who saw the need for the project and provided the funding. These interviews are a veritable treasure trove of individual experiences and perspectives and are now part of the historical legacy and narrative of this university.

Next, I want to thank a group of individuals who I met and came to know, some of them more personally and closely than others, during the mid- to late 1970s. These fourteen individuals regularly met for lunch in the downstairs cafeteria of the MSU Union, never all at one time but in various combinations daily. They deemed themselves the "Knights of the Round Table" and always sat at a round table in the north corner of the eating area. The six I came to know best were Lou Radelet, Bob Scott, Ralph Turner, and Leon Weaver (all from the School of Criminal Justice) and Harold Davidson of Horticulture, as well as Fred Honhart, mentioned above. Fred was my entrée into this group, and once he vouched for me, I was immediately accepted. These individuals provided my first connection to the university's past, as they had come here in the late 1940s and 1950s and knew MSU's history—formal and informal, sanctioned and unsanctioned, serious and comedic. All were great storytellers, and since they came from at least eight different areas of MSU, they all had different angles from which to tell their stories. Together, they did more for me than I am sure they ever realized, making me feel welcome, showing personal interest in me, and exhibiting friendliness and egalitarianism that were the hallmark of faculty and staff hired in the Hannah era. In a way, this book is dedicated to their memory. In the Union cafeteria the economists also had their lunch table (with a few historians thrown in) with Walter Adams presiding. Since I was a sports historian, Walter would call out to me: "Now, Noverr, what's going to happen in Saturday's football game? You're the big expert. Tell me." That Union cafeteria lunchroom was a great place to meet people and experience part of the university's enterprise and remarkable collection of talent.

Lastly, I have three special individuals to recognize. Gabriel Dotto, director of the MSU Press, read all the chapters as they were finished and provided encouragement and positive feedback. Diana Shank, who handled the typing and electronic formatting of my hand-printed manuscript, is one of the great possessors of "bilities": ability, likability, personability, and flexibility. She is one of the most reliable and dependable persons I have ever met, and I count her as a good friend and an indispensable part of this project. And finally, I express my deepest thanks to my wife, Betty, for her support, enthusiasm, and many considerations. She was unfailing in her interest in what I was discovering as I progressed through the writing of the book and liked to hear details and stories about individuals. She helped keep me organized and focused and sent me out the door in the morning in a positive frame of mind. For all these things and the fruits of forty-five years of marriage I thank her.

1

The Emergence of the Research University in the 1950s and 1960s

In a letter dated 2 November 1964, Charles P. McCurdy Jr., the executive secretary of the Association of American Universities (AAU), wrote to Michigan State University President John A. Hannah: "It is with a great deal of pleasure that I, among others, welcome you to the Association of American Universities. The entire membership looks forward to your first meeting with them when you may be assured of a very warm welcome to an Association of Presidents which I am certain you will enjoy to the fullest." On 4 November 1964, Hannah responded to McCurdy that "Michigan State is very happy to be included among the members of the Association of American Universities."

On 12 November, McCurdy wrote to Hannah again and enclosed the minutes of the 27–28 October 1964 meeting of the AAU, "confirming, among other things, the good news that Michigan State University was elected to membership in the Association." As Hannah reviewed the enclosed minutes, he would have learned that the Membership Committee had reviewed the "statistics for sixteen institutions which are the largest producers of the Ph.D. degree and which are not members of the AAU at this time." Speaking for the Membership Committee, Gaylord P. Harnwell, president of the University of Pennsylvania, stated to the AAU members that "there was sufficient evidence that one of these sixteen institutions is outstanding." The committee's recommendation was unanimous, as was the vote of approval by the members. Michigan State University (MSU) became the thirty-ninth member of the top tier of research and doctoral-granting institutions. It had been six years since a new AAU member had been accepted.

The same day President Hannah learned these details, he wrote to William W. Whitehouse, then president of Albion College, who had penned a handwritten note to Hannah congratulating him and the institution on the AAU membership. Hannah responded: "Michigan State University is indeed pleased to be included in the Association of American Universities. It is a recognition that we should have had earlier, but some of our colleagues in an institution not very far from where both of us live have delayed it as long as they could." No doubt Hannah remembered the efforts of the University of Michigan to block then–Michigan State College's (MSC's) entrance into the Big Ten Conference and to prevent it from being designated a university by the state legislature. Rankled by the unfairness of these delaying tactics and an injustice that he saw as motivated by power and influence, Hannah wrote frankly and bluntly to his counterpart at Albion College. Michigan State University was the last of the Big Ten Schools to be accepted into membership in the AAU, and its close land-grant counterparts Purdue, Penn State, and Iowa State had each become part of the elite group back in 1958. The minutes of the meeting of the board of trustees for 19 November 1964 under "Special Miscellaneous" read: "Report that the Michigan State University had been unanimously elected to Membership in the American Association of Universities."

Hannah would no doubt have taken some small pleasure in noting that Harlan Hatcher, then president of the University of Michigan, was also president of the AAU at the time of the 27–28 October 1964 meeting at which Michigan State was unanimously elected to membership. MSC's football teams under Clarence "Biggie" Munn had been able to claim national greatness with unbeaten seasons in 1951 and 1952 and a co–Big Ten championship in its first year of qualification for a conference title, as well as a win in the 1 January 1954 Rose Bowl. But matters like athletic prowess were settled differently than recognition of research prominence and distinction of doctoral programs. Hannah was justly proud of the high-quality faculty that had been recruited or found their way to East Lansing, and their record of conducting noteworthy research and making contributions to their fields. Clearly, he deeply felt that recognition as a research-intensive university had been earned much earlier than 1964.

In examining why and how MSC, now MSU, became a major research institution and how it moved into the national and international forefront of graduate education, it is necessary to look back into the late 1940s, and especially at the 1950s. Here the foundation for recognition and success was laid and the scaffolding for successive decades of prominence was erected.

During the 1950s, MSC produced almost one thousand PhDs (992 to be exact) compared with 145 in the 1940s. In the period from 1946 through 1950, 1,171 master's degrees were granted. In 1956–57, when 152 doctorates were granted, there were 586 graduating with MAs. This surge in the numbers of advanced degrees was accompanied by the development of strong departments with faculty who already had reputations and recognition as researchers, and who had a facility for balancing their overall duties with an added load of graduate students needing supervision and monitoring. Of the 992 doctorates awarded in the 1950s, 127 of them were graduate students in the Department of Chemistry. A snapshot examination of this department in the 1949–50 academic year illustrates its strengths as well as its resources for sustaining an expanding graduate program.

In 1949–50 the Department of Chemistry had twenty-two tenure-system faculty, with five full, seven associate, and ten assistant professors. Only two had their PhDs from MSC. Two of the faculty, Ralph Chase Huston and Bruce Edwin Hartsuch, had joined the department in 1911; Dwight Tarbell Ewing joined in 1914, and Charles D. Ball in 1919. As one might expect for this era, their academic credentials varied as far as attained degrees, ranging from a BA (Hartsuch), to an MS (Ball), to PhDs Huston and Ewing, both full professors. Two of the assistant professors on the department roster for 1949–50 did not stay with the department, but for those who did, or who were continuing or finishing out their careers, the average number of years in the Chemistry department per faculty member at MSC/MSU was exactly thirty-five (with forty-four years as the longest and eighteen as the shortest). This demographic denoted a department with stability and continuity, and its size meant that in the 1950s it could spread out the load for producing MS and PhD degrees. In the 1950s six professors directed 10 or more dissertations, with Max T. Rogers directing 15, Robert M. Herbst and Harold Hart 13 each, Dwight Tarbell Ewing and Lawrence L. Quill 11 each, Robert D. Schuetz 10, Richard U. Byerrum 10. Of this group, all but Quill and Ewing (who passed away in 1954) were hired in 1946 and 1947. This fact illustrates how quickly certain faculty could move into the role of graduate professor and take on

Harold Hart combined a remarkably prolific career as a published scholar in the field of organic chemistry with his dedicated commitment to advanced graduate students, directing 69 doctoral dissertations between 1951 and 1986. He and his wife were generous supporters of the arts on campus. Courtesy of Michigan State University Archives and Historical Collections.

Richard U. Byerrum established himself as a productive researcher in the field of plant metabolism, publishing widely and coauthoring a report to the National Science Foundation titled *The Structure and Stability of the Gull Lake Zooplankton Community*. Courtesy of Michigan State University Archives and Historical Collections.

advanced students, and how opportunities presented themselves as other faculty concentrated on teaching or working with MS students.

Certain faculty excelled in the role of directing dissertations. In the 1960s Harold Hart directed 29 of them, with Robert D. Schuetz and Max T. Rogers directing 18 and 14 respectively. In all, during his career at MSC/MSU Professor Hart would direct 69 doctoral

James L. Dye joined the Chemistry department in 1953 and in an over forty-year career became a distinguished national scholar as well as a mainstay of dissertation supervision, with 58 directed between 1959 and 1996. He was also highly active as a leader in academic governance, chairing the Consolidation Evaluation Committee, and was named a University Distinguished Professor in 1990. Courtesy of Michigan State University Archives and Historical Collections.

dissertations between his first in 1951 and his last three, all in 1986. It was a remarkable commitment to graduate students that was combined with a scholarly publication record of more than 175 papers. Hart distinguished himself in the synthesis of new compounds and chemical rearrangements and bondings. From 1967 to 1977 he served as editor of *Chemical Reviews*, the internationally preeminent chemistry review journal. Professor James L. Dye, who joined the Chemistry department in 1953, became a prolific and distinguished scholar, producing over 225 research papers over his career. Dye would direct 58 dissertations between 1959 and 1996 and 22 master's theses. Hart and Dye were one of the best organic-inorganic chemistry combinations ever at any American university, with their illustrious careers overlapping for thirty-four years.

Another factor that kept promising and productive faculty at MSC/MSU was faster movement to tenure and promotions and availability of funds for research, lab assistants, and graduate assistants. In the Chemistry department listing for 1949–50 there are thirty-nine graduate assistants and fifteen women who are designated as temporary assistants. However, the key factor in the department's growing strength was effective appointments in the period of 1945 to 1955 and beyond. Lawrence L. Quill, who came in 1945 at the age of 44, soon became the department chair, and Richard U. Byerrum, who joined the department in 1947, became a productive researcher in plant

Lawrence L. Quill was appointed professor and head of the Department of Chemistry in January 1945, serving as head for sixteen years while also serving as director of the Division of Physical Sciences. His volume titled *The Chemistry and Metallurgy of Miscellaneous Materials: Thermodynamics* (1950) is included in the National Nuclear Energy Series and was part of Quill's research on the Plutonium Project of the Manhattan Project. MSU trustee Blanche Martin cited Quill as an important mentor. Courtesy of Michigan State University Archives and Historical Collections.

Ralph Chase Huston joined the Department of Chemistry in 1911 and served as a faculty member until his death in 1954. He was key in the department's early development as a granter of PhDs, directing 23, and its important role of producing MS degrees, supervising 25 theses. Courtesy of Michigan State University Archives and Historical Collections.

metabolism, and authored or coauthored more than 90 publications. He would serve as assistant provost and then, from 1962 until 1986, as the first dean of the College of Natural Science. Ralph Chase Huston became dean of Graduate Studies, and his *A Correlation of Some Physical Properties of Alkanes and Alkenes* (1947) was the first scholarly scientific monograph published by the Michigan State College Press and was supported by a grant from the All College Research Committee. The MSC Press also published Elmer Leininger and Kenneth G. Stone's *Elementary Quantitative Analysis: A Practical Approach* in 1948. MSC also had the advantage of an increasing number of PhDs available nationally in this period, as well as a reputation as an institution with a progressive president who was known to favor science and support it.

To those faculty at MSC working in the sciences, it was no surprise that their departments were gaining in stature and had earned national reputations. Professor I. Forest Huddleson put the Department of Bacteriology and Public Health on the scientific map of the United States with his study of brucellosis, a disease found in animals as well as humans. Huddleson published major scientific works on brucellosis in 1934 and 1943, and his studies traced the disease from organism to pathology to detection, and to immunology and treatment. He developed means of detecting the disease as well as a product for treating it, with that product made at MSC and distributed worldwide. Traveling to other countries, Huddleson served as a consultant to governments seeking to bring the debilitating (for affected humans) and costly (for farm animals) disease under control, and in the process received many awards and honors for his work.

Huddleson started his career at MAC as a research assistant in 1915, and except for the period from 1917 to 1918, when he served in the U.S. Army, he would spend fifty-six years as a scientist in a department that would change names twice (in 1943 and 1954) and at an institution that would have three different names during his tenure. Huddleson's loyalty to MAC/MSC was absolute and abiding. He came to East Lansing from a small college in Oklahoma, and between 1916 and 1937 he earned MS, DVM, and PhD degrees—all from the school where he worked and distinguished himself as a world-class researcher.

I. Forest Huddleson came to East Lansing from Oklahoma and received three advanced degrees from MSC, with the third being a PhD in 1935. His career here spanned fifty-six years, and in that time he became the international expert on brucellosis and received many international awards and honors for his dedicated work. Courtesy of Michigan State University Archives and Historical Collections.

Henrik Joakim Stafseth, who became the chair of Bacteriology and Public Health as well as full professor in 1948, was, like Huddleson, a remarkable success story. Born in Norway in 1890, Stafseth came to the United States at the age of 21 and by 1915 had received a BA from North Dakota Agricultural College. In 1917 he received a DVM degree from MSC, and later he took an MS degree in 1930 and a PhD in 1935, writing his thesis on tapeworm infestation in chickens. He became a national expert on veterinary public health, poultry diseases, and the relationship between disease and poverty. In 1945–46 he served as the chief veterinarian for the United Nations Relief and Rehabilitation Administration in postwar China. Interestingly, the top two professors in the Department of Bacteriology and Public Health both had

Henrik Joakim Stafseth came to East Lansing from North Dakota in 1915 and received a DVM, MS, and PhD from MSC, becoming one of its most prominent faculty members and researchers. He was an internationally recognized expert on poultry diseases and veterinary public health and in 1945–46 served as the chief veterinarian for the United Nations Relief and Rehabilitation Administration in postwar China. Courtesy of Michigan State University Archives and Historical Collections.

all their advanced degrees from MSC, and both brought national and international recognition to their department through their research, extensive publications, and their travels or foreign assignments. Their work connected their department to public health as well as to animal and human health.

A key connection between MSC and the community was, of course, the bulletins of the Extension Division. Members of the Department of Bacteriology and Public Health regularly authored these, and in them conveyed valuable and practical scientific information to the county extension agents and to farmers' organizations and co-ops, as well as to individual farmers. Frederick William Fabian published one bulletin on the making of honey vinegar, issued in 1926 and reissued in 1935, and in 1943 he commercially published what became a standard book on home food preservation. Henrik Joakim Stafseth's 1935 PhD thesis on tapeworm infestations in chickens was issued as "Technical Bulletin No. 148" in December 1935 by the Michigan Agricultural Experiment Station. In 1952 the station issued *Studies in Brucellosis, III: A Series of Five Papers* collecting the work of I. Forest Huddleson.

This flow of scientific findings and applications had as its purpose increased efficiency, productivity, management, sanitation, and hygiene of Michigan farms. The publications also provided opportunities for professor scientists to convey their research to an audience of nonspecialists who had immediate practical need for the information (some more than others certainly, depending on what type of farming they did). The extension agents played important roles as mediators and translators of the information when needed, since farmers came to them and not to professors in East Lansing. "Scientific farming," then, included more than farming methods or fertilizers or pesticides. It involved understanding the scientific basis of infections or diseases or conditions that resulted in livestock mortality or low productivity, as well as affecting the health of the farm family. This is the area where the faculty researchers, aided by able and dedicated lab assistants, excelled and where they made essential scientific contributions.

Another essential ingredient in the advancement of research at MSC was the development in 1956–57 of MISTIC (Michigan State Integral Computer System), completed under the direction of Professor Lawrence W. Von Tersch. When a request in 1954 from MSC to the U.S. Army for the donation of a computer failed, a group of professors from East Lansing went to see the Illinois Automatic Computer (ILLIAC) at the University of Illinois. Convinced that a counterpart computer system and facility could be built, they made a recommendation to the Board of Agriculture and President Hannah, which was quickly approved. MSC was poised to launch a project that would cost an estimated $150,000 and required ongoing technical-staff salaries as well. Some unusual connections and timing resulted in the combination of factors needed to produce the desired result. The dean of the College of Engineering, John D. Ryder, had come to MSC in 1954 from Illinois, where he had been involved in the construction of the computer there, and before that he taught at

John D. Ryder came to MSC in 1954 from the University of Illinois and became the dean of the College of Engineering, serving as dean from 1954 until 1968. He recruited Lawrence Von Tersch to come to MSC from Iowa State to build the MISTIC computer. Dean Ryder was an expert in the field of electronics and circuits, and traveled the world because of his interest in international education systems. Courtesy of Michigan State University Archives and Historical Collections.

The MISTIC computer completed in 1957 achieved an almost legendary status on campus, as did electrical engineering Professor Lawrence Von Tersch, who built it with three of his graduate students. It weighed over a ton and had storage cabinets ten and eleven feet long. It worked, its memory was expanded from 5K to 20K in 1960, and it established computation and a new, revolutionary field at the Computer Center. Courtesy of Michigan State University Archives and Historical Collections.

Iowa State University. Lawrence W. Von Tersch had taken electrical engineering classes at Iowa State from Ryder, and Ryder recruited Von Tersch to come to East Lansing, which he did in 1956 with the construction of MISTIC as his first job. After just ten months the computer was fully operational. An important part of its development was Dean Ryder's desire to create a research program and a strong undergraduate curriculum, and Ryder saw the computer system as an essential part of that process.

In his Sesquicentennial Oral History Project (SOHP) interview, Von Tersch noted that the MISTIC computer "created more business than it could handle," even with its somewhat limited programming

The MISTIC computer with its 2,610 vacuum tubes was followed by the transistor-based Control Data Corporation 3600 in 1963, which was an investment of $1 million. Large-volume, fast computing became the driver of scientific, mathematical, and medical research, and computer coding became a central course for many undergraduate and graduate students. Courtesy of Michigan State University Archives and Historical Collections.

capabilities, and even after its magnetic core memory was added to in 1960, giving it 20K memory compared to its original 5K. Von Tersch noted that when they "asked Hannah for a million dollars to buy a commercial machine," the request "didn't shock him a bit." Hannah told Von Tersch that if he "could get half of it from someplace else to prove it was a good move, he'd see what he could do, which meant he'd do it."

In his interview for the Sesquicentennial Oral History Project, Henry Blosser, who came to MSU in 1958, noted that one of the main reasons he left Oak Ridge, Tennessee, to come to East Lansing was "the existence of the MISTIC computer which Von Tersch and his group of bright young men had built. It was not quite as big as the computer we were using in Oak Ridge, but it used the same language, so it was very easy to transfer codes and things to that computer." Blosser noted that the computer modeling work they did with MISTIC was the key to getting funds to build the first version of a cyclotron laboratory.

Von Tersch got $500,000 from the National Science Foundation (NSF), and true to his word, Hannah matched it. In 1963 a Control

Lawrence W. Von Tersch came to MSC in 1956, recruited by Dean John D. Ryder of the College of Engineering, and built the MISTIC computer in the year the institution became a university. When Dean Ryder retired in 1968, Von Tersch was appointed his successor and served until 1989. Together, Ryder and Von Tersch led the institution into the computer age. Von Tersch (*standing*) is shown here with Gerald Laatsch, data processing supervisor. Courtesy of Michigan State University Archives and Historical Collections.

Data Corporation 3600 was purchased, and only five years later a new CDC 6500 was operating in the Computer Laboratory. As Von Tersch noted, by this time the university had developed good contacts with the National Science Foundation through John W. Hoffman, director of the Division of Engineering Research, and through Henry Blosser. Hannah had challenged Von Tersch to go after a big grant and to learn how to develop a grant proposal that convincingly made the case for the purchase of a million dollar computer. This was a case of scientific intersection and overlap, as the cyclotron's and computer's futures became interconnected. In terms of academic and business computing, the large-capacity university computer was essential to support the enrollment growth of the university in the 1960s.

As Professor Blosser described it in his interview for the Sesquicentennial Oral History Project, funding for the cyclotron came

Henry Blosser came to Michigan State in 1958 after three years at the Oak Ridge National Laboratory. As director, he and his team designed and built four different cyclotrons, including the National Superconducting Cyclotron Laboratory, beginning in 1980. Widely published in the field of nuclear and accelerator physics, he also held five patents on various accelerator-related inventions. Courtesy of Michigan State University Archives and Historical Collections.

initially with $150,000 from MSC and then a grant from the Atomic Energy Commission (AEC) for $186,000. In this case, interschool rivalry and competition again emerged. After it learned about MSC's proposal to build one, the University of Michigan decided it wanted a cyclotron and used its connections in Congress to get an earmarked appropriation from the AEC designated to Ann Arbor, with MSC passed over. As Blosser notes, a team led by Professor Milton Muelder, who was vice president for research, made numerous trips to Washington, DC, to meet with officials at the AEC, the Office of

Milton Muelder served as dean of the College of Science and Arts from 1952 to 1959 and became the first vice president for research and dean of the Graduate School, guiding the university through its most dramatic period of growth as a research-intensive and graduate studies institution. He is known for his fifty-five years of dedicated service and his exceptional generosity to the university. Courtesy of Michigan State University Archives and Historical Collections.

Naval Research, and the NSF. Their case for Blosser's cyclotron was successful, and in 1961 the NSF made a grant to MSU for $700,000, which was designated as the first half of the total grant. The project resulted in the first set of appointments in the nuclear physics faculty as Morton M. Gordon, Philip Barnett, David Johnson, and others came together as a remarkable team to establish what would become a world-class center of nuclear physics research.

In the same period, the Biophysics department was born when Barnett Rosenberg, Ronald Mason, and Leroy George Augenstein were recruited. As Rosenberg discusses in his Sesquicentennial Oral History Project interview, the three of them were looking for permanent positions and "got together and decided we would try to set up a biophysics department at some university." At the same time President Hannah designated a "committee of different scientists to search out for a biophysicist. Well, we met with them, and they were pleased with us and offered us the job, all three of us." The three scientists had offers from four other major universities, but two of them chose MSU. Mason did not accept the appointment and returned to his native England, where he had an illustrious scientific career that resulted in a knighthood. Augenstein was chair of the Biophysics department from 1962 until his untimely death in November 1969 in a plane crash. Rosenberg noted that he chose MSU "because of John Hannah. He made a very simple statement. 'You do what you want to do. There are no restrictions on you. Set up any system you want. You're totally free!' Now that's a statement you rarely ever get." Rosenberg credited this assurance of "complete freedom" with providing the essential condition that "allowed me to do the experiments that led to the discovery of the drug cisplatin and the anti-cancer activity." Rosenberg also gave credit to Milton Muelder for his ability to work effectively with the scientists and to understand their plan to build a "science complex, commercial, around the university to take advantage of it."

During the 1960s the Department of Biophysics grew steadily as a graduate-level program, with new appointments and various visiting research professors cycling through. John Irwin Johnson Jr. became a noted scholar of the anatomy and neurobiology of mammalian brains, and William C. Corning published important books on invertebrate learning and the chemistry of the human mind and learning.

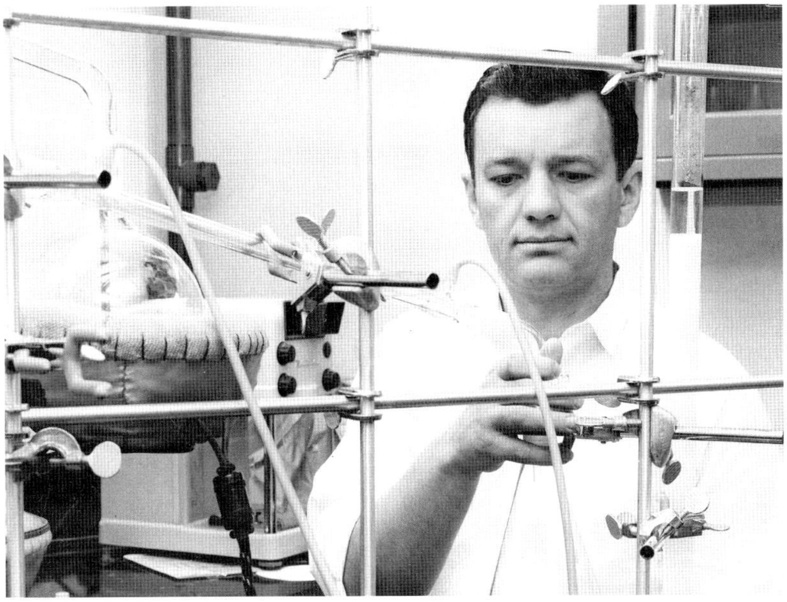

Leroy George Augenstein was one of the first members of the Department of Biophysics, established in 1962 as a research-focused graduate studies unit, and served as its first chairman. He was a member of the State Board of Education and was campaigning for a seat in the U.S. Senate when he was killed in an airplane crash in 1969. Courtesy of Michigan State University Archives and Historical Collections.

H. Ti Tien's research in cell biology, specifically lipid membranes, was noteworthy and influential in the field.

Hannah's passion for expanding the "bricks and mortar" facilities is well known, especially his skill at funding new building projects without legislative appropriations. The Sesquicentennial Oral History Project interviews with Lawrence Von Tersch, Henry Blosser, and Barnett Rosenberg provide rich information on Hannah's remarkable vision for the expansion of the sciences in new directions, and on his ability to create opportunities that resulted in new programs that had the necessary personnel base and combinations of expertise to succeed. Recognizing that the university needed new areas of science, Hannah brought in the individuals needed to develop research programs in computer science, nuclear physics, and biophysics. Henry Blosser told the story of how a research officer with the Atomic Energy Commission came to East Lansing to do a site review for the proposed cyclotron and asked for a meeting with Hannah. In the meeting the AEC representative asked Hannah, "Well, in this proposal, you say you're going to provide money to build a building. I'd like to know where you're going to get the money." Blosser described a classic Hannah moment: "Hannah kind of glared at the guy and said, 'Young man, this is a large university that has many resources, and if you put your money on the table, I'll put mine.'"

Barnett Rosenberg came to MSU in 1961 and was soon joined by another biophysicist, Leroy George Augenstein. Rosenberg credited President John A. Hannah with giving him the scientific freedom that eventually resulted in his research team's development of compounds that became the anticancer drug cisplatin, first marketed in 1978. Courtesy of Michigan State University Archives and Historical Collections.

This photograph of scientific laboratory equipment used by Barnett Rosenberg in 1965 at the new Chemistry Building was taken the year that Rosenberg, Loretta Van Camp, and Thomas Krigas published their now famous article "Inhibition at Cell Division in *Escherichia coli* by Electrolysis Products from a Platinum Electrode" in the 13 February 1965 issue of *Nature*. They demonstrated that cell division in *E. coli* was inhibited by certain platinum-containing compounds, which later led to development of the anticancer drug cisplatin. The photograph is a vivid illustration of what is termed "bench science," meaning science conducted in a laboratory. Courtesy of Michigan State University Archives and Historical Collections.

What Hannah and others at MSU understood was that in order to compete for federal grant money, the institution needed research teams in new fields like nuclear and theoretical physics and biophysics; it needed computing power and programming to facilitate the research; it needed to be able to generate and allocate funds internally for projects to give them a chance to secure federal grants; and it needed to provide a supportive atmosphere that had little administrative intrusion and allowed for "free" scientific investigation. In addition to competing for federal grants, the university vied for science development funds from the federal government. As Roger L. Geiger has documented, in 1973 MSU was seventeenth in the top twenty universities nationally, receiving $7,132,000 in development funds from 1963–64 to 1972–73 and increasing its share. The range

G. Malcolm Trout came to Michigan State in 1928 from West Virginia University and was on the faculty until his retirement in 1966. His pioneering research into the chemical and physical properties of homogenized milk brought him national attention. His 1950 book *Homogenized Milk: Review and Guide* (published by the MSC Press) and his Extension bulletins were widely read and used in the industry. Trout has an annual lecture, Visiting Scholar program, scholarship, a foundation, and a campus building named for him. Courtesy of Michigan State University Archives and Historical Collections.

for the top twenty was $6.5 million to $11.9 million (Geiger 207). This certainly indicates, as Geiger notes, that "Michigan State was nevertheless perceived to be an advancing and promising research university in the 1960s" (216).

Geiger's "nevertheless" qualifier relates to his observation that even though by 1970 MSU was the sixth largest producer of PhDs nationally (granting 633 doctorates in 1972), "few of its departments in arts and sciences achieved national rank," and his observation that the departments or programs that had the highest national standing were those in "applied and professional subjects like Hotel and Restaurant management." In his analysis, Geiger states that the university relied on the accelerated growth of the undergraduate body "to build its faculty and its graduate programs" (216) and, one could

Sylvan H. Wittwer served as director of the Agricultural Experiment Station from 1964 to 1983 after coming to MSC as an assistant professor in horticulture in 1946. His work focused on food production, and he coauthored *Feeding a Billion* (1987) on the success of Chinese agricultural methods. The AES prospered and expanded under his directorship through increased funding and the addition of the Pesticide Research Center. Courtesy of Michigan State University Archives and Historical Collections (*Wolverine* 1958).

add, to make strategic investments that required the outlay of fairly large amounts of money up front. Geiger argues that funds at MSU were too limited to hire "academic stars" and that professorial salaries were not nationally competitive. The full-time graduate student cohort with ongoing support was not large enough. All of these matters will be taken up in subsequent chapters as the story of MSU as an AAU Research Institution unfolds. At this point it is sufficient to note that the funding flow model had serious limitations that would become evident when state expenditures on higher education began to level off, stagnate, and decline.

With regard to national rankings in the American Council of Education's *A Rating of Graduate Programs,* compiled by Kenneth D. Roose and Charles J. Anderson (1970), the following departments/programs at MSU ranked among the highest nationally for 1969:

- Botany and Plant Pathology tied for 9th (up from 13th in 1964)
- Entomology tied for 12th (not ranked in 1964)
- Population Biology 13th (not included in 1957 and 1964 surveys)
- Sociology tied for 17th (17th in 1964)
- Zoology tied for 18th (not ranked in 1957 and 1964)
- Psychology tied for 20th (up from 22nd in 1964)
- Chemistry tied for 24th (not ranked in 1957 and 1964)
- Electrical Engineering tied for 24th (not ranked in 1964)
- Microbiology and Public Health tied for 25th (not ranked in 1964)
- Physiology tied for 25th (not ranked in 1964)
- Biochemistry tied for 28th (not ranked in 1964)
- Biochemistry and Molecular Biology tied for 29th (first ranking of this area)

These rankings were based on the "rated quality of graduate faculty." In the category of "Leading Institutions by Rated Effectiveness of Doctoral Programs," Botany and Plant Pathology was top tier, while the departments from Entomology on down to Biochemistry and Molecular Biology (with the exception of Electrical Engineering) were ranked in the second tier. The following other departments were rated second tier for "Quality of Graduate Faculty": English, Philosophy, Anthropology, Economics, Geography, History, Political Science, Mathematics, Physics, Civil Engineering, and Mechanical Engineering. All of these departments received third-tier ratings for "Effectiveness of Doctoral Programs."

More will be discussed later about national rankings, but the results in the Roose-Anderson ratings require commentary at this point. Botany and Plant Pathology's rise from a 13th ranking in 1964 to a tie for 9th in 1969 is certainly noteworthy, with Psychology moving from 22nd to 20th. A number of departments that had not been ranked in 1957 or 1964 made strong showings and ranked in the top thirty for "rated quality of graduate faculty." A second-tier rating in the area of "effectiveness of doctoral program" was, in fact, a strong ranking,

William B. Drew arrived at Michigan State in 1945, and from 1948 to 1973 served as chairman of the Department of Botany and Plant Pathology. He wrote an important history of the department in 1973 and in 1974 traveled to Thailand as a member of the Midwest Universities Consortium for International Activities team evaluating agriculture and veterinary higher education. Courtesy of Michigan State University Archives and Historical Collections.

as the first-tier listings often included fewer than ten institutions. One can conclude that many departments at MSU had good-quality faculty for their graduate programs, but in terms of the perceived and reputational quality of the effectiveness of the programs they were seen as third tier. It was as difficult to challenge or to put programs in the company of long-standing, highly recognized graduate programs as it was to wrest federal research funds away from the top-tier established schools. Geiger's critique of MSU and his charge that "few of its departments in arts and sciences achieved national rank" needs to be considered in light of these realities as well as the fact that when examined more closely, the Roose-Anderson/American Council of Education rankings for 1969 definitely qualify Geiger's conclusions at this point in time.

A look at the Department of Botany and Plant Pathology, the highest ranked department in the Roose-Anderson/ACE 1969 ratings, moving from a ranking of 13th in 1964 to a tie with Cornell at 9th in 1969, illustrates how the unit distinguished itself in research and graduate studies. In the 1950s the department used retirements of full professors to make strategic hires at the associate professor level, and continued to benefit from strong movement up through the ranks of those initially appointed as assistant professors. By 1960–61 the department had twelve full professors, with half of them having moved quickly from associate to full. By 1967–68 the department had eighteen full professors, nine associate professors, and ten assistant professors, with almost fifty supported graduate students in various roles. Botany and Plant Pathology was steadily and ably guided by Professor William B. Drew, who was head of the department from 1948 through 1973.

In 1962–63 the Division of Biology and Medicine of the Atomic Energy Commission selected Michigan State University as the site for a plant research laboratory after an evaluation that started with forty-two universities and eventually was narrowed down to four. The program involved multidisciplinary research in such fields as biochemistry, biophysics, genetics, microbiology, and others, and focused on research and graduate, as well as postgraduate, training programs. In 1965 Professor Anton Lang was appointed the first director of the MSU-AEC Plant Research Laboratory along with seven new faculty members. This facility would later be known as the MSU–Department of Energy (DOE) Plant Research Laboratory. By 1969 there were twelve faculty members connected with the laboratory, and they held joint appointments in other departments. The laboratory quickly became a national center of research activity and seminars with postdoctoral research associates regularly affiliated. As Director Lang described the "corollaries" that guided all work at the laboratory: "The appointees should be able to convey their own enthusiasm for research to their younger co-workers; there should be some overlap in their research activities to ensure a common language; and they should have a broad, non-possessive attitude toward research, being willing to share ideas and undertake cooperative work."

Here and at the National Superconducting Cyclotron Laboratory directed by Professor Henry Blosser, the new age of science was emerging: that of collaborative and cooperative multidisciplinary work that focused on an overall program that pushed the boundaries of science out, and that served educational purposes of training new generations of scientist-researchers. As Lang has noted in his invaluable "History of the Plant Research Laboratory," the resulting facility and program began with the commitment of President Hannah and key administrators "to strengthen plant biology on campus, including construction of the necessary new building." What resulted was an expanded department of senior faculty with the national reputations needed to attract top-notch graduate students, to vie successfully for a premier laboratory facility, and to gain a distinguished national ranking.

On a different scale and in a different manner, the Department of Entomology, which was tied for 12th in the 1969 ACE rankings (in its first national ranking) went from thirteen funded graduate students in 1964–65 to twenty-six in 1967–68. Gordon E. Guyer, who began as an assistant professor in the department in 1953, moved up the ranks and by 1964–65 was a full professor and took over as chair from Ray Hutson, who retired. This was a department where faculty moved up through the ranks, and the unit that had just three full professors in 1960–61 had seven by 1967–68. Roland Fischer, one of those full professors, had become curator of the Insect Collection in 1952, and for forty years until his death, Professor Fischer added to the heritage and legacy collection that originated with Albert J. Cook in 1867 In the 1960s this collection more than tripled to well over 300,000 specimens. The Albert J. Cook Arthropod Research Collection (so designated in 2000) now features close to 1.5 million specimens.

Anton Lang was a preeminent plant physiologist whose career began in Germany and took him to Canada and the United States. After fifteen years at UCLA and Cal Tech, he came to MSU as the first director of the MSU–Department of Energy Plant Research Laboratory. His pioneering work included heading the National Academy of Sciences committee investigating the effects of the U.S. use of herbicides in the forests of North Vietnam as a chemical defoliant during the Vietnam War. Courtesy of Michigan State University Archives and Historical Collections.

As director of the Cyclotron Laboratory, which became the National Superconducting Cyclotron Laboratory, Henry Blosser realized his dream of building and expanding his own facility and becoming one of the most prominent nuclear physicists in America. His fingerprints were on every part of the cyclotron in its successive stages of development for over thirty years. For him, it was a tool of research, and he knew every part of that tool intimately and fully.
Courtesy of Michigan State University Archives and Historical Collections.

The MSU Department of Psychology's history starting in the early 1960s illustrates its transformation into a large graduate-degree program and its developing national reputation for noted and influential scholars. In 1961–62 the department's tenure system complement was twenty-nine faculty (seventeen of them full professors with just one female faculty member). The unit had at least five full professors with strong scholarly credentials. Harold H. Anderson was the most extensively published, with eight major books on topics such as child psychology, personality development, and teacher and child relationships in the classroom. S. Howard Bartley had published books on experimental psychology, fatigue, and the principles of perception and the study of vision. Milton Rokeach was beginning a brilliant scholarly career with a 1960 book on the nature of belief and

Gordon E. Guyer (*right*) and Max M. Mortland (*left*) both began their faculty careers at Michigan State in 1953, Guyer joining the Department of Entomology and Mortland the Department of Crop and Soil Science. Both progressed through the ranks quickly and became experts and active consultants in their fields. They were part of a large group of scientists who advanced the reputation of MSC and made university status and AAU membership possible. Courtesy of Michigan State University Archives and Historical Collections.

The Albert J. Cook Arthropod Research Collection was established by Professor Cook in 1867 and has grown from 1,200 locally collected specimens of insects used for instruction to a research collection of close to 500,000 families and species, native and foreign. The collection has grown and become more diverse due to the generous contributions of its curators, faculty, and private citizens. Courtesy of Gary Parsons, Albert J. Cook Arthropod Research Collection manager.

Harold H. Anderson came to MSC as professor of psychology and head of the department in 1933 and became known nationally for his studies of the behavior patterns and personalities of teachers and their effects on classroom interactions. He helped organize the 1957–58 Interdisciplinary Symposia on Creativity at MSU and edited its report titled *Creativity and Its Cultivation*. Courtesy of Michigan State University Archives and Historical Collections.

Milton Rokeach was born in 1918 in Poland but received all of his education in the United States. His work in schizophrenia involved a study of three patients at the Ypsilanti State Hospital, each of whom believed himself to be Jesus Christ, and resulted in *The Three Christs of Ypsilanti* in 1964. In the 1984 edition of the book, Rokeach apologized for "playing god." He is best known for the Rokeach Value Survey, which could be used to measure values and predict a wide range of behavior. Courtesy of Michigan State University Archives and Historical Collections.

personality systems. He would become an eminent social psychologist, studying human values and developing a widely used system to measure them. Frederic R. Wickert, who had been part of the Vietnam Project from 1955 to 1957, was establishing himself as a prominent voice in the field of industrial and organizational psychology and had international teaching experience, with the ability to teach in German, French, or English. Henry Clay Smith had published in the field of personality and the psychology of industrial behavior. By any standard Psychology was a solid department with both a clinical psychology laboratory and an animal studies laboratory needed for a graduate program. There were definite strengths on which to build, as well as opportunities to bring in promising researchers as senior faculty retired. Faculty moved up quickly in rank as their scholarship and reputation developed.

By 1971–72 the department had a tenure-system complement of fifty-seven, with thirty-one full and nineteen associate professors. In 1981–82 the roster would include forty-one full professors,

Frederic R. Wickert joined the Psychology Department in 1947 and retired in 1982. He served as deputy adviser in the Vietnam Project from 1955 to 1957, working with Professor Wesley R. Fishel. In the photograph Wickert (*back center*) is shown with Stanley K. Sheinbaum (*left*), coordinator of the Vietnam Project at MSU, Ralph H. Smuckler (*back right*), assistant dean of International Studies and Programs at MSU, and three South Vietnamese professors. Wickert was part of a long line of faculty with nationally recognized expertise in organizational and industrial psychology. An inveterate traveler with his wife, Wickert mastered several languages and had a working familiarity with many others. Courtesy of Michigan State University Archives and Historical Collections.

LEFT: Neal Schmitt's published research has focused on a wide range of subjects across the field of personnel selection and staffing in organizations of all kinds, and his work on the labor force and business climate for the state of Michigan has been extensive and influential. His more recent scholarship has dealt with college students and their success in their studies.

CENTER: Daniel R. Ilgen came to MSU from Purdue University in 1983 and was appointed John A. Hannah Distinguished Professor of Psychology and Management, a position and title he held until his retirement in 2007. His books on industrial and organizational psychology and on motivation and performance are considered standards in the field, and he served as a consultant to major corporations as well as the armed forces.

RIGHT: Coming to MSU after earning his PhD in experimental child psychology in 1967, Hiram E. Fitzgerald established himself as a leading scholar of every aspect of infant development and health, with a particular focus on the effects of alcohol use on the family. He has also studied race, culture, social class, and ethnicity as factors in psychological development and socialization. He served as department associate chair for twelve years and became a University Distinguished Professor in 1998. Photos courtesy of Michigan State University Photography Services.

seven associates, and twelve assistant professors for a complement of sixty. Four women were full professors, and eight of the twelve assistant professors were women. By 1991–92 the number of full professors had decreased to thirty-four, with thirteen associate and nine assistant professors. Thirteen department faculty were listed as emeritus. In the 1960s and '70s Frederic R. Wickert, Henry Clay Smith, Neal Schmitt, and Carl F. Frost extended and strengthened the department's reputation in industrial and organizational psychology. In 1983 Daniel R. Ilgen came to MSU as the John A. Hannah Distinguished Professor of Psychology and Management, and he and Professor Schmitt became two of the nation's most prominent experts on hiring, training, and evaluating workers.

In the same period of time, Lucy Rau Ferguson published important books on child rearing and personality development. Ellen A. Strommen also focused on developmental psychology. William

J. Mueller and Bill L. Kell published important work on counseling and psychotherapy. Bertram P. Karon published on the effects of racial discrimination and on schizophrenia, and Robert A. Zucker (at MSU from 1968 to 1994) became a distinguished national expert on alcoholism and drug addiction, mental health in youths, and prevention programs for addictive behaviors. Hiram E. Fitzgerald published a series of studies on children from various racial and ethnic groups, conditions, and situations. His work is deeply rooted in developmental psychology at every phase or stage, with a focus on infancy and mental health. Eclectic and deeply humanistic, Professor Fitzgerald has been a strong voice and advocate for infants and children, and for programs that not only benefit them but are committed to the development of their full possibilities. The research and work of the Department of Psychology (and its counterpart in Psychiatry) have always had the imprint of President John Hannah's belief that a university has to respond to and address the problems of society, and that it must weigh the "health of the University. . . . in the same balance" (*Report to the President* x).

Michigan State's dramatic growth and maturation as a comprehensive institution in the 1960s can be attributed to the momentum generated in the 1950s and to the influence and efforts of the most significant single report in the institution's history. This was *A Report to the President of Michigan State University from the Committee on the Future of the University*, forwarded to President Hannah on 28 July 1959. In March 1959 Hannah had appointed seventeen members to this committee and requested that they be released from "part or possibly, in some cases, all their current responsibilities to enable them to devote to this assignment the time and attention it deserves." In the process of doing its work, the committee held sixty-seven meetings, had five open meetings with faculty and two with students, met for an evening with the members of all the college committees, and had a dinner meeting with selected alumni. A questionnaire was distributed to about 11,000 students, with 7,500 completed and returned.

What turned out to be a 74-page report (including nine annexes) is a remarkable document characterized by its succinct and clear style, its scope, and its articulate expression of the future of MSU as expressed in its aspirations and goals. In the report's "Summary," that future is described as one in which the university

1. Achieves international distinction by emphasizing research, graduate, and professional programs;
2. Develops and maintains vigorous four-year undergraduate programs and off-campus programs of ever increasing quality which gain strength from and contribute to these research, graduate, and professional programs;
3. Carefully selects the programs in which it will be distinguished and allocates its available resources in a fashion that will best achieve them.

The key emphasis in the report is on "greater selectivity in the program it [the university] maintains or develops" and the marshaling of the "physical and financial resources of the University to bear in terms of the new emphasis and new priorities envisaged here" (xii). Clearly,

ABOVE: President Hannah's vision of building MSU into a research-intensive university took shape and form in the 1950s and 1960s and was aided by the report and recommendations of the 1959 Committee on the Future of the University. Hannah's keen interest in all the sciences and his understanding of the work of scientists created a climate that drew top researchers to East Lansing. Courtesy of Michigan State University Archives and Historical Collections.

OPPOSITE: The seventeen-member Committee on the Future of the University produced a remarkably comprehensive report to President Hannah on 28 July 1959, just five months after Hannah appointed them. This document shaped the future of MSU and guided its development as a research-focused land-grant institution. Courtesy of Michigan State University Archives and Historical Collections.

Professor Dale E. Hathaway of the Department of Agricultural Economics served as chair of the 1959 Committee on the Future of the University. He was a consultant to several federal-government committees and won numerous awards for his published research. Courtesy of Michigan State University Archives and Historical Collections.

Professor Arthur E. Adams served as the executive secretary of the Committee on the Future of the University and was a noted historian of Russia and Eastern Europe. He served as the chairman of the 1967 Committee on Undergraduate Education that issued the first of three comprehensive reports on the undergraduate curriculum. Courtesy of Michigan State University Archives and Historical Collections.

the recommendation is to let the research, graduate, and professional programs drive the university, and to develop undergraduate programs that "build upon" the graduate and advanced professional programs. As knowledge is advanced through research focused on "fundamental areas," then these areas can be applied to the "problems of men." Thus, not only does the principle of selectivity apply to the programs in which the university seeks to be "distinguished," but also "some selectivity in choosing areas of knowledge for emphasis is necessary for any university that does not have completely unlimited means" (1). For the committee, the process meant "concentrating our total University research, teaching, and off-campus efforts upon these programs in which there can be a continuum of integrated effort." In order to be of service to the people of Michigan, Michigan State should not attempt to develop or claim expertise in a large number of areas or fields of knowledge, nor should it continue to do what other institutions could now at this point do adequately, such as the two-year certificate or other special programs (5). The focus should be on the "fundamental disciplines" and on "the necessity of selectivity among programs to insure distinctiveness and quality."

In order to advance research and put increasing emphasis on it, the report recommended that department heads be responsible for promoting research by creating more time for faculty to do this activity. Productive scholars should have lower teaching loads or have flexible loads from quarter to quarter. Large lecture classes could be established in order to provide released time for research, and rotating research professorships with a minimum of a one-year assignment should be established with endowment funds or savings through efficiency. There should be "marked salary differentials for the outstanding scholar-teacher" (32). Everything possible should be done to support the research workers' needs.

In the Spring quarter of 1960, President Hannah asked the Committee on the Future of the University to prepare a progress report on steps taken to implement the recommendations made in their 1959 report. Their progress report was forwarded to Hannah on 7 November 1960, and Hannah shared the nine-page document with all the faculty. In the areas of graduate programs and research, the progress was solidly encouraging. Graduate assistantships had been increased from 512 in 1959–60 to 577 for 1960–61, with the stipend

A REPORT TO THE PRESIDENT OF MICHIGAN STATE UNIVERSITY FROM THE COMMITTEE ON THE FUTURE OF THE UNIVERSITY, EAST LANSING, MICHIGAN, 1959

IV Research

Research is one of the most important activities of every great university. Through their research, the nation's scholars make invaluable contributions to knowledge, to health and productivity, and to the survival of the nation. Increasing emphasis upon research is an absolute essential, therefore, if only because of its value to our society at large.

Research should be emphasized for another important reason. The main functions of a university can be defined as teaching and research, and the ideal we have established elsewhere in our report is the ideal of the professor as teacher-scholar. It is our belief that the active research scholar, excited by the quest for knowledge, will be the truly outstanding teacher. We would add that the research scholar must always be aware of not only his responsibility to discover new knowledge but also his duty to disseminate it to the best of his ability in the classroom. If the nation is to increase its staff of great teachers, it must provide the facilities, time, and incentives necessary for research.

At Michigan State University, with its increasingly excellent faculty and its growing professional and graduate school populations, the need to expand and improve our research performance in the future is imperative. Significant changes must be made if research is to be given adequate emphasis in such a way that it will enhance and complement the fulfillment of our other obligations.

The task is neither easy nor simple. Our manifold obligations complicate the problems we must solve. Our administrators and professors are burdened with a multitude of duties, many of them the unavoidable consequences of our rapid growth. We must decide upon the proper emphases to be placed upon research in relation to our other responsibilities. We must overcome serious shortcomings in our library holdings and our laboratories and in a variety of technical facilities. At the same time we are endowed with special strengths in certain areas of knowledge, and the decisions we make concerning fields to be emphasized should take advantage of these strengths. Research has mounted in cost until some areas are almost too expensive to enter, yet too vital to ignore. All segments of our faculty and administrative personnel must realize the integral relationship between teaching and research. The general public which does not fully understand the immeasurable value of research to society must be better informed; and, because research is hard and slow, often with results not immediately discernable, and always expensive in terms of money and time and thought, public support must be increased. Great care must be taken to assure that research is not sacrificed to activities which do not make those sound contributions to knowledge and teaching which every great university must consider its first duty.

The Committee views the task of stimulating and encouraging research as a complex problem which involves at least three main factors, each of which appears to be almost inseparably related to the others. These factors are: (1) policy-making for research; (2) recruiting and holding outstanding research scholars and facilitating their work; (3) financing research.

Large lecture classes for introductory courses became a part of the instructional delivery system in the 1960s at places like the Erickson Hall Kiva or the lecture classrooms in Wells Hall, which opened in 1967. Certain professors gained recognition as "star" professors to larger groups of students as the size features of a "megaversity" became established. Courtesy of Michigan State University Archives and Historical Collections.

increased significantly. Graduate fellowships were increased from 38 to 61, with the award increased from $1,000 to $2,750. Fifty additional waivers of out-of-state fees for winners of graduate scholarships were made. The increase in the awards was possible due to funds made available by the National Science Foundation and the National Defense Education Act.

In the area of research, the new Office of Research Development (ORD) was serving to put research activities and policies at the forefront. The Research Liaison Committee worked with the vice president for research development to create a comprehensive research policy. The ORD worked with the AEC, the Office of Naval Research, and the NSF to attract new support for research, focusing its efforts on the proposal for the cyclotron. Notable progress was made toward the goal of doubling funds by 1965 for the purchase of library materials.

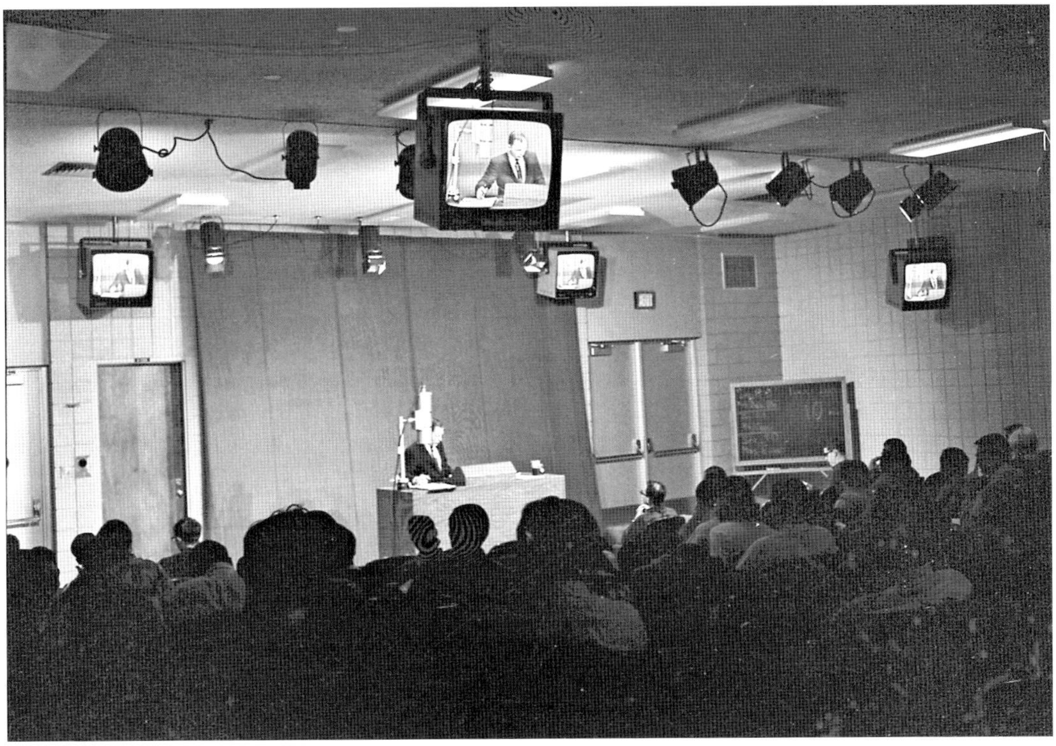

University of the Air Telecourses began at MSU in 1954–55 with five credit and eleven noncredit courses involving 162 enrolled students. WKAR-TV worked with coordinators in the schools and departments. Courses could be only by television or television-assisted, with monitors showing close-ups of calculations or scripting by instructor. WKAR-TV also made instructional and enrichment shows available to public schools. Courtesy of Michigan State University Archives and Historical Collections.

By far the most significant progress was made in the area of budgeting procedures and policies as more flexibility was introduced at the department and college level. Academic units had been encouraged to reorganize programs in order to achieve savings through greater scheduling efficiency, increased use of large lectures in introductory courses, more streamlined curriculums and requirements for majors, and decision making based on information supplied by the Office of Institutional Research. Academic units were asked to prepare five-year plans of goals, needed resources, and projected budgets. A major portion of savings achieved by new economies and efficiencies would be kept by the department to expand "higher priority programs." The 1960 progress report notes that this increased budget flexibility had resulted in released time for scholarly activities, purchase of research equipment, and retention of key faculty with salary increases. The introduction of five-year plans brought faculty and administrators (department heads and deans) together in collaboration and planning. The committee report contained some points of caution and warning, noting that the five-year plans were at that point uneven, with varying levels of essential faculty involvement evident. It warned against giving "all units the same percentage increase or decrease." "It was the strong feeling of the Committee on the Future that the latter procedure is not in the best long-run interests of the University, for it perpetuates and expands programs of dubious value at the same rate as those most essential to the University and enables the University as a whole to avoid making difficult but essential choices between programs" (*Progress Report* 9).

This was a key reassertion of the principle of selectivity emphasized in the 1959 report. "Therefore, there must be selectivity both as to the activities and areas of knowledge emphasized and as to the kind of strength appropriate to those activities and areas." The follow-up report of November 1960 also reemphasized the importance of the widespread involvement of all faculty in the process of moving into the future—a future with a substantially increased student body and the "likelihood of continued financial drouth" (9). Only by vigilant monitoring of course offerings to prevent subject duplications and fragmentation of areas of knowledge, and by faculty awareness and concern over this matter, could the economies and efficiencies continue to generate funds that could be directed toward research, needed research materials, and higher salaries. The committee expressed concern that there was "As yet, . . . little indication of widespread faculty concern on this subject."

Here, then, was the crux of the problem and the challenge. During the 1960s departments expanded in order to handle increased undergraduate and graduate enrollments. New faculty came with specializations and specialized research interests that required support in the form of laboratories, equipment and tools, availability of published research literature in books and scholarly journals, and clinical and professional practice facilities. Opportunities to gain funds from federal agencies had to be taken advantage of, and when competitions were won or proposals gained approval, it was a sign of growing prestige.

MSU surged ahead in the 1960s as it became a "megaversity" or "multiversity" with an enrollment on the East Lansing campus in Fall 1966 of 38,107 undergraduate students and another 7,354 in graduate studies. Federal funds and agency grants stimulated research and research facilities as higher education was seen as a bulwark of democracy and the site of scientific advancements needed to compete in the Cold War with the Soviet Union. In 1959–60 the Ford Foundation made a research grant of $1,000 to MSU "to add to the international dimension of the University and its faculty through the selective development of areas in which the university has already demonstrated strength, particularly in relation to problems of under-developed countries" in Latin America, Africa, and South and South-East Asia (*Progress Report* 7). The competition between democracy and Soviet Communism was seen as a struggle between systems and involved the transformation of countries and peoples that could be "won over" by solving their basic problems. Through its many technical assistance programs, MSU had distinguished itself with expertise that could address agricultural, educational, and infrastructural problems. Its record was one of repeated successes where expertise and problem-solving were transferred to native citizens who would then sustain the progress. As Hannah had said repeatedly, the university should never become disconnected from the basic problems and conditions of society. Its land-grant heritage or commission was to remain connected to the people—the people of the State of Michigan, the nation, and parts of the world where MSU could be of beneficial assistance.

As Hannah had written to the members of the Committee on the Future of the University in a letter given to them on 12 March 1959: "The University is a social institution, and its role cannot be assessed without reference to the society—state, national, and world—in which it rests. This fact has meaning for its instruction, its research, its service. How to keep it respondent to those social needs is of vital importance" (qtd. in preface to *Report to the President*).

Hannah placed ready responsiveness to social needs above anything else, including national rankings for research and graduate programs. It was this condition of responsiveness, this outward-looking orientation and connection, that validated the university's role. All research, of course, did not have to be instrumental or pointed at a specific problem, question, or set of conditions. It did not have to answer or respond to a program or an agenda or a time frame for solution. It might take some extended period of time for a scientific discovery to happen or develop. However, the overall value of the university, its value as a "social institution," was that it had the resources, the trained expertise, the tradition and practice of inquiry, and its sense of connectedness to society to respond to social needs. It could and should address problems or conditions that have hindered human progress. Discoveries or advances in knowledge added to that body of understanding in a field and therefore had intrinsic value. But when turned in the direction of society and its needs, that new knowledge was multiplied by the number of people it affected and benefited. For Hannah, "the health of the society and the health of the University are being weighed in the same balance" (qtd. in preface to *Report to the President* x). He called this relationship of a public university to the rest of society "symbiotic."

The Committee on the Future of the University endorsed and reaffirmed Hannah's updated philosophy of the land-grant public university. On the one hand, the land-grant identity was an ongoing heritage and legacy, while on the other hand, it was a flexible and expandable philosophy that could take in new challenges and be applied to rapidly changing circumstances. Certainly, not everyone necessarily agreed with Hannah's land-grant and public university views. Some felt it imposed obligations or expectations on the university that it could not fulfill because it was not given the resources or support to do so. Some believed that it tied the university too closely to society and its needs, and that these could be addressed by others, such as the government agencies founded to deal with them and funded to do so. Others believed that external programs, particularly international ones, were fraught with political complications or drew valuable teaching and research personnel away from the central goal of educating enrolled students and meeting their needs.

Hannah was certainly aware of all these reservations and critiques, and he believed that the land-grant identity needed to be refreshed and adjusted periodically. However, his central or core beliefs about the land-grant public university never wavered. In 1969, as he was ending his presidency, he had the *Report* of 1959 reprinted and redistributed. It served as a reminder of how a report could provide the basis for remarkable change and progress, as it did in the 1960s as a research and graduate-studies university developed its potential, was confirmed as "excellent" by its selection for membership in the American Association of Universities in 1964, and attained its standing as the sixth largest producer of PhDs by 1967. For Hannah, as well as for others, the 1959 report could readily serve as a guide to the future of the 1970s. It was reprinted for use, not just as a historical document at the conclusion of Hannah's remarkable service to his institution. The university would enter its next phase of development as a research university with major graduate programs under new leadership and facing challenging economic circumstances.

The Critical Piece: The MSU Main Library and Its Growth

After Michigan State entered the Big Ten and achieved university status, it was clear that the library was inadequate to meet the needs of its students and faculty, and in fact, it was an embarrassment to an institution with growing aspirations for recognition and achievement. As President Hannah stated in his *A Memoir* (1980), the library was "pretty puny" and a "poor tenth" among the Big Ten (52). Hannah characterized the library as "the heart, nerve center and intestinal track of a university" and was not satisfied with the management of the library or what he saw as its outdated philosophy of preserving books and protecting them from use. What was needed were more

Richard E. Chapin served as director of the MSU Libraries from 1960 to 1989 and guided it through its greatest period of growth in space and size. He also oversaw a diversity of collections as MSU became an AAU institution in 1964 and its international role and presence expanded, with International Studies and Programs leading the way. The MSU Libraries' organization evolved to match and mirror the strengths of the university. Chapin also served as the director of the MSU Press. Courtesy of Michigan State University Photography Services.

books of the right kinds, more space, significantly more money, and "a different kind of management" that stressed circulation and use. For Hannah, the goal was to develop a "top level" library that served the needs of expanding graduate programs and stimulated as well as supported faculty research in all fields.

Into the picture came Richard E. Chapin, who was appointed associate director of the library in 1955 with the clear understanding that he would succeed Jackson E. Towne, who had been head librarian since 1932. Chapin came to Michigan State with two doctorates, one in library science and the other in communications from the University of Illinois, "figuring that library science was not going to be library science that much longer" (SOHP interview, 9 November 1999). One of his first jobs was to supervise the move of the library from the present museum building to the new library building in the fall of 1955. As he remembered the physical move, fraternities provided the hands and arm power to move the books, and young coeds brought food and Cokes with everybody having a "good time."

When Chapin became director of libraries upon Towne's retirement in 1959, the library had 750,000 volumes. By 1973 the collection included two million volumes. The student population also grew during this time period; from 1955 to 1965 undergraduate enrollment increased from 15,801 on-campus students studying in 78 different fields to 29,003 students studying in 161 fields, and graduate

In 1965 students organized a protest over the low rating the MSU Library received in the Big Ten, and their signs revealed their displeasure. The low quality and quantity of the Library's holdings were widely recognized and a source of embarrassment to a university with high aspirations in research and graduate studies. Courtesy of Michigan State University Archives and Historical Collections [*Wolverine* 1966]).

enrollment increasing from 2,089 in 52 departments to 6,421 in 77 departments (Chapin and McCoy 267). The library's expansion, however, was not adequate to close the gap with the holdings of other Big Ten schools. In 1965 students held a protest in front of the library with signs that read "9th in the Big Ten" and "We Want a Better Library Now." By the time of Chapin's retirement from the director's position in 1989, the collection had grown to three million volumes.

Behind this story of the dramatic growth and expansion of the MSU Libraries was, of course, the hard work of gaining sorely needed additional revenues, gathering support from deans, and making strategic decisions about the development of collections. A new building (the East Wing) was opened in early 1968, and initially the two parts of the main library were designated Undergraduate Wing (west) with open stacks, and Graduate Wing (east) with closed stacks.

The construction of the East Wing of the Main Library is shown here in a shot from near the Red Cedar River, with the foundation of the Administration Building, under construction, visible in the foreground. The university's resourceful ability to build new buildings or expansions at the time of need (and to do so within its budget and resources) has been one of its signature strengths and a legacy of John A. Hannah. Courtesy of Michigan State University Photography Services.

Within a year all the library was open to users. What had been a divisional based library was changed when the emphasis shifted in 1968 to providing reference services to large numbers of students and faculty. The strategic decisions made by Chapin and his staff proved the wisdom of his choice as associate director/director-in-waiting in 1955, since the libraries became what John Hannah envisioned and knew were necessary for a library where "what counts is the use of what is there" (*A Memoir* 52).

In his 1966 article for *Library Trends* and in his 1999 Sesquicentennial Oral History Project interview, Chapin credited his staff for the successful transformation of the library. He cited the work of Henry Koch, who was head of Collection Development and Special Services and head of the Humanities Division, serving MSU for twenty-eight years; William Stoddard, social sciences librarian; Mladen Kabalin, science librarian, who came to MSU the same year as Chapin; Catherine Muhlbach in education and psychology; Carolyn

McMillen in technical services; Florence Hickok in reference. The single most important contribution of this group was to change "the nature of the collection from one strong in biological science to one [strong] in many fields" (Chapin and McCoy 269). Eugene deBenko developed resources for the non-Western areas of study with the support of Ford Foundation funds. An African Area Language Study Center's development in 1960 with the U.S. Office of Education, and MSU's role in supporting the development of the University of Nigeria prompted the acquisition of materials initially on West Africa and the Congo and then all of Africa. These resources supported and enabled the research and published scholarship of an internationally prominent group of Africanists at MSU, as well as anchoring the work of doctoral students in this field. MSU soon became the most nationally prominent producer of African PhDs and has maintained that distinction.

Chapin's central role in the transformation of the library system cannot be overstated. As the numbers and quality of undergraduate and graduate students increased, the library steadily improved and changed to meet pressing needs. Chapin knew that library science was changing and that the new order necessitated changes and adjustments, that is, responsiveness to the needs of users and graduate programs. He traveled to MSU projects in Pakistan, Vietnam, and Brazil, connecting the library to international programs and expanding his network of campus supporters. In the early 1960s he took time to go to the IBM Management School, and in 1989 he did away with the card catalog and took it fully online. He also went to the National Agricultural Library to learn automation systems using IBM cards. His ability to anticipate change and to meet it served MSU well for the thirty-five years he guided the library's development. He also served as the director of the MSU Press and helped it survive a difficult period financially and begin to grow once again.

The main library became the hub of academic life for many students. It was the preferred place for studying, either alone or on a "study date." Copies of reserved assigned readings necessitated visits to the library, as did the assignment of research papers. In the American Thought and Language curriculum, the third quarter was devoted to the formal research-paper assignment as first-year students learned the mechanics of "bib cards," note-taking, citation

Henry Koch served as the head of the Collection Development and Special Services of the MSU Libraries. He was involved in the acquisition of the Russel B. Nye Popular Culture Collection and the History of Veterinary Medicine Collection, among others. His work included the establishment of the Art Library. His *Catalogue of Rare Veterinary Books and Allied Subjects in Animal Husbandry in the Michigan State University Library* was a magnificent work of descriptive bibliography that covered in full detail more than 1,400 manuscripts and rare books in the MSU collection dating from the fifteenth century. Courtesy of Michigan State University Archives and Historical Collections.

Mladen Kabalin began his career at MSU in 1955 as the science librarian, and in 1972 became the assistant director of libraries. His work in strengthening the Science Library was critical to the success of growing graduate programs in all the sciences. He was an inveterate sketch artist who did portraits of all of the regular and emeritus faculty of the School of Criminal Justice at the time of its 50th anniversary. Courtesy of Michigan State University Archives and Historical Collections.

of sources, footnoting, and essential research. Thousands of students descended upon the library and learned how helpful and invaluable reference librarians can be.

Starting in January 1956 when the new main library building opened, it became a destination site, a place associated with quiet and purposeful study, with research, or with the completion of assignments that required the location of information. Couples on "study dates" frequently took a break for soft drinks or snacks at the nearby Student Union or finished their evening there. Singles did the same. The social element of a college experience has always been a constant, one of seeing and being seen, of learning to play social roles and finding one that is comfortable. Like the classroom, the main library was a place for students in the location of the university's books and gathered academic resources. Allowing for some degree

The expansion of the MSU Libraries in 1967 involved the addition of the East Wing to the main library building, which tripled the shelf space. The East Wing became the Graduate Library, with closed stacks. Between 1963 and 1973 the collection doubled from one million to two million volumes due to the expansion of undergraduate and graduate enrollments. By 1995 the collection had reached four million volumes. Courtesy of Michigan State University Photography Services.

of socialization there, the library was a place where students "got serious" about their studies and found an environment conducive to intellectual work and discovery of knowledge. It was a place where one learned how to use certain tools (books, reference works, volumes of data and reports, bibliographies, etc.) to do that work. With the advent of online electronic sources and libraries of e-books, those discoveries can come in other venues and via other means, and libraries have significantly less of a monopoly on information and knowledge holding than they previously did. However, for many successive generations of Michigan State students (and the more recent ones), the main library holds a special place in their memories, a place where as students they came and studied and learned.

2

The University in the Vortex of History and Social Change

Early Monday morning, 17 March 1969, MSU Board of Trustees chair Don Stevens appeared unexpectedly at the Marshall Hall office of Walter Adams, professor of economics. Stevens, who had been elected to the State Board of Agriculture and began serving in January 1959, was the chair of a nine-member board. Under the new state constitution of 1964, the political parties nominated individuals to run as party candidates for the Board of Trustees at MSU, the University of Michigan, and Wayne State University. In 1960 MSU had moved from being governed by the State Board of Agriculture to oversight by the Board of Trustees.

As Adams soon learned, the purpose of trustee Stevens's visit was to sound out Adams on who he thought would be a good interim successor to President John Hannah, who had announced his retirement on 4 February 1969 with an effective date of April 1. Stevens actually wanted to see if Adams could be interested in assuming the position in just two weeks. When Adams mentioned Provost Howard R. Neville as the "obvious and logical choice," Stevens indicated a change was in order. In his autobiography *The Test* (1971), Adams remembered: "Stevens agreed that Neville was well qualified, but hinted there were other considerations—that there ought to be a clean break with the past administration, that the time required a personality different from that suitable in the last decade. Hannah's understudy [Neville], he said, would be difficult to sell to the trustees. . . . Stevens believed that a member of the faculty who could command the respect of both his colleagues and the students might be the best choice, especially at this juncture in the history of the university when rumblings of faculty and student power were beginning to make themselves felt" (23).

Before leaving, Stevens managed to get a commitment from Adams that he "would not refuse the call" if the Board of Trustees

Howard R. Neville received a PhD in economics from MSU in 1956, became director of Continuing Education Service in 1959, and provost in 1964. With Hannah's retirement Neville seemed the logical choice to succeed him, but the Board of Trustees decided to make a break with the past. Neville became president of the University of Maine in 1973 and served until 1979. Courtesy of Michigan State University Archives and Historical Collections.

As president from April through December of 1969, Walter Adams faced the challenges of organized student protests at the Placement Bureau and the Wilson Hall cafeteria with a calm and ready willingness to talk and listen, and a sense of shared responsibility for all parties to reach resolution on issues. He loved the give-and-take of informed arguments as central to the university culture. Courtesy of Michigan State University Archives and Historical Collections.

could not find another "suitable faculty member" and agreed upon Adams's selection as interim president. By Thursday, 20 March 1969, the board was prepared to name Adams, and Stevens called Adams, who had gone to a professional conference in Spokane, Washington, and informed him that he was needed in East Lansing by 9 a.m. Friday, 21 March, to be formally introduced at the Board of Trustees meeting.

As Don Stevens remembered the circumstances in his Sesquicentennial Oral History Project interview, Clair A. White, another member of the Board of Trustees, was a "great pusher" for Professor Adams, and even though Stevens had his "questions as to whether or not he [Adams] was the right guy to be president of the university," Stevens realized he "was outnumbered on that one" and agreed to cast his vote in favor of Adams. This made the vote 5 to 3, since Provost

Walter Adams (*seated*) was a prolific and influential scholar of economics and government economic policy and teamed with James W. Brock, a former student of Adams, on a number of books. He specialized in the study of monopolies and trusts and frequently appeared as an expert witness in national congressional hearings. Courtesy of Michigan State University Archives and Historical Collections.

Neville received the votes of the three trustees who were affiliated with Michigan's Republican Party.

Stevens's point to Adams about making "a clean break with the past administration" was an essential and important one, and it certainly played into the selection of Adams over other possible faculty candidates. As Adams noted in his 1971 book *The Test,* he was "by instinct and temperament . . . an admirer of the Wayne Morses and Estes Kefauvers more than the Franklin Roosevelts and Dwight Eisenhowers of this world," and that he "had always been a critic of

MSU trustee Don Stevens approached Walter Adams in March 1969 to see if he would entertain accepting the presidency, and five days later Adams was introduced as Hannah's successor. Stevens also played a major role in Clifton R. Wharton Jr.'s being named president, as Stevens had to resist intense political pressure to support former governor G. Mennen Williams for the job. A labor activist and prominent AFL-CIO leader, Stevens served on the Board of Trustees from 1958 to 1979. Courtesy of Michigan State University Archives and Historical Collections.

the establishment—on campus and off" (24). Adams's politics were that of a professor whose mindset was to be inquiring, questioning, and criticizing as warranted. In 1968 he had led a student demonstration protesting high textbook costs, earning him credence and support with the students.

Adams had other than political differences with Hannah. With John A. Garraty, a professor in the History Department, he published two books that brought into question the effectiveness of American faculty abroad and the technical assistance programs of the university that Hannah believed in so deeply and that he touted as the university's significant contribution to the world. The two books, *From Main Street to the Left Bank: Students and Scholars Abroad* (1959) and *Is the World Our Campus?* (1960), were published by the Michigan State University Press and were part of a grant from the Carnegie Corporation to examine "the organized activities of American universities all over the world." In the second book, Adams and Garraty raised serious questions about technical assistance programs in Europe and Turkey (and by implication elsewhere) in terms of impact and effectiveness, and in terms of the question of their being a drain on university resources and a misdirection of mission.

Adams had also expressed serious personal concerns about the growth of the "multiversity" and the shifting institutional priorities to research and graduate education. While he was initially appointed to serve on the Committee on the Future of the University, he was on leave during the Spring quarter 1959 when the committee did its work, and thus was not one of the signers and endorsers of the report forwarded to President Hannah on 28 July 1959. His work during that leave resulted in *Is the World Our Campus?* Adams's concerns were that the university was neglecting its mission to educate its on-campus students with the best of its resources, and that in reaching out to far-flung nations it was neglecting the people and immediate conditions in the State of Michigan. Further, he believed that the university-government contract system could skew or even corrupt the independence of the university and compromise its independent search for the truth or solutions to human problems.

In his discussion with Adams, trustee Stevens had also emphasized that what was needed was "a member of the faculty who could command the respect of both his colleagues and the students" in light of the "rumblings of faculty and student power." In other words, the interim president had to understand why and how faculty were pushing for more power, and had to be able to respond to the "rumblings" with flexibility and skilled negotiation. Adams had achieved a well-deserved reputation for objective analysis and independent viewpoints and had a passion for teaching and learning in a university setting where anything could be freely questioned and openly discussed.

Adams had another virtue as interim president: not being G. Mennen "Soapy" Williams. Soon after Hannah had announced his resignation, a movement began to maneuver Williams into the MSU presidency. He had served as the state's governor for twelve years from 1949 to 1961, built the Mackinac Bridge linking the two peninsulas, and served as assistant secretary of state for African Affairs from 1961 to early 1966 in the Kennedy and Johnson administrations. Having lost a U.S. Senate race in 1966 to the incumbent Republican, Williams was available and, by all reports, interested in heading the university.

However, as Walter Adams notes in *The Test*, the campus balked at Williams being maneuvered or rumored into the presidency despite his credentials, experience, and name recognition. The campus preferred some degree of separation from politics, and this movement on behalf of Williams was a test of the university's autonomy and its capability to decide on the "right" or best person to lead it. To take Williams because his supporters wanted him to have the position would compromise a process of selection that was one for the university community to carry out and conclude. Appointing Walter Adams interim president allowed for some needed time, and it was a popular and well-received move. The Williams candidacy did not, however, disappear entirely, and came back into play later.

Adams's year as interim president was, as he characterized it in *The Test* (1971), one of a series of challenges, unexpected developments, and demanding situations, and a "test" of how he and the university would respond. He came into the position with no administrative style or philosophy and no specific experience. In fact, he saw himself as a "critic" of the university for its "bigness" and its inability or unwillingness to change with the times. What Adams did have were insights into the problems a university bureaucracy could have when it became disconnected from its students, especially in a tumultuous time like the Vietnam War, and when it tried to stifle dissent with authoritarian measures. As an experienced and savvy professor of economics, Adams also knew that teaching students involved challenging them and respecting them. As a practitioner of the Socratic method in the classroom, he knew that questions and reflective and analytical thinking about answers leading to the refinement of conclusions was preferable to lecturing. His strategy was to be visible and accessible as president, to respond to each new situation on its own terms with its own players, and to rely on instinct and intuition.

Adams was tested twice by the radicals from the Students for a Democratic Society (SDS) during incidents at the MSU Placement Bureau, where they tried to prevent the Oakland, California, Police Department and then the General Electric Company from recruiting job candidates. He and others had to respond to a Black Student Association occupation of the Wilson Hall cafeteria for 72 hours. The situations at the Placement Bureau proved relatively short-lived and did not involve a great many people. However, the situation at Wilson Hall was infinitely more complex and difficult. The immediate issue of the alleged mistreatment of two black cafeteria workers by two white supervisors brought out all the underlying issues of race and racism. These included discrimination without recourse or processes to prevent it; the lack of employment opportunities, especially supervisory positions, for black students; and the sincerity of the university's commitment to resolving racial issues. The situation at Wilson Hall received extensive media coverage, and the settlement that was finally reached to resolve the crisis was widely criticized as a "caving in" to the students' demands. Adams came under sharp criticism from a number of quarters, and the *Detroit News* editorialized that Adams "complied" with the takeover of a campus building and that he had given "amnesty" to "insurgents" and tolerated as well as rewarded "anarchy" (qtd. in Adams 73–74).

Adams's perspective was that something instructive and valuable had been learned from what had been a tense, confusing, and exhausting three days. A group of students and university officials had been tested to see if they could resolve an immediate problem and return a cafeteria to its full, daily use by black and white students.

But the situation involved a whole range of white responses to black militancy and activism. The action could be seen as a threat or an unlawful occupation or obstruction of university space, or it could be seen as the opening act of a series of challenges that called upon the university to deal with underlying issues of race. Adams believed that the Wilson Hall situation "showed the impossibility of ignoring the realities of the world in which even academicians have to live. It forced the faculty to confront the race question squarely—on center stage" (Adams 75). The Wilson Hall cafeteria occupation and its resolution helped MSU inch ahead on the matter of race and racial relations.

One of the major developments in Adams's time as interim president was the unanimous commitment made at the Board of Trustees meeting on 19 April 1969 "that the Board appropriate sufficient funds to support the Equal Opportunities Program and the Center for Urban Affairs for the fiscal year beginning July 1, 1969 as may be adequately substantiated before July 1, up to the total of $1,500,000, and that the President be authorized to begin such employment in this fiscal year as may be necessary to support this program." This motion was introduced by Blanche Martin, who as the first African American to serve on the board was just beginning a term of service that would span from 1969 to 1985. Just before this motion, the board had heard from Robert L. Green, associate director of the Center for Urban Affairs, and from two black students who read a statement that addressed a number of issues related to perceived racism and discrimination on campus. The board also unanimously approved a motion made by trustee Don Stevens establishing a "policy of requiring proof of equal employment practices from all university contractors."

Adams made these developments the focus of an address to the faculty at an Academic Senate meeting on 8 May 1969. In it he challenged the faculty to become directly involved in "innovative change" and reform, and to focus on the urban crisis and the needs and challenges of the cities. He saw the Center for Urban Affairs functioning as a catalyst and instrument for change, with the full involvement of departments and colleges with curriculum, research, and pedagogy directed toward the urban mission. In his scheme for "self-renewal and self-regeneration" he saw the land-grant philosophy redesigned and revitalized.

Charles Curry came to MSU in 1963 as a member of the freshman admissions office. Along with Gordon A. Sabine, Curry developed programs that attracted large numbers of National Merit scholars and provided them with Alumni Distinguished Scholarships. He left for three years from 1968 to 1971 to work at Hope College, but returned to MSU in 1971 to head the Admissions Office until his retirement in 1993. From 1981 to 1993 he determined the eligibility for all incoming freshmen athletes under NCAA and Big Ten guidelines. Courtesy of Michigan State University Archives and Historical Collections.

The October Moratorium march, or the March for Peace, on 15 October 1969 made its way from campus down Michigan Avenue to the State Capitol, after teach-ins that morning and a mass meeting in the MSU Auditorium addressed by U.S. Congressman Don Riegle Jr., U.S. Senator Philip Hart, and President Walter Adams. The march of some eight thousand people was peaceful and orderly. Courtesy of Michigan State University Archives and Historical Collections.

Adams also believed in acting on matters of immediate urgency. One of the issues raised by Samuel "Sam" Riddle Jr. and Jason P. Lovette, the two black students who addressed the Board of Trustees on 18 April 1969, was the "humiliation of two young black women who courageous [*sic*] went out for the MSU cheerleading squad." The cheerleader issue went back to 1968, and Adams took the suggestion of a student who said that if cheerleading was moved to student government from intercollegiate athletics, the students would resolve the problem. Two black cheerleaders were soon selected and became part of the team at football games. Adams also worked to get Professor Irvin E. Vance, a black mathematics professor, put on the slate of nominees for membership on the Athletic Council and then appointed him. Even when faced with the opposition of the Board of Trustees to the nomination of Robert L. Green as director of the Center for Urban Affairs, he refused to withdraw the nomination and Green was appointed (Adams 88–90).

One more instance of Adams's leadership needs discussion: his role in the Vietnam or October Moratorium march from campus to the State Capitol building on 15 October 1969. In the front line of the marchers with Board of Trustees chair Don Stevens, two black state representatives from Detroit, the president and vice president of MSU Student Government, and Josephine Martin, the wife of MSU trustee Blanche Martin, Adams joined about eight thousand others who made their way down Michigan Avenue in a show of solidarity for peace. Adams, Green, and the new provost John E. Cantlon each gave speeches to the marchers at a rally before they left East Lansing. According to Kenneth J. Heineman in his *Campus Wars: The Peace Movement at American State Universities in the Vietnam Era* (1993), "the local Moratorium was anything but harmonious and moderate." Adams's economic analysis of the war was attacked and rejected by Professor Norman Pollack, a member of the History Department and faculty radical, and the student government took sharp issue with Adams's decision not to suspend classes for the November Mobilization March on Washington, DC.

Like every other president of a large state university, Adams was caught in the pull and tug of ever-shifting politics and outside forces exerting pressure on the campus: state legislators, parents, local media, alumni, and national war-protest organizations, each with a presence on campus. At best, he could steer a course or respond to developments so that violence and property damage did not occur, university property was not occupied or shut down, and potentially explosive situations were defused. As long as the war continued, the campus would continue to be a flash point and a contested ground for radicals and activists.

All in all, Adams had stood up to his "tests" rather well and was appreciated for the way he had led the university. A movement began for his selection as the "regular" president, with editorials of endorsement being published and petitions circulating. At the same time, the Board of Trustees moved a national search forward in anything but a smooth, bipartisan, and professional way. Former governor G. Mennen Williams reemerged as a candidate, but he had not gone through the formal application/nomination process and was therefore not on the official list under consideration. The list of four finalists was leaked to the press, resulting in one finalist's withdrawal. As the board was unable to make a decision, the external pressure to appoint Williams increased, and Adams was urged to reconsider his well-known position that he was a faculty member doing a necessary but temporary job. In the end, two Democratic board members, Don Stevens and Blanche Martin, joined their three Republican colleagues to select Clifton R. Wharton Jr. as the next MSU president. Trustees Frank Hartman, Warren M. Huff, and Clair A. White remained staunch supporters of Williams in the final vote. Hartman and White would be gone from the board by 1973 and Huff by 1977.

Walter Adams was now able to move back to the Economics Department and full-time teaching. He had in fact continued to teach while president and never taken on the trappings of the office, such as a box at Spartan Stadium or the on-campus president's house. As he concluded in his *The Test*, he was "distrustful of power and its corrupting influence, and cynical about the transitory achievements of administration." In "being what I am and believing as I do," he concluded that the classroom was where he made his most effective and long-lasting contribution to students, and where he could be the critic of whatever needed criticism or logical examination. His greatest published works of scholarship in economics were still ahead of him: *The Structure of American Industry, The Bigness Complex, Dangerous Pursuits: Mergers and Acquisitions in the Age of Wall Street*, and *Adam Smith Goes to Moscow: A Dialogue on Radical Reform.* On campus with his cigar and ever-present at the athletic events as a devoted fan, in the Union Cafeteria at his table with his colleagues engaged in spirited conversations, he became more than a recognizable, constant figure; he became an iconic figure who was in his element and who relished the life of a professor who loved his university (even with its faults) and who was deeply loved, respected, and honored in return. In the period between John Hannah's last day as president and the first day of President Wharton's term, Walter Adams made significant contributions to MSU and was part of critical and much needed top-level changes that created a climate where Clifton R. Wharton Jr. could be elected president.

Wharton came to MSU with the strongest and most impressive credentials of any president in the university's history. A graduate of Harvard, he earned an MA in international affairs from the Paul H. Nitze School of Advanced International Studies at Johns Hopkins and then took MA and PhD degrees from the University of Chicago. From 1958 through 1964, he lived in Southeast Asia and supervised the Rockefeller Foundation's programs in Thailand, Vietnam, Laos, and Cambodia; he was also a professor of economics at the University of Malaya. He served as a member of President Johnson's Presidential Mission to Vietnam in 1966. His research focused on the crops of Southeast Asia, agricultural development in the context of subsistence agriculture, economic development possibilities in world trade, and the training of native agricultural economists. His 1958 doctoral dissertation was a case study of the economic impact of technical assistance on the agriculture of Minas Gerais, Brazil. This was a location where MSC had conducted a research project in 1954 "studying the rate of adoption of new agricultural practices and technologies" (Smuckler 48). When he came to East Lansing, Wharton had just been on a Rockefeller Foundation mission to Latin America, and *Subsistence Agriculture and Economic Development*, a book he edited and contributed to, had been published. In short, he had all the qualities and experience the premier land-grant university could want: administrative and budget experience with the Rockefeller Foundation; political connections in Washington, DC; knowledge of international agriculture and published research; connections to Southeast Asia and South America; and a remarkable record of personal educational achievements. His wife, Dolores, was well known as an advocate for the arts and had, during their years in Southeast Asia, conducted a survey of contemporary Malaysian artists. They were a team, and came to be referred to as "the Whartons" in recognition and appreciation of their closeness and their mutual interests.

Of the four finalists who were considered by the Board of Trustees, Wharton was the youngest by five years at age 42. Trustee Don Stevens recalled in his Sesquicentennial Oral History Project interview of 19 April 2001 that when the board interviewed Wharton at the Waldorf Astoria Hotel in New York City, "He made a good impression on me, and some of the others." That "good impression" proved to be critical in Stevens's resistance to the intense political and

Dolores and Clifton Wharton Jr. were a cosmopolitan and international couple with a quietly sophisticated Eastern style. They both served on numerous corporate and foundation boards and were deeply committed to fostering the fine and performing arts and bettering the opportunities for women and minorities. Courtesy of Michigan State University Archives and Historical Collections.

personal pressures exerted on him to vote for G. Mennen Williams, including a one-on-one meeting with Soapy where Stevens had to explain that he would only vote for a candidate approved by the university-wide committee. Williams was not on that list and knew it. Stevens also recalled that the Democratic trustees who did not vote for Wharton gave the incoming president a difficult time, but that Wharton handled it well. In no other selection of an MSU president did party politics swirl around and in the process as this one.

When Wharton took office in 1970, he could not have predicted or anticipated national and state developments that would affect the university. The passage of the 26th Amendment to the U.S. Constitution (ratified on 1 July 1971) set the voting age at 18, with students now being eligible to vote in their college town. While that was a positive step that promised changes in local politics, for male college students, the draft lotteries held by the Selective Service System from 1 December 1969 through 1975 introduced the randomness of fate (the order of the draw) and the irony of having one's birthday be the source of the call by "Uncle Sam." Rather than appearing to be fairer or more impartial than local draft boards, the national lottery actually increased opposition to the Vietnam War and its mechanism of continuation—the draft. Further, the national age for legal drinking and the power to make contracts was lowered to age 18 effective 1 January 1972, creating two full generations of college students (the seven years from 1972 through 1978) who could buy liquor and drink in bars as soon as they hit East Lansing.

National and state economic developments would also have their impact. Between 1965 and 1966 the U.S. inflation rate almost doubled from 1.59 to 3.01 percent, and the same thing happened between 1973 and 1974 with a 6.16 rate soaring to 11.03 percent. The nation would have three years of double-digit inflation from 1979 through 1981 with rates of 11.22, 13.58, and 10.35 percent. The Arab oil embargo, subsequent rise in Organization of the Petroleum Exporting Countries (OPEC) oil prices in late 1973, and the 1973–74 stock market crash resulted in increased unemployment and sent shockwaves through Michigan's automobile industry, as it took U.S. automakers some time to respond to the competition of smaller imported cars with four-cylinder engines and smaller, lighter bodies. The first in what would become a regular pattern of budget cuts in the State of Michigan by the governor occurred in 1971–72, a development discussed later in this chapter.

However, the national development with by far the most impact on the campuses across the United States was the announcement made by President Richard M. Nixon on 30 April 1970 that U.S. troops were invading Cambodia in an effort to strike at the routes used through Cambodia by the North Vietnamese to move more troops into South Vietnam. This action came after Nixon had announced on April 20 the withdrawal of 150,000 U.S. troops from Vietnam.

This incursion by the U.S. troops came during somewhat of a lull in campus protests against the war, since Nixon's stated policy had been to "Vietnamize" the war and replace U.S. troops with South Vietnamese soldiers.

On Monday, May 4th the unthinkable happened on the campus of Kent State University when Ohio National Guardsmen opened fire and killed four students and wounded nine. At MSU the response to this tragedy was to organize a strike that aimed at shutting down the campus. On May 5th, three thousand students surrounded the Hannah Administration Building and demanded that President Wharton honor the dead Ohio students and go on record urging Nixon to withdraw U.S. troops from Cambodia. In a brief statement to the press, Wharton responded by declaring the university flags would fly at half-staff in mourning for the students' deaths and that students were free to hold an antiwar sit-in. That evening about seven thousand people spent six hours in the MSU Auditorium debating and voting on strike issues (Heineman 251). The strike went ahead, and for about two weeks, more than twelve thousand students observed the strike, which had the endorsement of the student government and other groups. As Heineman notes in *Campus Wars*, the strikers represented "only 32% of the student body" and were "largely social science and humanities majors, while very few hard science and business majors, who constituted 46% of the student body, participated in the strike" (252).

The strikers' aim of shutting down the campus was not achieved, but the visible numbers of war protestors and activists had substantially increased. The Vietnam War and its continuation not only divided university campuses across the nation, it divided the nation itself. Faculty and students were caught up in a whirl of conflicting loyalties and positions on the war. However, the majority of students continued to attend classes and move towards the end of the semester. Privately, they might have misgivings or doubts about the war, or might even have been touched by the war in terms of family members serving in the military or fighting in Vietnam. Or they might know one of the American soldiers who was killed or wounded. The same was true also of the activists and protestors. There was a wide spectrum of attitudes and feelings, and what made a student a radical or a hard-core supporter of the war was a complex matter.

Mass demonstrations at the Hannah Administration Building during the Vietnam War featured speeches by various leaders of antiwar and peace groups, handmade signs, and singing and chanting well-known slogans. Student radicals faulted the university for not taking a firm position against the war, for trying to maintain "business as usual," and for an unwillingness to meet student demands. Courtesy of Michigan State University Archives and Historical Collections (*Wolverine* 1971).

All experienced the same national and campus developments, and each reacted differently or saw in them different issues or personal connections.

What can be said about this period from the fateful day of 4 May 1970 at Kent State through the end of the month is that the MSU campus did not experience the rage, heightened confrontations, and battles and fire bombings that occurred at places like Kent State or the University of Wisconsin. Part of that can be attributed to the

The fatal shootings of four Kent State University students and wounding of nine other students on Monday, 4 May 1970 by Ohio National Guardsmen sent a shock wave through college campuses and the nation. In response there was a strike of four million students as well as demonstrations protesting the "massacre" and the callous responses of the Ohio governor and the Nixon administration. At MSU students marched with signs bearing the victims' names. The war protest movement took on a new sense of urgency and justification. Courtesy of Michigan State University Archives and Historical Collections (*Wolverine* 1971).

fact that the majority of the students did not participate in the mass demonstrations or boycott classes during strikes that were called. In *The Test* (1971), Walter Adams credited Michigan governor William Milliken with a calm leadership: "Whenever public feelings ran high, Governor Milliken could consistently be counted on to defuse tension and counteract fear. His attitude, I think, had much to do with the fact that Michigan's universities avoided disruption, bloodshed, and mass unrests which occurred in other states governed by lesser men" (158).

Adams's conclusion after a year in the president's office was: "So long as we must fight an unpopular, seemingly endless war and neglect our domestic problems, it is idle to hope for lasting campus peace" (Adams 129).

As President Wharton would learn firsthand, this proved to be true through 1972 and into 1973. Another round of campus unrest and demonstrations came in response to the escalation of the bombing of North Vietnam and Nixon's order to mine North Vietnamese ports. On Wednesday, 10 May 1972, Wharton met with about four to five thousand students at Beaumont Tower and indicated the university was willing to make four concessions to the nine student demands. Not satisfied, the crowd headed to Grand River Avenue, where they had blocked traffic the night before. All that night the

Student protesters occupied a five-block section of Grand River Avenue on Thursday night and Friday morning, 11–12 May 1972, after students had occupied the Hannah Administration Building for about three hours. The developments received heavy media attention as the war protest movement neared its conclusion. Courtesy of Michigan State University Archives and Historical Collections.

students occupied the main thoroughfare, holding what a *Lansing State Journal* reporter called a five block party with marijuana, beer, and wine (11 May 1972). A rock band provided music, and students played Frisbee and planted flowers and shrubs in the cinder blocks they had laid across the street. On Friday morning Mayor Wilbur B. Brookover told the remaining occupiers of the street to leave or face arrest. An estimated five hundred policemen moved down Grand River and reclaimed the street, with garbage and trash trucks moving

President Clifton Wharton Jr. had ongoing encounters and discussions with student war protesters and activists, and tried to steer a moderate course that listened to students but kept the university open and operating. His and others' patience ran thin when students occupied and shut down Grand River Avenue and briefly took over the Hannah Administration Building on 11 May 1972. Courtesy of Michigan State University Archives and Historical Collections.

behind them to clear the debris and makeshift gardens. The standoff was over, and the last major act of trying to "stop business as usual" had been played out.

President Wharton steered a middle course with the protestors and listened to their demands, meeting or accommodating ones to which the university could reasonably respond. He had been widely criticized for calling in the State Police, who used tear gas on those protestors gathered at Demonstration Hall on 15 May 1970 during the student strike. In May 1972 he told protesting students that he would contact members of the Board of Trustees to see if they would adopt an institutional resolution condemning the Vietnam War. On 21 April 1972 the board passed on a 6-1 vote two resolutions on the war in Indochina urging "our national government to bring American military involvement in this conflict to a speedy end, without further expansion."

But the temperate language of this resolution had not satisfied the antiwar activists. The East Lansing City Council created a similar resolution with liberal council members who had been elected by students under their new voting rights. Wharton was, of course, criticized and second-guessed by many groups, and like Walter Adams, he found himself in a difficult position where no action on his part could fully satisfy any one group. He was determined to keep the university operating, with classes being regularly taught and university property protected, while allowing for a reasonable measure of dissent and protest. However, when about five hundred students stormed the Hannah Administration Building on the afternoon of Thursday, 11 May 1972, gained access to it, and were riding bicycles inside and claiming the MSU Board Room on the fourth floor as the "people's headquarters," Wharton told the occupiers to leave or face arrest. When a small group refused to leave, they were removed by a large contingent of State Police who marched across the library bridge and sealed off the building after about a three-hour occupation by students (*Lansing State Journal*, 12 May 1972). Unlike Adams, who had set limits on his term as president, Wharton had to think about the years of his presidency beyond the first two, which meant, on occasion, taking some strong measures with radical faculty and students in order to set some limits. In doing so, he necessarily incurred some unpopularity with certain segments of the campus community. On the other hand, he was appreciated by others for guiding the university through a period of trial when other campuses experienced violence and property destruction.

Wilbur B. Brookover joined the faculty in 1946 after service in the navy during World War II and was a professor of sociology, social studies, education, and urban and metropolitan studies. He served as an expert witness in the *Brown v. Board of Education* Supreme Court case and was involved in national studies of school desegregation. From 1971 to 1975 Brookover served as mayor of East Lansing, following Gordon L. Thomas, a communications professor, who served from 1961 to 1971. Courtesy of Michigan State University Archives and Historical Collections.

Economic Developments

On 15 August 1971 President Richard M. Nixon imposed wage and price controls in an effort to combat an inflation rate above 4 percent; it had been 5.46 percent in 1969 and 5.84 percent in 1970. The freeze was presented as a ninety-day program, but lasted almost a thousand days until April 1974. On 15 September 1971, President Wharton released an eight-page report to the faculty and staff detailing how the university was "taking every step we can to minimize the impact on our faculty and staff and to provide them equitable treatment while

MINUTES OF THE BOARD OF TRUSTEES, APRIL 21, 1972

Resolutions on War in Indochina

Trustee Stevens presented the following resolution:

The Michigan State University Board of Trustees is a constitutional body elected to represent all the people of Michigan in the governance of the University. As such, our official duties and responsibilities are confined to the welfare and furtherance of this institution of higher education.

We are, however, citizens of this state and nation, and we cherish our individual rights to speak out on major issues which confront us. Such an issue is the war in Indochina, and particularly the continued American military involvement.

In our collective years as Trustees, working closely with the youth who attend this University, we have seen with growing alarm the divisiveness, the cynicism and the widening gap of credibility which this war has instilled in so many young people. We deplore this serious breakdown in our society and loss of confidence in our democratic system—all caused by a war which has long since lost all context or meaning for the majority of the American people. The latest expansion of this conflict only furthers the sense of frustration.

The campus is the catalyst by which the youth of today become the nation's leaders of tomorrow. It must remain a forum—and not itself become a battlefield.

Therefore, as individual citizens speaking together, we urge our national government to bring American military involvement in this conflict to a speedy end, without further expansion. We urge our students to use, to the fullest, the new right of the ballot which is the most effective weapon we have. By such use, they can begin to constructively shape their nation as they would have it be.

Motion was made by Trustee Stevens, seconded by Trustee Hartman, to approve the above resolution. *Carried* by a vote of 6 to 1, Trustee Merriman voting "No."

Mr. Robert Bowling, representing the Vietnam Veterans Against the War, the Veterans for Peace, and other concerned citizens of the University community, requested permission to address the Trustees and urged that the Trustees adopt the following resolution.

Resolution on the Resumption of Bombing in North Vietnam

We, the publicly elected Trustees of Michigan State University, while we cannot speak for all our students, faculty and staff, personally deplore and oppose the escalation of the bombing and naval war in Indochina.

We believe that the President's action in stepping up the war will not protect our troops being withdrawn, nor will it bring home the American prisoners in North Vietnam. It will only serve to prolong a futile war and to increase the number of U.S. Prisoners held by Hanoi.

We urge President Nixon to declare an immediate cease fire, to set a specific date for withdrawal of all air, naval and ground forces from Indochina, and to enter into meaningful negotiations for the release of our prisoners when all U.S. forces are out of Indochina.

Trustee White, supported by Trustee Carrigan, moved the adoption of the above resolution. *Unanimously carried.* Trustee White requested that the two resolutions be transmitted to President Nixon by President Wharton.

complying with the spirit and letter of the freeze order." The report included Wharton's 9 September 1971 memorandum to the Board of Trustees ("Subject: Review of Actions under the Price-Wage Freeze") and the text of two letters Wharton had written to the Federal Cost-of-Living Council and John B. Connally, secretary of the Treasury, the first applying for an exemption to the freeze so that wage increases at MSU scheduled for 1 July 1971 could go ahead, and the second asking for a ruling that promotions in rank would "qualify for normal pay increases" that come with "an advancement with greater and different responsibility." It was an unusual release of documents by the president, but showed his concern that faculty and staff have full and current information on economic matters directly affecting them.

However, it was economic developments in the State of Michigan that, in fact, created the most concern and disruption in the university. Into the first week of October 1971, the state legislature had failed to approve an appropriation for higher education, and Governor William Milliken announced on 29 September 1971 that he was authorizing up to 3 percent of the funds in the appropriations bills to be withheld for a state contingency fund. In a frank and direct letter from Wharton to MSU faculty and staff on 6 October 1971, the president noted that a full 3 percent withholding amounted to a reduction of $2,282,640, and that in 1970 the university was "forced to cut more than $800,000 from our appropriation."

On top of these dire developments, Wharton had recommended an average 7 percent salary increase for faculty retroactive to July 1. After reviewing the choices available, Wharton indicated that he would recommend to the Board of Trustees that in the "best long-term interests of the university" a retroactive 7 percent increase be carried out "as originally planned, with no strings, making up any later internal deficit through forced savings and perhaps painful program reallocations." Wharton made it clear that "Efforts already are underway to identify the various operational and program reductions which may be necessary over the short and long terms."

Several developments are noteworthy here, and were momentous for MSU. First was the delay into the next fiscal year of the state appropriations for that year, introducing uncertainty and a constantly shifting target for the operating budget. Second was the magnitude of the potential withholding from MSU's budget, almost $2.3 million,

Robert Repas was a professor in the School of Labor and Industrial Relations whose work focused on collective bargaining and contract administration. In 1972 Repas and trustee Clair A. White released the faculty salary list to the *State News*, the first time it had ever been made public, and it was the talk of the campus for some time. Courtesy of Michigan State University Archives and Historical Collections.

and that after an $800,000 cut taken the previous year. On top of this, the governor put a freeze on vacancies. Third was the introduction of the reality that planned salary increases could necessarily involve program reallocations and reductions and that some of these might be permanent. A new pattern had been set, establishing financial contingency and uncertainty as budget realities that could not be avoided, and that when faced were, as Wharton stated, "never easy." The expansion and operation of MSU as a "multiversity" or "megaversity" had been predicated on steady, reliable (and for the most part increasing) annual appropriations from the legislature within the structure of the fiscal year. The question now was whether an era of contraction had begun or if this was an economic bump that would be smoothed over and forgotten.

The crux of the problem for MSU was the reduction of the original state appropriation in 1971–72 from $65,318,000 down to $64,011,640, or a loss of $1,306,360 in operating funds. State appropriations to MSU had increased about $5 million each year, so the loss of critical funds in 1971–72 was a hard one, since salaries and labor costs were increasing yearly. President Wharton and the board were committed to providing annual salary raises and pulling faculty salaries up from their low status. Improving salaries and benefits, especially for senior faculty, was a key to recruitment and retention. After this one drop-down year, the state appropriations found their former incremental pattern and even improved, except for the period from 1974–75 through 1976–77.

In response to the budget cuts and their impact on faculty salaries, the first effort to unionize the faculty came in 1972. The Michigan Employment Relations Commission scheduled an election in October 1972 on the question of organizing a faculty union and instituting collective bargaining. Subsequent elections were held in 1978 and in 1981, as the Michigan Education Association (represented by Faculty Associates on campus) and the American Association of University Professors (AAUP) vied for the role of representing the faculty. In all three elections the faculty union was voted down by a margin of about 2 to 1, with senior faculty and faculty in the sciences and medical school strongly opposed to a union. While the union advocates were defeated in each vote, the effort to bring collective bargaining to MSU had the effect of bringing salary inequities or

Table 1. Appropriations to MSU from the State of Michigan

1972–73	$70,839,000
1973–74	$77,325,100
1974–75	$85,665,800
1975–76	$88,635,893
1976–77	$89,752,925
1977–78	$99,382,900
1978–79	$109,614,225

disparities, work conditions and protections for faculty, benefits, and general economic issues into the open for more public discussion. When the faculty salary list was released to the *State News* in 1972 by Professor Robert Repas and trustee Clair A. White, many faculty were surprised to see how low some of the salaries were and how much disparity existed between colleges and departments. The union movement also allowed for visible faculty leadership to develop, as individuals could and did take strong positions on issues outside the normal committee system and faculty representation. In the context of these open discussions, there were several salutary developments, including the adoption of a grievance procedure, new Bylaws for Academic Governance in 1974, the institutional settlement of a lawsuit brought by certain MSU women faculty, and wide circulation and analysis of budget and salary figures.

In August 1974 it was announced that money for an 8 percent raise would be available for salary changes. However, by early 1975 departments were asked to submit a budget incorporating a 4 percent cut in expenses, as well as one reflecting an 8 percent budget cut. These cuts were ordered by Governor Milliken and aimed at the next year's budget. Provost John E. Cantlon announced that cuts would vary from unit to unit. However, the state's economy and revenues improved in the period from 1973 through 1976, and for 1975–76 the state's appropriation for higher education was $556.8 million.

Michigan had proudly built what was until 1967–68 the second largest state system (after California) of higher education in the nation. By 1967–68 Michigan was fourth behind California, New York,

Trustee Clair A. White voted for former governor G. Mennen Williams for the MSU presidency, as did trustees Frank Hartman and Warren M. Huff. However, Democratic Board of Trustees members Don Stevens and Blanche Martin broke ranks with their Democratic colleagues and voted for Clifton Wharton Jr. to become MSU president. Courtesy of Michigan State University Archives and Historical Collections.

William Milliken (*center*) served as Michigan's governor from 1969 to 1983, taking over when George Romney resigned to join President Richard M. Nixon's cabinet. Milliken was elected to four-year terms in 1970, 1974, and 1978. A moderate Republican, Milliken was widely respected and supported by members of both political parties and known for his support of education at all levels. Walter Adams credited Milliken's calmness and sound judgment with keeping Michigan's college campuses free of the extremes of destructive riots, bloodshed, and mass arrests during protests against the Vietnam War. Courtesy of Michigan State University Archives and Historical Collections.

and Illinois. Under the governorship of George Romney (1963–69) Michigan had moved from expenditures for higher education of $101 million in 1960–61 to $343.7 million in 1970–71 (Chambers 5). Although state expenditures increased in actual dollar amounts in the period from 1971–72 through 1976–77 the overall percentages of increases declined and became smaller and smaller each budget year. At the same time the state universities faced revenue cuts, inflation was jumping from 3.27 percent in 1972, to 6.16 in 1973, to 11.03 in 1974. The state's economic "bounceback" brought feelings of relief, and the state's strong commitment to higher education resumed. William Milliken was a strong pro-education governor, and figures in the state legislature such as Dominic Jacobetti from Marquette, Morris W. Hood Jr. from Detroit, Perry Bullard from Ann Arbor, and

Lynn Jondahl from East Lansing worked tirelessly and effectively to gain appropriations and building funds for the universities in their districts. As the universities became more accessible because of increasing capacity, and as the junior-college system grew, a strong pro-education consensus developed and was reinforced.

International Developments

Wharton's firsthand knowledge, administrative work, and research in South America and in Southeast Asia gave him a remarkable international reach. As Ralph H. Smuckler notes in his book *A University Turns to the World*, published by the MSU Press in 2003, Wharton and international experts from MSU were turned to by the federal government in the formulation of the 1975 Title XII amendment to the Foreign Assistance Act, with a program aimed at strengthening the alliance between MSU and the Agency for International Development (AID) and AID's ability to deal with famine and hunger prevention. Wharton was appointed the first head of the Board for International Food and Agricultural Development (BIFAD), and a number of MSU faculty served on committees created by Title XII (47).

Smuckler also provides the story about how President Wharton's reputation for Rockefeller Foundation work in Brazil, as well as MSU's experience in working there on technical assistance programs, brought the Brazilian government to East Lansing when they were selecting a technical assistance partner for improving management in their universities. Smuckler credits Wharton's detailed knowledge of the needs of Brazil, his credibility, and his fluent Portuguese as key factors in assigning the project to MSU's leadership. Smuckler also credits Wharton with always sound judgment and discretion in handling sensitive international matters and providing strong support to International Studies and Programs.

In the 1970s the African Studies Center (established in 1960) and the Asian Studies Center (established in 1962) came into their maturity as vital and nationally recognized area studies centers. They sponsored research, fostered the teaching of languages, promoted the development of undergraduate and graduate courses in a variety of departments and programs, and furthered the development of Study

Ralph H. Smuckler came to Michigan State in 1951 as a political science professor and spent several years in Saigon, South Vietnam, as part of the MSU Vietnam Project. He became dean of International Programs in 1969 and held the position until 1991. His book *A University Turns to the World* (MSU Press) is a rich account of his leadership and the growth of international programs and contributions of MSU expertise to other countries. Courtesy of Michigan State University Archives and Historical Collections.

Abroad programs. Most importantly, these centers (and the others that developed in International Programs) brought together scholars from various disciplines in a concentration of expertise that brought them Title VI support and resources from grants and foundations. As Ralph H. Smuckler, dean of International Programs from 1969 to 1990, notes, the African Studies Center was frequently ranked first nationally because of its productive and influential faculty, which included Professors Ruth Simms Hamilton (Sociology), Harold G. Marcus and David Robinson (History), John M. Hunter and Harm J. de Blij (Geography), Michael Bratton (Political Science), and Carl K. Eicher (Agricultural Economics) (Smuckler 78–79). Such clusters of excellence had a different kind of analytical and explanatory power than, say, Henry Blosser and his team at the Cyclotron, but they were no less important in terms of their contributions to knowledge and understanding of conditions and developments.

MSU and Africa

Michigan State's connections and activities in Africa began with the 1958 trip of President Hannah and Dean of International Programs Glen L. Taggart to Nsukka, Nigeria, to survey the site for a new university, which would become the first fully fledged university in Nigeria and would open in October 1960 in conjunction with the country's independence from Great Britain. The decision was made by the institution's planners to make it devoted to the needs of the region and the new country with a focus on agriculture and education (Smuckler 68). Starting from scratch and working with a number of different national groups, the MSU team focused its efforts on establishing a broad and full curriculum, organization and administrative management, and physical plant. A second campus at Enugu developed when the Nigerian College of Arts, Science and Technology was incorporated into the new university.

The chief of party was Professor George Marion Johnson, an African American who had served with Hannah on the U.S. Civil Rights Commission and who was dean of the Law School at Howard University. Johnson served as vice chancellor of the University of Nigeria from 1960 to 1964, guiding it through its formative years and providing leadership of extraordinary quality. Glen L. Taggart followed Johnson and served as vice chancellor from 1964 to 1966. The project was coordinated by George Axinn, and from 1965 to 1967 George and Nancy Axinn relocated their family to Nigeria.

What made the Nigerian Program solidly successful was the dedication of the MSU resident team, which included up to thirty people who lived there with their families without most of the comforts or basics to which they were accustomed (Smuckler 68–69). Those faculty, administrators, and staff who went had to adjust quickly and make do, but did so resourcefully. In 1961 Michigan State contracted with the Peace Corps to train volunteers who would serve in Nigeria, and as Ralph Smuckler notes, "a good number of them were stationed at Nsukka, working closely with the University of Nigeria and MSU faculty" (75).

The effects of the Nigeria experience were far-reaching there and back on campus. Individuals' careers were determined and defined as well as changed. Carl K. Eicher, who was a visiting professor at the University of Nigeria from 1963 to 1966 (and later at the University of Zimbabwe from 1983 to 1987), helped to establish the Economic Development Institute at the University of Nigeria and served as director of the institute from 1964 to 1966. Eicher's over fifty year career in agricultural economics has focused on the development of agricultural research and education throughout sub-Saharan Africa (MSU Agricultural, Food, and Resource Economics). George and Nancy Axinn used their Nigeria experience to establish their mission of fostering rural development in Third World nations, and moved on from Africa to Nepal to India, working with foundations and United Nations organizations (George and Nancy Axinn International Scholarship Fund). Joseph L. Druse, who came to Michigan State as a humanities instructor in 1955, participated in the Nigeria Project from 1962 to 1964, and his papers in the MSU University Archives and Historical Collections contain valuable lecture notes for the courses he taught, as well as slides documenting his experience. He also collected a wide range of Nigerian cultural artifacts and, upon his return, donated this collection to the MSU Museum. With others, Druse helped develop a Humanities Department curriculum that by the mid-1970s included 200-level courses titled "The Cultural Traditions of Islam" and "The Cultural Traditions of Sub-Saharan Africa."

George Marion Johnson served as MSU's chief of party for the Nigerian Program, and once the University of Nigeria was established, he served from 1960 to 1964 as its first vice chancellor. He served as a member of the U.S. Commission on Civil Rights during the time that Hannah served as its chair from 1957 to 1964. Hannah persuaded Johnson to move from his position as dean of the Howard University School of Law to Michigan State. His book *Education Law* was published by the MSU Press in 1969. Courtesy of Michigan State University Archives and Historical Collections.

One of MSU's notable agricultural economists in a long history of notables, Carl K. Eicher served three years at the new University of Nigeria, where he helped establish the Economic Development Institute, and four years at the University of Zimbabwe. Professor Eicher worked to improve agricultural research and education in sub-Saharan Africa. Courtesy of Michigan State University Archives and Historical Collections.

Cole S. Brembeck, who joined the education faculty in 1955, was part of the Nigeria group that focused on both formal and nonformal education, and published major works on the social foundations of education, nonformal education, and the educational systems of Pakistan, Africa, and India. He served as director of the MSU Center for International Studies in Education, which became and has remained a robust center for research, grant activity, and programs.

The success of the Nigerian Program demonstrated the flow-back benefits of committing faculty, experts, and program administrators to the project in a major way. This program went far beyond technical assistance, although, of course, it involved that. The university gained invaluable experience working with the U.S. Agency for International Development (USAID), with the Nigerian government, and with the Peace Corps. Later, in the early 1970s, MSU was involved in a Midwest Universities Consortium for International Activities, Inc. (MUCIA) project in Ethiopia aimed at upgrading the national university (Smuckler 76).

Other programs and cooperations in Africa begun to be established, and all fields from agriculture to medicine were involved. Zimbabwe became a major site, as did Sudan, Burundi, and Senegal. When President John A. DiBiaggio made his two trips to Africa, he renewed ties with universities and officials in these countries (Smuckler 76). Zambia, Mali, Mozambique, and Kenya eventually became part of the MSU-African network. Other generations of MSU experts in food policy and security, distribution and marketing, agricultural development and diversification have continued the university's research and assistance in African countries and regions, working with international aid organizations and governments as well as with USAID. Those working in sub-Saharan Africa have included John M. Staatz and Michael Weber, Agricultural Economics and African Studies, and Duncan Boughton of Ag Economics. As time and political developments have shown, change has been a constant factor in African governments, with the geopolitical map radically changed from what it was. Between independence for Nigeria in 1960 and the end of apartheid and white rule in South Africa, thirty-five years passed. In 1978 the MSU Board of Trustees, at the urging of many in the university, voted to divest the university of investments and financial interests in South Africa. That set the stage for a growing

MINUTES OF THE BOARD OF TRUSTEES, 30–31 MARCH 1978

The resolution as approved reads as follows:

RESOLVED, that after December 1, 1978, the Board of Trustees shall commence a program of prudent divestiture of its stock holdings in firms doing business in the Republic of South Africa unless the Board of Trustees received sufficient evidence of assurances that the affected firms have adopted and are implementing positive measures to withdraw from the Republic of Africa.

RESOLVED, further, that the Board of Trustees requests that the University Committee on Academic Environment in consultation with interested persons or groups establish indices of corporate policy and accomplishment to enable the Board of Trustees to reach its decision, including but not limited to: (1) no new investment in South Africa, (2) no reinvestment of profits in South Africa, (3) no expansion of facilities and operations in South Africa, (4) no new licenses, affiliates or subsidiaries in South Africa, (5) no operations in Bantustans, homelands, or Namibia, (6) no importation of technologies, processes or equipment for use by the police, military, or for social control.

RESOLVED further, that the University shall withdraw its deposits from and not invest in banks granting or renewing loans to the Republic of South Africa.

RESOLVED further, that the University shall vote its proxies in support of proposals to withdraw from the Republic of South Africa.

MSU relationship with South Africa, and a new set of connections and relationships that have proved to be as vital and significant as the ones established during the Nigeria Program in the 1960s.

In the 1970s the number of MSU courses focused on non-Western societies and cultures expanded greatly and richly. The majority of students took their core courses (writing, natural science, social science, and humanities) in what was designated University College. In the Humanities Department of University College, students could take courses on the cultural traditions of China, or India, or Japan, or Islam, or sub-Saharan Africa. Students could take a "Survey of Sub-Saharan Africa" or a "Cross-Cultural Relations in the Modern World" course. In Political Science, students could take courses on African politics or on political institutions and behavior in East and Southeast Asia. A network of interdisciplinary courses was developed, and this fuller internationalization of the curriculum brought new faculty to campus as well as provided a growing group of international students with the opportunity to study their own cultures and societies.

Also bringing international and national attention to MSU was a Rockefeller Foundation grant to fund summer humanities institutes

David D. Anderson received a PhD in English from MSU in 1960, and while teaching in the Department of English and then in the Department of American Thought and Language became a nationally recognized scholar in American literature and the founder of the Society for the Study of Midwestern Literature and its publications. He published 37 books and hundreds of articles as well as creative writing. As chairman of the Humanities Coordinating Committee of the MSU Humanities Institute, he coordinated Rockefeller Foundation–supported summer humanities institutes on campus aimed at introducing non-Western materials into the curriculum. Private collection.

for faculty in 1975 and 1976, with a focus on the wider introduction of non-Western materials and courses into the curriculum. The institutes were coordinated by Professor David D. Anderson, who became chair of the Humanities Coordinating Committee of the MSU Humanities Institute in 1974 and who had twice been a Fulbright professor to Pakistan, in 1963–64 and 1969–70. Prominent artists and writers from non-Western nations were invited to campus as speakers for the institutes. Four campus-wide symposiums were held in April and May 1976 with such titles as "The Golden Age of Islamic and Jewish Culture" and "Images of Man."

New Groups and Developments

Wharton's presidency coincided with the development of a number of advocacy and identity groups that formed associations so as to consolidate strength and present a united voice. These developments came out of the ferment of the civil rights movement as well as the radical antiwar movement. Change—whether it was a willingness to change or change forced by confrontation—was the desired order of the day for those who saw institutions, laws, social and economic structures, and inflexible leaders as needing reform and, for some, even revolutionary transformation.

Higher education was one of the institutions that came under scrutiny and experienced a series of challenges on a number of fronts. During the Vietnam War, the university was criticized for being part of the military-industrial complex with its government-directed contracts and research, or it was faulted for its unwillingness to take an institutional stand on the continuation of the war and to condemn it on moral and ethical grounds.

Race and race relations were another area where the university was found wanting. In 1965 black students were 4.5 percent of the total enrollment in American higher education, and by 1973 black students constituted 7.3 percent and numbered almost 800,000 students nationwide. Ibram X. Kendi has termed this the period of the "Black Campus Movement," and he has shown how black student requests necessarily turned to demands and protests, which were met with repressive measures as well as with reforms (Rogers).

As more black students entered MSU and became more visible and responsible for the success of athletic programs, issues and concerns came to the fore. The issue of black cheerleaders and the so-called Wilson Hall cafeteria "crisis" have already been discussed. However, the concerns of black students went far beyond these specific matters and had to do with the actual instances of racism and/or discrimination experienced by black students on campus; the lack of curriculum reflecting the African American experience and contributions; the relatively small number of black professors and administrators, and of employment opportunities; and the need for advising, tutoring, and counseling to meet their specific needs.

The MSU Black Student Association (BSA) was organized in the mid-1960s to address these issues and to provide racial solidarity. In 1968 the BSA leaders met with the administration of the Department of American Thought and Language, which agreed to require a text on black studies in each of the three quarters of the first-year writing requirement, an agreement that became part of the department's regular reading list. Students would read primary historical documents of the black experience as well as works by such noted writers as Frederick Douglass, W. E. B. Du Bois, George Washington Carver, Malcolm X, Richard Wright, Ralph Ellison, and others. In his *A University Turns to the World*, Ralph H. Smuckler recalls how the African Studies Center became a target for demonstrations and sit-ins because black student leaders believed that the teaching about Africa was from "a biased and white racist perspective" (77–78). What happened was that the African Studies Center clarified its mission and developed "a regular relationship with faculty and students who were interested" in the possibility of the development of a Black Studies Program (78). The Black Student Association continued to press aggressively for changes throughout the 1970s and took what others saw as overly militant and radical positions with sometimes sweeping, condemnatory rhetoric. Looking back on it, one sees that it was part of the tug and pull occurring in the university over minority rights and treatment. On its own turf and in the context of the academic culture, the civil rights movement was played out, as were identity politics. There was much to learn from this process, even though at times it was contentious and confrontational as well as seemingly irresolvable.

Another group asserting its voice comprised students of Chicano background. The first issue, which brought out concerned students demanding to speak at a Board of Trustees meeting, had to do with the classification of some Chicano students as out-of-state because a determination on their status as Michigan residents seemed difficult to make. At their 21 April 1972 meeting, the Board of Trustees developed a policy statement and process. A student would be considered a Michigan resident "if the parent or legal guardian of a minor student or a student who has reached his majority has been employed as a migrant worker in Michigan for a minimum of 2 months each year for 3 of the past 5 years" with "proof and verification of employment." This eligibility formula allowed for the usual length of migrant-worker seasonal employment and the fact that such employment might not be possible or available each year. Another issue was university lettuce purchases in light of a national boycott against certain companies in California and Arizona. Three trustees put forth a resolution that MSU observe this boycott except for the lettuce harvested under union labels. The motion failed by a tie vote, 4-4.

At the same time that the Black Campus Movement for students developed, a slowly increasing number of black faculty came to MSU and formed the core of what would become the Black Faculty Association and a truly remarkable generation of black leaders on and off campus. Some of them, like William Harrison Pipes (American Thought and Language and University College) and Irvin E. Vance (Mathematics), were already established. Pipes, who earned his PhD at the University of Michigan in 1943, was the foremost national authority on the rhetoric and traditions of African American preaching. Vance developed the MSU Inner City Mathematics Project and published an influential and widely used study of pedagogy for algebra and geometry teachers in 1970. Professor James B. Hamilton (Chemistry) and Professor Ruth Simms Hamilton (Sociology) joined the faculty in 1968. James Hamilton's contributions to the university would include cofounding with Judy K. Gentile the Office of Programs for Handicapper Students in 1972, the promotion of the Federal TRIO Programs and other educational opportunity programs to develop research and data to support programs and services for low-income and first-generation students, and leadership as assistant provost. Ruth Simms Hamilton was a professor of sociology and affiliated

LEFT: Irvin E. Vance joined the Department of Mathematics in 1966 and was selected by the Black Student Association as cochair of the committee that investigated the complaints of black students regarding discrimination in the Wilson Hall cafeteria, resulting in a 72-hour takeover of the facility. Professor Vance directed the MSU Inner City Mathematics Project, as well as obtained funding for a number of projects focused on math learning in the Detroit Public Schools.

CENTER: James B. Hamilton joined MSU in the Department of Chemistry in 1968, as did his wife, Ruth Simms Hamilton, who was a sociologist. With Judy K. Gentile, he cofounded the Office of Programs for Handicapper Students, and as assistant provost, he did important work on minority and first-year student retention as well as academic support programs. His 1995 autobiography, titled *What a Time to Live*, describes his career and his last years living with amyotrophic lateral sclerosis. Courtesy of Michigan State University Archives and Historical Collections.

RIGHT: Ralph W. Bonner joined the faculty of the School of Criminal Justice after completing a PhD in MSU's College of Social Science in 1977. He became the director of Affirmative Action, Compliance and Monitoring, and later director of the Department of Human Relations. His in-service workshops on affirmative action and diversity goals were important to all administrators. Photos courtesy of Michigan State University Archives and Historical Collections.

with the Urban Affairs Programs, the African Studies Center, and the Center for Latin American and Caribbean Studies. Her work focused on the African Diaspora, and she was one of the leaders in interdisciplinary studies on campus. Robert L. Green came out of the Educational Psychology program at MSU, earning his PhD in 1963, and became the first black dean at MSU when he was appointed head of the College of Urban Development in 1972. Green was strongly supported by both Walter Adams and Clifton R. Wharton Jr. and he was one of the most outspoken of the black faculty on campus, unafraid of taking what some would see as a radical position on civil rights and affirmative action. Ralph W. Bonner (Criminal Justice) became director of Affirmative Action, Compliance and Monitoring and influenced several generations of administrators by educating

LEFT: Florence Harris graduated from MSU in 1971, joined the Office of Supportive Services, and became its director from 1979 to 2000. She served as an influential advocate for accessibility and academic-support programs, and she was a key link between MSU and inner-city schools and students of low-income families. Courtesy of Michigan State University Archives and Historical Collections.

CENTER: Ruth Simms Hamilton came to MSU in 1968 and joined the Department of Sociology along with her husband James B. Hamilton, who was appointed in the Chemistry department. She served as director of the African Diaspora Research Project from 1987 to her death in late 2003 and planned an 11-volume series on the African Diaspora. She was a core faculty member in the African Studies Center and Center for Latin American and Caribbean Studies, an energetic teacher of courses on comparative race relations and topics of inequality, Third World urbanization, and world diasporas. She was known as a generous mentor and scholar who loved teaching and connecting with students. Michigan State University Press.

RIGHT: Judy K. Gentile was one of the first wheelchair users on campus as an undergraduate student, and she was a strong activist for campus-wide accessibility and accommodations for students with disabilities. She became the first director of the Office of Programs for Handicapper Students in 1972, and for twenty-one years led the unit in its commitment to providing resources and services that promote academic success and access for disabled students. The atrium garden in the east part of the office wing in Bessey Hall is named in her honor. Courtesy of Michigan State University Archives and Historical Collections.

and guiding them in the institution's goals of affirmative action, and doing so with a positive and supportive approach that served these goals well. Florence Harris, who started with the Office of Supportive Services as a graduate, eventually became director from 1979 to 2000 and fostered the development of the College Achievement Admissions Program (CAAP). She became a key link between the university and inner-city schools and low-income students, and then a source of support for these students in their transition to MSU.

Black leadership at Michigan State developed in the athletic program, but not as fast as it needed to and not to the degree it was needed as coaches recruited more talented black athletes. At issue was the complete absence of black coaches and an apparent lack of interest in hiring any. Militant black students and their organization (the Black Student Association) took the case to the public and to the Board of Trustees. Recruiting and playing black athletes was not enough. A "white" institution could not continue to benefit from talented athletes, as MSU clearly had done, without including black professionals in its ranks of administrators, coaches, professors, and staff. Reality had caught up with MSU. It had moved forward on the racial front as far as recruiting and playing black athletes without providing the beginnings of a changing racial face institutionally. Black athletes and students needed black advocates, spokespersons, academic counselors, mentors and mediators, and individuals with standing and position in the university community.

In April 1968, Don E. Coleman joined Coach Hugh "Duffy" Daugherty's staff as an assistant coach. As a tackle on the MSC teams from 1949 to 1951, Coleman emerged as a premier national player due to his quickness and blocking skills against opposition players who frequently outweighed him by 30 to 50 pounds. In 1951 he was Michigan State's first unanimous All-American football player and its first black All-American. From 1952 to 1954 he served in the U.S. Army, including a year of service in Korea. Instead of pursuing a professional football career after his military service, he returned to his hometown of Flint, Michigan, and became a teacher and principal at Flint Central High School.

As a two-way star lineman for three seasons from 1949 to 1951 on the Spartan football team, Don E. Coleman was the first black All-American at MSC and a member of the national championship team of 1951. He returned to Michigan State in 1968 after serving in the U.S. Army in Korea and working as a teacher, coach, and counselor in the Flint Public Schools. After his one year as an assistant football coach, he served as an administrator of various minority-student support programs for more than twenty years. Courtesy of Michigan State University Archives and Historical Collections.

Coleman's hiring was a response to growing unrest among a group of black athletes who were threatening to boycott all sports in protest against the university's unresponsiveness and apparent inability to recognize a situation that had been many years in the making. When Coleman joined the football coaching staff, he had effectively been disconnected from football for fourteen years, and he joined a staff and team coming off a 3-7 record in 1967, which was a sharp drop-off from the 1966 team that had won nine and tied one (the 10-10 "Game of the Century" against Notre Dame that concluded the season). After ten months as an assistant coach, Coleman resigned and took a position in the residence hall program. In 1971 he completed a PhD in the Department of Administration and Higher Education with a dissertation titled "The Status of the Black Student Aide Program and the Black Student Movement at Michigan State University." Starting in 1968 Coleman began an administrative

Jim Bibbs was a world-class sprinter at Eastern Michigan University from 1949 to 1951 and turned to coaching high school track in the Detroit school system and then in his hometown of Ecorse, Michigan. He founded the Detroit Track Club and worked with amateur runners. From 1968 on as a coach at MSU, Bibbs's sprinters brought excitement and press coverage to his teams wherever they competed and succeeded. In 1977 he became the first black head coach in MSU history and remained head coach until his retirement in 1995. Courtesy of Michigan State University Archives and Historical Collections.

career at MSU that took him to assistant director of student affairs, director of the Minority Comprehensive Support Program of the College of Osteopathic Medicine after 1974, and assistant dean of the Graduate School. He retired in 1992 at age 64 due to heart problems. Like Jacweir "Jack" Breslin, Don Coleman achieved recognition as an honored and celebrated athlete and then made MSU a place to shape a career and become a campus leader.

With less fanfare and media attention than Coleman received, Jim Bibbs was appointed an assistant track coach in 1968. He had no connection to MSU, having earned All-American recognition as a sprinter in the 100 and 220 yards at Eastern Michigan University and led his teams to three consecutive conference titles. He taught physical education and coached track in the Detroit and Ecorse school systems from 1959 through 1967, building a successful program at Ecorse, Michigan, and working with the Detroit Track Club, the Detroit Amateur Athletic Union (AAU) club, and the U.S. Women's Track Team. Athletic director Clarence "Biggie" Munn called Bibbs and offered him a position, and after Bibbs was convinced the offer was genuine, he accepted and began what would be a twenty-seven year career at MSU.

Bibbs was a consummate sprinters' and speed coach who taught techniques with one-on-one intensity and motivational psychology. Once he found out what performance level an athlete was capable of, he worked with her or him to set goals and develop a program for achieving them. Early in Bibbs's career he was fortunate to coach the two fastest outdoor and indoor sprinters in MSU track history: Herbert Washington and Marshall Dill, both members of the MSU Athletics Hall of Fame. Washington was a four-time All-American from 1969 to 1972, won seven Big Ten titles, was a National Collegiate Athletic Association (NCAA) indoor champion in 1970 in the 60-yard dash, and tied or broke the world record in the 50- and 60-yard dashes a number of times. Dill was All-American in 1972 and 1973, was eleven-time Big Ten champion, won the 1973 NCAA outdoor 220-yard dash and two years straight in the outdoor 100-yard dash. In the indoor 300-yard dash, Dill won three straight conference titles. These two remarkable athletes brought excitement and recognition to MSU with their record-setting performances. In addition to Washington and Dill as well as other sprinters, Bibbs worked with female sprinters, such as Karen Dennis and Judi Brown Clarke. Whoever had talent and potential, male or female, received Bibbs's attention to their style, technique, and mechanics. Judi Brown Clarke, an NCAA champion and 1984 Olympic silver medal winner in the 400-meter hurdles, described Bibbs as a "life coach" who helped her and others set track goals that were transferred into professional and career goals ("MSU Athletics Hall of Fame Class of 2010: Jim Bibbs"). After he retired from MSU in 1995, he continued as a volunteer track coach at East Lansing High School and was a volunteer instructor of health and physical education at the MSU Black Child and Family Institute. No other coach in any sport at MSU coached as many All-Americans as Jim Bibbs. Like Don E. Coleman, Bibbs was a highly respected individual who had been a talented and successful college athlete, who had first worked in the public school systems, and who was called to Michigan State at a critical time when black leadership was needed in the university community.

Clarence Underwood came to MSU in 1955 fresh out of his service in the U.S. Army paratroopers, arriving in Lansing by train with his wife Noreese and their three-week-old daughter. He quickly learned that rental of an apartment in East Lansing near campus was impossible due to the fact that he was black. What he had anticipated would be a receptive campus for a black veteran turned out to be anything but that, as he reveals in his autobiography, *Greener Pastures*. Faced with blatant segregation and racism, Underwood stayed and pursued his degree in physical education with the goal of being a high school coach. His career at MSU began in 1969 when he was hired as an assistant ticket manager. He worked for the Michigan Department of Education from 1970 to 1972, but came back to MSU in 1972 as assistant athletic director for academic services. He was responsible for academic counseling of each of the seven hundred student-athletes, finding tutors, and developing support services programs. By 1982 he had earned a PhD in the MSU Department of Administration and Higher Education with his dissertation titled "An Investigation into the Values of Selected Football Players and Nonfootball Players at Michigan State University as Determined by the Rokeach Value Survey Instrument." In 1984 the Michigan State University Press published Underwood's *The Student Athlete: Eligibility and Academic Integrity*, a virtual handbook of best practices and bad practices for

At age 22, Clarence Underwood came to East Lansing in 1955 as an undergraduate after two years of service in the U.S. Army. He worked at MSU for three different periods of time in various roles related to athletics, the third period including his service as athletic director. He is known and respected for his integrity, clear sense of purpose, and high standards for the athletic program and its athletes. Courtesy of Michigan State University Archives and Historical Collections.

athletic department administrators and academic advisory personnel. He left MSU again, this time for a period of eight years, to serve as deputy commissioner for the Big Ten. In 1990 he returned to MSU again, and in his last three years he served as athletic director.

Underwood's success at MSU—from his beginnings in 1955 as a 22-year-old army veteran starting out as a freshman while married and with his first child to his retirement as athletic director—is a story of persistence, hard work, dedication to whatever job he held, adherence to high standards and principles, and ability to survive loaded political situations. He talked candidly and honestly with student athletes to make them aware of their responsibilities in the classroom and stressed the importance of earning their degree. His greatest pride has been not in his own achievements but rather in the student-athletes who have gone on to be productive citizens, professionals, and family people. What Don Coleman, Jim Bibbs, and Clarence Underwood brought to their positions and careers at Michigan State were experience, maturity, a commitment to bettering society by small-scale individual acts, and a dedication to an institution that could, at its best, foster individual development and racial understanding needed by administrators, faculty, staff, and community.

These individuals came to prominence as leaders who advanced a culture of improving race relations and affirmative action. Much of the work they did went on behind the scenes of their official roles, such as mentoring and advising black students, serving to resolve conflicts and issues informally, influencing white colleagues through actions and conversations, playing roles and making contributions in the community. This is not to say that their own situations were always easy or that they found ready success and acceptance. Well into the early 1960s, it was hard for black faculty to find housing in East Lansing, and that hurt the university in recruiting black faculty. However, what is evident is that the black faculty who came to MSU and stayed (or stayed on because they had been graduate students here) accepted a role of leadership and the challenge of making the campus a place of increasing equality and racial diversity. They influenced others by their persistence, their refusal to accept halfway measures, and their dedication to a goal. The social and ethical maturation of the university was in many ways dependent upon their commitments.

The College of Urban Development was approved by Board of

Trustees action on 19 May 1972, and on 16 March 1973 the board approved the establishment of the Department of Racial and Ethnic Studies and the Department of Urban and Metropolitan Studies as joint creations of the College of Urban Development and the College of Social Science. The courses and curriculum for the two departments became operational in the 1974 catalog. The Racial and Ethnic Studies curriculum was not a black studies program as such, and in fact courses on American Indians, Chicanos, other minorities, and women were part of the offerings. The curriculum expanded to include courses on human rights in the modern world, urban housing problems of minorities, ethnic groups of Michigan, human rights violations in the contemporary world, and housing policies in selected industrialized countries.

Professor Robert L. Green was dean of the College of Urban Development (CUD) from 1972 to 1981, after serving as director of the Center for Urban Affairs. During his graduate studies at MSU, he served for a year with the Southern Christian Leadership Conference (SCLC) and worked with Martin Luther King Jr. Just before becoming dean, Green served as a visiting lecturer at Hebrew University in Jerusalem and at the University of Nairobi in Kenya. His research and publications ranged across the whole field of race and educational reform. He coauthored key reports on the Detroit Police Department and the desegregation of the Kalamazoo Public Schools. He was a national expert on urban educational reform, pernicious effects of discrimination on urban minorities and the poor, and the development of effective learning programs for disadvantaged students to increase achievement. He also published a series of popular biographies on Louis Armstrong, Perry L. Julian, Daniel Hale Williams, Benjamin Banneker, and Charles Richard Drew to provide young black and white readers with stories of talented and successful black Americans. He understood and studied the challenges faced by minority students in college. In all his efforts, Professor Green emphasized political action and the need to organize and assert power directed at needed changes and reforms. For over twenty years he was an influential presence and voice on campus, as well as an influential educator at the national level.

However, by 1984 the College of Urban Development and the two new departments were gone—eliminated by the budget cuts

Robert L. Green received a PhD in educational psychology from MSU in 1963 and held appointments from 1960 to 1983, including dean of the College of Urban Development created in 1972. Green was a prominent campus activist for civil rights and affirmative-action hiring programs as part of a group of important black faculty and administrators that turned the university toward greater racial diversity and a larger public commitment against racism and discrimination.
Courtesy of Michigan State University Archives and Historical Collections.

forced by the financial crisis in 1981–82. In President Walter Adams's December 1969 commencement address, he stated: "Now again we face a major challenge—the crisis in the long neglected urban centers of our society. In order for the University to remain the same—to serve the purposes of the land grant philosophy which has been our central value system from the beginning—we must change because our society has changed, the world has changed" (Adams 238).

The new college and departments were part of the change Adams and Wharton believed necessary and incumbent upon the university: to address the problems and challenges of urban society, which meant talking about racism, discrimination, poverty, unequal education/opportunities, housing, and so forth. The university needed to be connected to Lansing, Flint, Detroit, and Benton Harbor. The larger, long-term questions were weighty. How long would this commitment need to be maintained to make a difference? What additional resources were required? Was the university capable of being an agent of change, and how would its traditional mission be changed with a focus on urban centers? Was the university capable of sustaining such an effort and could it change in the ways required by such a new direction? The answers would take some time in coming and were, in the end, shaped or determined by economic necessity and the need to make a "continue or stop" decision in 1980–81 regarding programs that were not yet a decade old.

Women Faculty and the Case of the College of Human Ecology

The greatest single concentration of women faculty of Michigan State was, of course, in the Division of Home Economics, which in 1944 became the School of Home Economics and then, beginning in 1970, the College of Human Ecology. A snapshot of the faculty in 1949–50 indicates ninety-four women serving as faculty or support personnel, such as lab technicians and research assistants, graduate assistants, extension specialists, or food and dormitory directors. The Library had twenty-five women on its staff in 1949–50, and the Physical Education, Health and Recreation for Women section had nineteen faculty.

Marie Dye came to Michigan Agricultural College in 1923 with a PhD from the University of Chicago, became dean of the Division of Home Economics in 1930, and served as dean for twenty-eight years until her retirement in 1957. Her work focused on nutrition research and on the teaching of home economics at the college level, and in her retirement she wrote a history of home economics at the University of Chicago, published in 1972, two years before her death. Courtesy of Michigan State University Archives and Historical Collections.

Historically, the Food and Nutrition area was the strongest in terms of reputation and personnel. In 1949–50 there were five professors in that section, including Marie Dye, the School's dean, who in 1923 had been the first woman with a PhD (University of Chicago) appointed to Michigan State. Dye became dean in 1930 and served in that role until the year before her retirement in 1957. Food and Nutrition was such a strong department that in 1949 Edith Holloway Nason was appointed to it as a full professor at the salary of $6,500 a year. An important thing to note is that the School of Home Economics was a place where women faculty could move through the ranks and become full professors, where women at the highest ranks had doctorates, and where research and published scholarship gave them national visibility and recognition as well as brought them grant support. The School of Home Economics offered master's degrees in all four of its areas and a doctorate in food and nutrition. In 1949–50 it supported over ten graduate assistants. It carried out extension

Jeanette A. Lee came to Michigan State in 1937 as an instructor in foods and nutrition, and retired in 1971 after seven years of service as dean of the new College of Human Ecology. She led the college through a self-evaluation and consideration of its future role, which resulted in a transformed curriculum and new mission. Her concern for documenting the history of the college resulted in the establishment of a rich archive for the third oldest college at Michigan State. Courtesy of Michigan State University Archives and Historical Collections.

programs for women and girls in rural areas and the cities, and the faculty and staff operated the Spartan Cooperative Nursery School.

The critical turning point for the College of Home Economics came in the late 1960s when Dean Jeanette A. Lee, who became dean in 1964 after serving as assistant dean to Marie Dye for many years, led the faculty in a study of the college's role and direction as well as the decision about a new name. The 1960s and the early 1970s were a decade of almost continuous calls for curriculum reform and revision, especially curriculums that seemed time-bound or too traditional. With Home Economics, a perception was that it reinforced the home as a "separate sphere" for women, thus limiting their choices and options, and that it was a carryover from agricultural times. However, home economics had been changing and evolving over the years, but had been stuck with a name or popular image that many did not look past to see the realities. In 1970 the college became the College of Human Ecology, thus escaping the designation of the home and the economics of home management. Four new departments were established: Human Environment and Design, Family and Child Sciences, Family Ecology, and Food Science and Human Nutrition. The curricular emphasis shifted to larger and more inclusive categories and to the study and consideration of complex relationships of individuals to everything that defines and sustains life, society, and culture. The name change and reorientation were certainly in step with the larger ecology movement that stressed land use, preservation of ecosystems, food production, and harmony with natural cycles. This was part of a larger movement to integrate knowledge and direct it toward the well-being of human lives, societies, and cultures. What had been a traditionally and historically defined or delimited area (home economics) now became several areas with ever expanding and overlapping boundaries.

Two things happened with the changes in the college's name and its departments. The Food Science and Human Nutrition department grew to a complement of 111, which included nineteen full professors, eight associate professors, and forty-seven graduate-student teaching or research assistants. This one department was larger than the other three departments combined. Second, Lois A. Lund, who had been serving for four years as associate dean of the College of Agriculture and Home Economics at Ohio State, came to MSU in 1973 as the

As dean of the College of Human Ecology from 1973 to 1985, Lois A. Lund (*right*) presided over a college with an expanding enrollment and overall program improvement that gained the college a ranking of sixth nationally in 1985. From 1985 until her retirement in 1996, Lund returned to a professor's role and helped establish an undergraduate major in food science and business. Courtesy of Michigan State University Archives and Historical Collections.

next dean of the College of Human Ecology and would serve as dean until 1985. With her PhD from the University of Minnesota in 1966, Lund had established herself as a researcher in the field of consumer behavior regarding foods, and at Ohio State she oversaw a home economics program that had over 1,000 undergraduates and 180 graduate students (SOHP interview, 14 March 2000).

With the change to the College of Human Ecology, and early in Lund's tenure as dean, the enrollment increased by 40 percent, and by 1975 undergraduate enrollments hit a high of 2,200 with 250 graduate students. With the cutbacks in funding from the State of Michigan in the early 1970s and the beginning of a series of periodic budget crises for the university, Lund's college found its resources strained to the point where they could only manage 1,500 undergraduates. In the enrollment surge occasioned by a new name and mission, faculty had to instruct larger numbers of students as well as take on classes that necessitated increased planning time because of their interdisciplinary nature. Faculty had little time for research, and the fields had been reconfigured to demand interdisciplinary and multidisciplinary research. Lund notes that while research and publication lagged, program quality improved, and that in 1985 (the year Lund stepped down as dean) the undergraduate program was ranked sixth among 551 institutions offering a degree in home economics (SOHP interview, 14 March 2000). Lund worked hard to improve research productivity in the college, brought about a greater mix of women and men faculty, developed a college publications program that produced five books, and established significantly more undergraduate fellowships and student internships. Her twelve-year period as dean was characterized by vigorous attention to the college's needs and its steady and certain improvement.

In 1985 Lois A. Lund stepped back into the role of full professor and spent her last eleven years at MSU teaching. In her 14 March 2000 Sesquicentennial Oral History Project interview with Professor Jeffrey G. "Jeff" Charnley, she conveyed an optimistic view of the future of her college and had no inkling of what was to come. In early 2004 Provost Lou Anna K. Simon announced that the College of Human Ecology would be eliminated and its programs and faculty relocated. It was handled in essentially the same way as the earlier disbandment of University College by then provost Clarence L. Winder. Winder had eliminated University College by provostial fiat with no discussion or faculty input. Some faculty of the College of Human Ecology opposed its closing but many did not, and there was no hue and cry in the university community.

A study written by Robert J. Griffore and Lillian A. Phenice, both professors in Human Development and Family Studies at MSU, concluded that the college's fate was determined by several internal and external factors. Internally, the faculty in the college "lost their focus on a common intellectual core of ecological principles and concepts," and new faculty "did not always share an affinity for a core of ecological principles and concepts" (Griffore and Phenice). In other words, the philosophical and intellectual concepts that established the foundation of the college in 1970 did not have the hold they once did, and did not provide that cohesion and sense of direction and purpose.

Externally, Professors Griffore and Phenice believed, the college had lost the support of the central administration, which had once been favorably disposed. The two also concluded that what was unusual about the elimination of the College of Human Ecology was an effort "to eliminate all vestiges" of it. They also noted that a waning interest in ecology and less national attention to its concerns and issues paralleled declining support for human ecology programs.

There are, of course, other explanations and factors involved. It is challenging to maintain a faculty unified and cohesive in philosophy and pedagogy over time. On 17 October 1970, three and a half months after the College of Home Economics became the College of Human Ecology, the Foods and Nutrition Department of CHE and the Food Science Department of the College of Agriculture and Natural Resources became Food Science and Nutrition, a department jointly administered by both colleges. A snapshot of the faculty roster of the new department in 1981–82 reveals that four faculty who had been part of the College of Home Economics (full professors Dena Cederquist and Beatrice V. Grant and associate professors Faye Kinder and Mary L. Morr) are listed as emeritus faculty. New dynamics had been introduced with the merging of the departments of Foods and Nutrition and Food Science in October 1970. From its very beginning the College of Human Ecology was part of a reorganization.

Program reorganization and elimination have been an often painful part of Michigan State University's history that has left individuals with bitterness and often bewilderment as to decisions made, with negative feelings largely concentrated on the provost who made the call. Clearly, the College of Human Ecology attempted to do something different, to align itself with an emerging philosophy and science that sought new integrations and synthesis of the developing knowledge of all relationships. Interdisciplinary and cross-disciplinary work was demanding and required faculty to connect productively with others and learn to share credit. Dean Lund's viewpoint was that this 1970s "love affair" with interdisciplinarity and collaboration was "conceptually interesting" but did not work and was not rewarded by the university. Individual achievements remained the standard of advancement and reward (SOHP interview, 14 March 2000). She believed that once faculty figured this out, they worked independently along disciplinary lines, and the departments in the college began to

Marylee Davis received a PhD from MSU in the Department of Administrative and Higher Education in 1974 and held numerous administrative positions, including secretary to the Board of Trustees and executive assistant to the President, as well as associate vice president for governmental affairs. Her civic and community contributions were extensive and distinguished, and early in her career she was involved in establishing equal retirement benefits for women. Courtesy of Michigan State University Archives and Historical Collections.

look more like distinct disciplines. In the end, this made it easier to relocate faculty when the decision was made to eliminate the College of Human Ecology and, to some extent, accounts for the relative lack of vocal and public opposition on the part of the college's faculty. One thing is for certain. As new fields of inquiry and knowledge develop and as established fields intersect, overlap, and combine in new ways, these dynamics will be reflected in the university's curriculum and structural organization. This process has become accelerated, and it is difficult to predict what will have any kind of staying power. The College of Human Ecology's history (before and after 1970) offers a fascinating and complex study of this process.

Another group asserting its voice on campus was women faculty and staff who addressed long-standing concerns about their salaries, rates of promotion, maternity leaves, and lack of representation in the administrative ranks. The Faculty-Professional Women's Association (FPWA) became a more activist, issue-oriented group. One of the issues had to do with the unequal retirement benefits for women under the TIAA-CREF retirement program the university had adopted in 1973. After the matter had surfaced at Wayne State University, the case came before state legislative committees. Professors Elvira M. Wilbur and Patricia Ward D'Itri testified before the committees, and a law was passed mandating equal retirement benefits for women. Marylee Davis helped coordinate a statewide effort to set up an escrow fund separate from TIAA-CREF that would ensure equal retirement benefits for women. Eventually TIAA-CREF was forced into a position that resulted in a change in its policy. In May 1973 a maternity-leave policy for faculty women was established.

Many of the advances for women came about as a result of President Wharton's appointment in February 1972 of the Women's Steering Committee, charged with studying women's concerns on campus and proposing a structure that would address those concerns. The Women's Steering Committee report proposed that an Office of Women's Affairs be established with a director of Women's Programs, and that a Women's Advisory Council be created with direct access to the president. At its 27 September 1972 meeting, the Board of Trustees approved a new Department of Human Relations that reorganized the Office of Equal Opportunity Programs and placed the director of Women's Programs and the director of Minority Programs in Human Relations. A Women's Advisory Council and a Minority Advisory Council were also authorized.

Trustee Patricia M. Carrigan, elected to the Board of Trustees in 1971 and serving until 1979, was an effective and vigilant advocate for women faculty all during her term of service. For example, when the Board of Trustees agreed to release faculty salary information (without identifying recipients), she insisted that gender, years of professional experience, status in the tenure system, and term of appointment be included. She also expressed concerns about the low rate of women for tenure and promotion and status as full professors, as well as raised the issue of unequal retirement benefits for women in the TIAA-CREF system.

When trustee Don Stevens approached Walter Adams on 17 March 1969 about serving as interim president, Stevens stated that whoever was in the office would be there "at this juncture in the history of the university when rumblings of faculty and student power were beginning to make themselves felt" (Adams 23). The full weight of responsibility at this "juncture" in the university's history fell on the shoulders of President Clifton R. Wharton Jr. As many of those who worked with him have noted, he had a dignified presence and composure that carried him through challenges and times of testing. Trustee Blanche Martin, a strong supporter of Wharton, said of him: "He was fairly low key, decisive. He didn't back down too often. A lot of folks, because he seemed to be such an easy-going guy, they mistook kindness for weakness, but that was not the case. He was a strong guy. If he believed in something, he'd fight. He was a quiet warrior. Yes, he was" (SOHP interview, 11 March 2000). He had a great sense of responsibility for the university and its entire community and measured everything in terms of that largest scale. As a firm believer in the processes of analysis, weighing of options, and collective decision making, he trusted that the more groups were involved in discussion and recommendations, the clearer the best path would be. He trusted in the process of academic governance, which was, in fact, in its relative infancy and experiencing growing pains, especially in a time when multiple issues were being discussed and when various groups were contesting for changes and reforms.

In April 1975 the NCAA leveled charges against the athletic program, citing 90 alleged violations. On the surface, given the large

Patricia M. Carrigan received a BA in education from Michigan State in 1950 and received a PhD in psychology from the University of Michigan with a focus on the learning of special needs children. In 1970 she was the first woman elected to the MSU Board of Trustees, serving until 1978 and during that time becoming the first woman to chair the board. She was well known for her work on behalf of women faculty in terms of salary, advancement through promotions, and benefits. Courtesy of Michigan State University Archives and Historical Collections.

LEFT: Blanche Martin was a three-year letterman in football as a halfback and a starter on the 1957 Spartans team that finished 8-1. He studied dentistry at the University of Detroit with John A. DiBiaggio as a professor, and was influential in DiBiaggio's decision to take the presidency at MSU in 1985. As the first minority member of the Board of Trustees, Martin served from 1969 to 1985.

CENTER: After eight years as a local high school coach and six years as head coach at Alma College, Denny Stolz coached three seasons (1973–75) at MSU. When charges were made by the NCAA against the football program, after his investigation President Wharton fired Stolz and removed Burt Smith from his position as athletic director. Jack Shingleton served as athletic director for a year until Joseph "Joe" Kearney was hired.

RIGHT: Danny Litwhiler came to MSU as head baseball coach in 1964 after nine seasons of coaching at Florida State, following John H. Kobs, who had been the Michigan State coach since 1925. For nineteen seasons "Skip," as he was known to his players, led his teams to Big Ten championships in 1971 and 1979 and to berths in the NCAA tournament in 1971, 1978, and 1979. He was a great ambassador for the game of baseball and teacher of the sport, an inventor of the pitching-speed radar gun and other devices, and a developer of Major League talent. Photos courtesy of Michigan State University Archives and Historical Collections.

number of possible infractions of NCAA rules, it appeared that the athletic program, specifically the football program, was in serious disorder as far as maintaining compliance and operating within the rules. On 26 January 1976, MSU was put on three-year probation for 21 infractions. Athletic director Burt Smith and head football coach Denny Stolz (only in his third season) lost their jobs when they proved to be less than forthcoming to Wharton during the investigation. Wharton was criticized in many quarters for handling much of the probe himself, taking the responsibility for responding to the NCAA and becoming too immersed in the defense of the institution. From Wharton's perspective, it was a case of his thinking he could not trust anyone in or close to the Athletic Department, as well as his strong sense of responsibility for the image of the university.

What happened as a result of the "housecleaning" (which included basketball coach Gus Ganakas, who lost his job in 1976) was unexpected but truly remarkable. In 1978, Coach Darryl Rogers—in his third season as head football coach—led the Spartans to a co–Big Ten championship with the University of Michigan after starting 1-3 and then finishing with seven consecutive wins, including a 24-15 win over the Wolverines in Ann Arbor. George Melvin "Jud" Heathcote, in his third season as head basketball coach, took his team to a national championship in 1979, fashioning a 26-6 season record, with five of the six losses coming in the Big Ten season. Baseball coach Danny Litwhiler's team won a Big Ten title in 1979 (his second Big Ten title, with the first coming in 1971). Finally, the shadow of the three-year probation in football passed. Athletic director Joseph "Joe" Kearney (at MSU from 1976 to 1980) brought stability and consistency to the athletic program and worked smoothly with the coaches and their staffs. President Wharton's moves in response to the NCAA investigation had an outcome that resulted in perhaps the most miraculous and exciting academic year (1978–79) in Spartan athletic history.

John E. Cantlon served as provost from 1969 through 1976, and during his term the medical program expanded to four years and the College of Osteopathic Medicine was established. His research as a scientist focused on ecology and the mechanisms of biological communities, and after serving as provost, Cantlon served as vice president for research and graduate studies from 1976 to 1988, and his extensive connections in Washington, DC, aided MSU immeasurably. Courtesy of Michigan State University Archives and Historical Collections.

The Wharton Imprint and Legacy

As president, Clifton R. Wharton Jr. guided the university through a period of turmoil in the last years of the Vietnam War and through a challenging and necessary period of change and progress for faculty, staff, and students. The university became more responsive to the issues brought forth by minority students, students with disabilities, women, and faculty in general. Positive steps included an Affirmative Action program and office, new centers and directors focused on the needs of minorities and women, and the Office of Programs for Handicapper Students and the Center for Supportive Services.

John E. Cantlon, who served as provost from 1969 through 1976, was a major factor in the successes and the consistency of Wharton's presidency. Highly respected as a scientist and researcher, Cantlon worked with Wharton smoothly and easily. As Cantlon noted in his Sesquicentennial Oral History Project interview, Wharton delegated "all the responsibility and authority" Cantlon needed and held him accountable. Under Cantlon's leadership, the two-year medical

BOARD OF TRUSTEES MINUTES FOR 27–28 OCTOBER 1977

The following resolution was moved by Trustee Martin, supported by Trustees Radcliffe and Stevens.

WHEREAS, as early as 1935, the governing body of Michigan State College adopted a policy to provide equal opportunity to all students regardless of race or color; and

WHEREAS, the current Bylaws of the Board of Trustees of Michigan State University prohibit discrimination in employment or in treatment of students based on race, color, sex, creed or national origin; and

WHEREAS, since the adoption by the Federal government of laws and regulations promoting equal opportunity and affirmative action and prohibiting discrimination in higher education, Michigan State University has conscientiously sought to comply with the spirit and letter of such requirements; and

WHEREAS, the so-called "Bakke Case" now before the U.S. Supreme Court has raised concern in many quarters that an adverse decision could wipe out the concept of affirmative action and requirements that education institutions take affirmative steps to increase the representation of women and minorities among its faculty and staff; Therefore, be it

RESOLVED, that the Board of Trustees of Michigan State University wishes to go on record as strongly endorsing the nation's moral commitment to equal opportunity as embodied in the affirmative action concept and to further express its belief that the Supreme Court will recognize this commitment in its decision; and be it

FURTHER RESOLVED, that in any event, the Board of Trustees will not waver in its dedication to the principles of equal opportunity and that it will continue to take all such steps as it legally may to encourage and strengthen the representation of classes of individuals who have been denied in the past their full opportunity to participate in higher education.

Approved by a vote of 6 to 0. Trustees Carrigan and Stack were not in the room at the time the vote was yes.

program became four-year and the College of Osteopathic Medicine was established.

The most permanent reminder of the Wharton presidency is, of course, the Wharton Center for Performing Arts. Although its doors were not opened until 1982, the discussion of building a performing arts center came up in the 16 April 1971 Board of Trustees meeting, as did an all-events building. In the mix was also a new ice arena. At the 18 November 1971 Board of Trustees meeting, Richard E. Sullivan, dean of the College of Arts and Letters, and Wilson B. Paul, Sullivan's consultant, reviewed and displayed performing arts centers recently built. They proposed a facility that would have a 2,500 seat auditorium, an 800–900 seat recital hall, and a 700–800 seat theater. The probable cost was estimated at $12 to $15 million.

When the idea of a center first came up, the trustees tied the

The groundbreaking ceremony for the Wharton Center for Performing Arts (shown here with President Clifton Wharton Jr. [*left*], former president John Hannah [*center*], and MSU trustee John B. Bruff [*right*]) was an act of faith and a show of commitment that had been urged by Hannah in 1979, who had spearheaded fundraising for the facility at the request of President Edgar L. Harden. A second groundbreaking occurred in May 2008 with a 24,000 square-foot expansion aided by a $2.5 million gift from the MSU Federal Credit Union. Courtesy of Michigan State University Archives and Historical Collections.

funding for it to an all-university capital funds campaign. Dolores and Clifton Wharton were dedicated fundraisers for what was called the University Enrichment Campaign. President Wharton gave slide shows and pitches all over campus in April 1977. The dedicated effort on the part of many was unable to produce the needed funds, and in the end it was necessary to borrow money to build the Wharton Center.

Not everybody was convinced at the time that a first-class performing arts venue was needed or desirable. For many years the Auditorium, a Works Progress Administration project, was the cultural center of the campus, with Broadway shows, travelogues, and a wide array of musical events. The Department of Theatre provided a rich schedule of plays featuring faculty and student actors in the Fairchild Theatre, a separate theater within the Auditorium. Recitals were held at the Music Building. Complicating the matter was the question of whether a new performing arts center would house the music and theatre departments, and whether department programs would continue to be vital alongside the commercial and artistic interests of bringing in the best Broadway shows, classical

The Wharton Center for Performing Arts became one of the best-known places on MSU's campus, with its Broadway entertainment schedule and noted speakers. Photo by Gary Boynton.

and popular musicians and performers, and top dance companies. The inability to raise the needed funds, coupled with the necessity of borrowing money to complete the project, answered most of the internal questions. Because any overlap was eliminated in what had to be a scaled-down building, the Wharton Center was, in effect, free to develop along the lines of being a cultural and commercial magnet, able to take on the biggest and the best shows or acts and to deliver enthusiastic and large audiences for more than one hundred performances a season. The adage "If you build it, people will come" proved true. For thirty years now, the Wharton Center has been a jewel, a place as well known as Spartan Stadium and with larger annual patronage and equally enthusiastic fans.

Research and Graduate Studies

In *Research and Relevant Knowledge: American Research Universities since World War II*, Roger L. Geiger documents that of the state universities receiving $6 million or more in science development funds from 1963 to 1973, MSU ranked seventeenth out of the twenty state universities, with $7,132,000 in grants. The range of the top twenty was from $6.5 million to $11.9 million. The change in MSU's share from 1963–64 to 1972–73 was +20 percent, with the national range of percentage change running from –50 percent to +79 percent. These were federal funds made available for science infrastructure (labs, equipment, special research facilities) and research capacity. This illustrates Geiger's characterization that MSU was in the 1960s "perceived to be an advancing and promising research university" (Geiger 216).

The continuing push in research at MSU is evident in the budget figures for "recovery on research contracts" (that is, the overhead recovery). In 1970–71 this figure was $2.1 million. By 1974–75 it was $4.4 million, and in 1977–78 it was $6.4 million. These research dollars became part of the general funds available to the university. What these two sets of figures indicate is that MSU benefited reasonably well from federal development funds in science into the early 1970s, and that its research centers and individuals sought and were awarded grants at a regularly increasing level.

In terms of PhDs awarded, MSU went from a high of 633 doctorates granted in 1972 down to 504 in 1977 (Geiger 215). Geiger cites the fact that "Even at the peak of the boom in graduate study, only 45 percent of the Michigan State graduate students were full-time, and that figure declined thereafter" (216). Geiger believes that the commitment to "service and access" hurt MSU in terms of any aspirations to prominent national rankings; that is, its graduate programs met the increasing demand for doctorates and expanded, which was easier to do when over 50 percent of the graduate students were less than full-time and therefore did not require tuition and fees remission, or income and benefits from assistantships. As Geiger further notes, only limited funds at MSU were available to increase the level of full-time graduate student support, or to increase historically low professorial salaries, or to bring in "big name" scholars (216). MSU found itself increasingly in a triple bind: (1) a dependence on expanding undergraduate enrollments and increasing tuition in order to generate needed operational revenues (thus increasing the instructional delivery load at all levels); (2) a decreasing number of doctoral-level students; (3) constrained state appropriations that could not increase at the level needed to expand graduate-level support in terms of research or dissertation fellowships, assistantships and accompanying benefits, and support for field research. In 1970–71 student fees generated $29.9 million for general operating funds, and by 1977–78 student fees contributed $48 million. The effects of these factors will be discussed later in terms of the 1995 and 2010 National Research Council (NRC) rankings of graduate programs.

Campus and Local Culture

In the period from 1969 to 1977, campus culture was still largely a communal, shared experience. East Lansing had two major downtown movie theaters, and the Residence Hall Association (RHA) screened recent films on campus. X-rated films could be seen at Wells Hall on the weekend. The Midwest Film Festival, which began in the early 1970s, was well attended annually, and in January 1976 the Canadian Film Festival featured the work of the National Film Board of Canada. This was an era before VHS tapes of movies and before the shift to home viewing. Commercial films and art or experimental films were discussed widely with great interest.

Nationally prominent poets such as Gary Snyder or Richard Eberhart were regularly brought to campus by the English Department as part of their co-curricular offerings, and they read to large audiences in the Union. The Union Building cafeteria was a gathering place for people, as it offered both evening meals and a Sunday dinner that brought large crowds. Because of the lowered legal drinking age of 18, the bar scene was substantial. The Auditorium and Fairchild Theatre featured regular cultural events, with touring Broadway shows such as *1776* and *Hair* coming to the Auditorium. After the Vietnam War was resolved, a liberal and active period of culture and advocacy for change ensued. The Great Issues course and related symposiums sponsored by University College were popular with students and faculty, and in April 1973 there was a four-day conference on American foreign policy. The carryover of issues from the activism of the 1960s to early 1970s found expression in the advocacy activities of a large number of groups. The greater internationalization of the curriculum has already been noted, and in 1972 University College and the College of Arts and Letters launched their first Study Abroad program offerings. Arts and Letters would become the leading college in the university in offerings for study abroad and would maintain that position.

3

Financial Crisis and Its Impact

At the Board of Trustees' meeting on 21–22 June 1979, President Edgar L. Harden "welcomed President-elect M. Cecil Mackey and introduced President Emeritus John A. Hannah to give a progress report on the fundraising program for the Performing Arts Center." Harden had asked Hannah in the spring of 1978 to assume a leadership role in the fundraising, and as he did with everything connected to the institution, Hannah had responded to the request with zest and produced results. He was able to report that in six months in 1978, pledges had doubled from $3.3 million to $6.6 million, and that by June 1979 the total in cash gifts and firm pledges had risen to $10.6 million. In prefacing his report, President Hannah said he "was attending his first Board meeting in 10 years after attending them all for 35 years." In his presentation, Hannah compared the challenge of funding the Performing Arts Center to the "task of funding the construction of the University Auditorium four decades ago." Hannah also offered four options that the board could consider in addressing the remaining balance of needed funds, raised the possibility of naming the facilities for major donors, and suggested "a symbolic ground-breaking ceremony" to demonstrate the university's commitment to this project.

As President-elect Mackey sat and listened to Hannah's report, he was presented with the embodiment of the living history of the university as well as an example of an honored statesman and public figure. While Hannah represented a connection to the agricultural past and the institution's modest origins, he also represented the guiding hand and vision of a modern research university with ambitions to take its place as an agent of change and as a multiversity.

A Southerner born in Montgomery, Alabama, in 1929, Mackey received his BA and MA degrees in economics from the University

An economist and lawyer, M. Cecil Mackey (shown here with his wife Clare) became MSU president with unanimous support of the Board of Trustees and weathered the storms of a conflict with the MSU Alumni Association and a serious budget crisis resulting in program eliminations. He brought the first black and first female vice presidents to MSU. Courtesy of Michigan State University Archives and Historical Collections.

of Alabama. His one period of stay in the Midwest was his PhD work from 1953 to 1955 at the University of Illinois. While serving in the U.S. Air Force, he had his first of five faculty appointments, teaching economics at the U.S. Air Force Academy in 1956–57. He returned to the University of Alabama, where he taught business law while at the same time studying for a bachelor of laws degree. After being admitted to the State Bar of Alabama, he studied law at the graduate level at Harvard University. From 1959 to 1962 he was an assistant professor of law at the University of Alabama.

In 1962 he began what became a seven-year stay in Washington, DC. He started with a year's work for the U.S. Senate Subcommittee on Antitrust and Monopoly, followed by two years as director of the Office of Policy and Development for the Federal Aviation Agency, and two years as director of the Office of Transportation Policy for the U.S. Department of Commerce. Then from 1967 through 1969 he served as assistant secretary for policy and development for the Department of Transportation. In these seven years, Mackey worked in federal agencies where he was charged with developing programs and policies related to the major transportation infrastructures of the nation, and with the economics of operating and expanding systems contributing to economic growth. He moved readily between positions that offered increasing administrative experience and responsibilities. Instead of being a scholar studying these things from the outside or at a distance, he was working from the inside as a planner and policy formulator.

In 1969 he became a professor of law at Florida State University and was now back in the academic world with a wealth of federal government experience and perspectives as well as connections. In 1971 Mackey was selected as the second president in the history of the University of South Florida. He had the daunting challenge of following John S. Allen, who served as president from 1957 to his retirement in 1970. Allen was the "foundational" president, building the institution from the ground up, and within four years from its first classes offered in 1960, Allen introduced graduate degree programs at USF. Mackey's job was to build on the foundation and progress that President Allen had established and to guide the university in its chosen focus on research and scholarship. Mackey's presidency there was from 1971 through 1976, and in 1976 he became president of Texas Tech University. He again followed a popular president, Grover E. Murray, who in ten years had overseen the school's transition from Texas Technological College to Texas Tech University and brought a law school and medical school to an expanding campus. That Mackey was selected to follow such popular and beloved presidents as Allen at USF and Murray at TTU speaks to the strengths that search committees saw in his credentials. Those strengths included self-confidence, an ability to adapt to new circumstances and challenges, versatility in administrative positions, and a combination of expertise in law, business, and economics.

As MSU trustee Blanche Martin (in his Sesquicentennial Oral History Project interview of 31 March 2000) described the search process for President Wharton's successor, a campus-wide committee of over twenty people constituted the search committee, and the process grew frustratingly long, with almost two years passing. The committee had considered M. Cecil Mackey earlier in the process, but when contacted, Mackey indicated he was not interested. Certainly, the fact that Mackey was only in his second year then as president of Texas Tech was part of his indication of non-interest. Warren M. Huff, who served on the MSU Board of Trustees from 1960 to 1977, played the role of getting Mackey to reconsider, and as Martin noted, Mackey "was well thought of by the committee." The board hired Mackey with

FAMOUS PEOPLE WHO HAVE TAUGHT AT MSU

The following alphabetical list includes individuals who taught at Michigan State for a period of time in their careers but who were notable largely after they left East Lansing.

1. **Arthur E. Adams** came to Michigan State in 1952 and established himself as a prominent historian of Russia and Eastern Europe as well as an influential faculty member of university committees. For two years from 1961 to 1963 he worked as associate policy director for Radio Free Europe in Munich, Germany. In 1970 he became dean of the College of Humanities at Ohio State University, then associate provost and special assistant to the OSU president. His major historical works were published while he was at Ohio State, and he has a drive on campus named for him.
2. **D. W. Brogan** was appointed Distinguished Visiting Professor of History at a salary of $4,000 for the months of April, May, and June 1961. This Scottish historian published seven major books on American politics and national character and came to MSU just after his *America in the Modern World* was published in 1960. In 1963 he received a knighthood.
3. **Cathy N. Davidson** taught in the English Department from 1984 to 1996 and published major studies on the rise of the novel in America and a history of reading literature in the United States. In 1996 she moved to Duke University and served as vice provost for interdisciplinary studies from 1998 to 2006. She has become a national expert on digital literacy and learning and a strong promoter of information systems and their central role in the university. She serves as a presidentially appointed member of the National Council on Humanities.
4. **Richard M. Dorson** taught in the History Department from 1944 through 1957 and then at Indiana University from 1957 to his death in 1981. At IU he became the most prominent folklorist in the United States, published eighteen of his twenty-four major books, and headed the renowned IU Folklore Institute.
5. **Erich Fromm** was appointed as professor of psychology in 1957 at a salary of $3,000 and taught in East Lansing until 1961. Four of his influential books were published during his time in East Lansing, including *Zen Buddhism and Psychoanalysis* (1960) and *Sigmund Freud's Mission* (1954). Fromm was a well-known member of the Socialist Party of America in the 1950s.
6. **John A. Garraty** was a member of the Michigan State History Department from 1947 through 1958 and then went to Columbia University, where he spent thirty-one years. A prolific writer, Garraty published survey histories of the United States, studies of specialized subjects like the Great Depression and the Constitution, biographies, and historiography. During his time at Michigan State, Garraty coauthored two books with Walter Adams that were products of international grants they shared. He is best known for his editorship of the 24-volume *American National Biography* published in 1999.
7. **Russell Kirk** taught in the History of Civilization section of the Basic College in 1949–50 and took a series of leaves in order to earn a doctor of letters degree at the University of St Andrews in Scotland in 1953. Kirk had graduated from Michigan State in 1940. After leaving MSC, Kirk became a harsh critic of Michigan State's growth and of President John Hannah, claiming the university had all but abandoned academic standards and the core liberal arts. Kirk became one of the most widely read traditional conservatives in the United States.
8. **Joseph La Palombara** taught political science and was head of the department, as well as being assigned to overseas projects in Vietnam and Pakistan in 1961. He left MSU in 1964 for Yale University and published a series of notable books on international politics, multinational companies, and Italian politics. His four major books on Italy resulted in

his being awarded medals of honor by the Presidency of the Italian Republic and the Italian Constitutional Court.

9. Surrealist painter **Abraham Rattner** was appointed artist-in-residence at a salary of $4,000 for the period of April 1957 to 30 June 1957. Although the faculty directories have him listed as late as 1967–68, he apparently only taught the one academic quarter in 1957. In 1956, Rattner's *Farmscape No. 5* was the first American painting to enter the Art Department collection.
10. **Lawrence S. Ritter** taught as an instructor in the Economics Department in 1949–50 and went back to New York City and made his academic career at New York University. He was well known in the field of finance and was the coauthor of a college text (*Principles of Money, Banking and Financial Markets*) that went through twelve editions after 1974. However, he is best known and loved for a series of classic books on American baseball history, including the 1966 *The Glory of Their Times*, based on taped interviews with the game's greats.
11. **Milton Rokeach** came to MSC and to the Psychology Department directly after receiving his PhD from the University of California, Berkeley in 1947. He taught here until 1970, but his most important work on human values and value scales came during his fourteen years from 1972 to 1986 at Washington State University. While at MSU, Rokeach published his book *The Three Christs of Ypsilanti: A Psychological Study* (1964), a study of three men suffering from delusions of being Jesus Christ.
12. **David K. Scott** came to MSU in 1979 as the John A. Hannah Distinguished Professor of Physics and Astronomy and Chemistry, and for a year was director for research at the Cyclotron Laboratory. He became the university's associate provost in 1983 and then provost and vice president for academic affairs from 1986 through 1992. In 1993 he became the chancellor of the University of Massachusetts, Amherst, a position he held until 2001. His work in studying extreme states of temperature and pressure in nuclear systems and in collisions of nuclei has been substantial and important.
13. **Glendon Swarthout** earned a PhD in English from Michigan State in 1955. He held a position in the Basic College's Department of Communication Skills while also teaching in the English Department. In 1959 he resigned from a tenured associate professor's position to leave East Lansing for Phoenix, Arizona. He would become a best-selling novelist in Arizona and noted creative writing professor at Arizona State University.
14. **Barrie Thorne** was a member of the MSU Sociology Department from 1971 to 1985 who focused her research on gender and language and patterns of male dominance. She was involved in the creation of the MSU Women's Studies Program, and in 1987 she moved to an endowed chair appointment at the University of California, Berkeley. Her influential work on children and the family as well as school resulted in *Gender Play: Girls and Boys in School* (1993), her most widely read book. An academic feminist, Thorne was part of a generation that brought women and gender into the field of sociology.
15. **Linda Wagner-Martin** taught modern American literature in the English Department from 1968 through 1988, when she left to accept an endowed chair position at the University of North Carolina, Chapel Hill. She is a prolific scholar, publishing biographies of major women writers, critical studies of specific works, and edited collections of literary criticism—a body of work totaling over fifty books.
16. **George F. Will** was appointed assistant professor of political science at James Madison College in June 1967 and went on leave in 1968–69 and 1969–70 as he established himself as a Washington, DC, observer and political columnist for the *National Review* and the *Washington Post* and later *Newsweek*. He has become the most influential and best-known conservative writer in America.

MSU trustee Warren M. Huff (*left*), who served on the Board of Trustees from 1960 to 1977, was influential in convincing M. Cecil Mackey to become president and in generating a unanimous vote for him. Mackey maintained the strong support of the board for all but the last year of his presidency. Courtesy of Michigan State University Archives and Historical Collections.

a unanimous vote, and with enthusiastic confidence in his ability to address certain issues and what they saw as unattended business. He came to MSU with eight years of experience as a university president, seven years of experience in Washington, DC, and over seven years of being a faculty member. When hired by the board, he became a professor of economics, a position he assumed full-time in 1985 when he concluded his presidency.

Unlike President Clifton R. Wharton Jr., who had to deal his entire term with a 5-3 Republican to Democrat split on the board, President Mackey had a group that was solidly behind him and satisfied that he was the best available candidate for the position. It proved to be a solid and constant support that would serve Mackey, the Board of Trustees, and the university well in the trying and difficult times to come. If the search process had its points of contention and debate (and it did), if Mackey's selection raised some doubts and criticism (which it did in the university community), none of it found its way into the Board Room where Mackey and the trustees worked smoothly and collaboratively under what would become trying times.

The first challenge that Mackey faced came from the MSU Alumni Association and its president, Jack Kinney. At its 26–27 July 1979 meeting, the Board of Trustees considered a resolution approving "the goals and objectives of the MSU Alumni Association as stated [in materials submitted to the Board of Trustees], and in return for the services enumerated in this statement agrees to provide an allocation of $80,000 on a quarterly basis for the fiscal year 1979–80." That resolution was tabled until a "specific contract proposal" could be prepared and presented to the board. Earlier, at its 21–22 June 1979 meeting, the Board of Trustees had approved the incorporation of the Alumni Association as a nonprofit organization and approved arrangements for its separation from the university effective 1 July 1979. Mackey was at this meeting as president-elect and signed the board minutes as "President." The one unresolved issue was the contract that was to specify the services that the Alumni Association would perform for the university.

This unfinished legal business gave Mackey the opportunity he wanted to put issues before the board. He was not comfortable with the separation of the Alumni Association from the university and its incorporation as a nonprofit organization with its own budget, while at the same time it continued to occupy space in the Union Building and owned all "present Alumni Association furnishings, equipment, supplies and merchandise inventory." Mackey began to float the details of a contract relationship that would make himself, two MSU trustees, and the provost members of the Alumni Association board; that would stipulate that the Alumni Association president serve at the mutual pleasure of the Alumni Association board and the university president; and that would install editorial control by Mackey over the *MSU Alumni Magazine* (Crawley 42). For Mackey, these were central policy issues as well as organizational concerns. They had to do with centralized fundraising, with concerns over checks and balances between a university and an alumni association carrying the university's name, and with harmonious relations.

The Board of Trustees never wavered in their commitment to Mackey on this issue and acted quickly to demonstrate this. At their 29–30 November 1979 meeting, the Board of Trustees passed a unanimous resolution that "identified the President of the University as its principal executive officer with responsibility for promoting, supporting, and protecting the University's interests and for managing and directing all of its affairs." Alumni relations were directly connected to the president's responsibilities and directly delegated to him. The last part of the "Resolution on Alumni Relations" undid previous actions and gave Mackey authorization to act: "Accordingly,

Jack Kinney challenged M. Cecil Mackey over control of the MSU Alumni Association in a highly public way, creating a sensational media story as well as divided public opinion. However, the trustees backed Mackey fully and he prevailed in the end. Courtesy of Michigan State University Archives and Historical Collections.

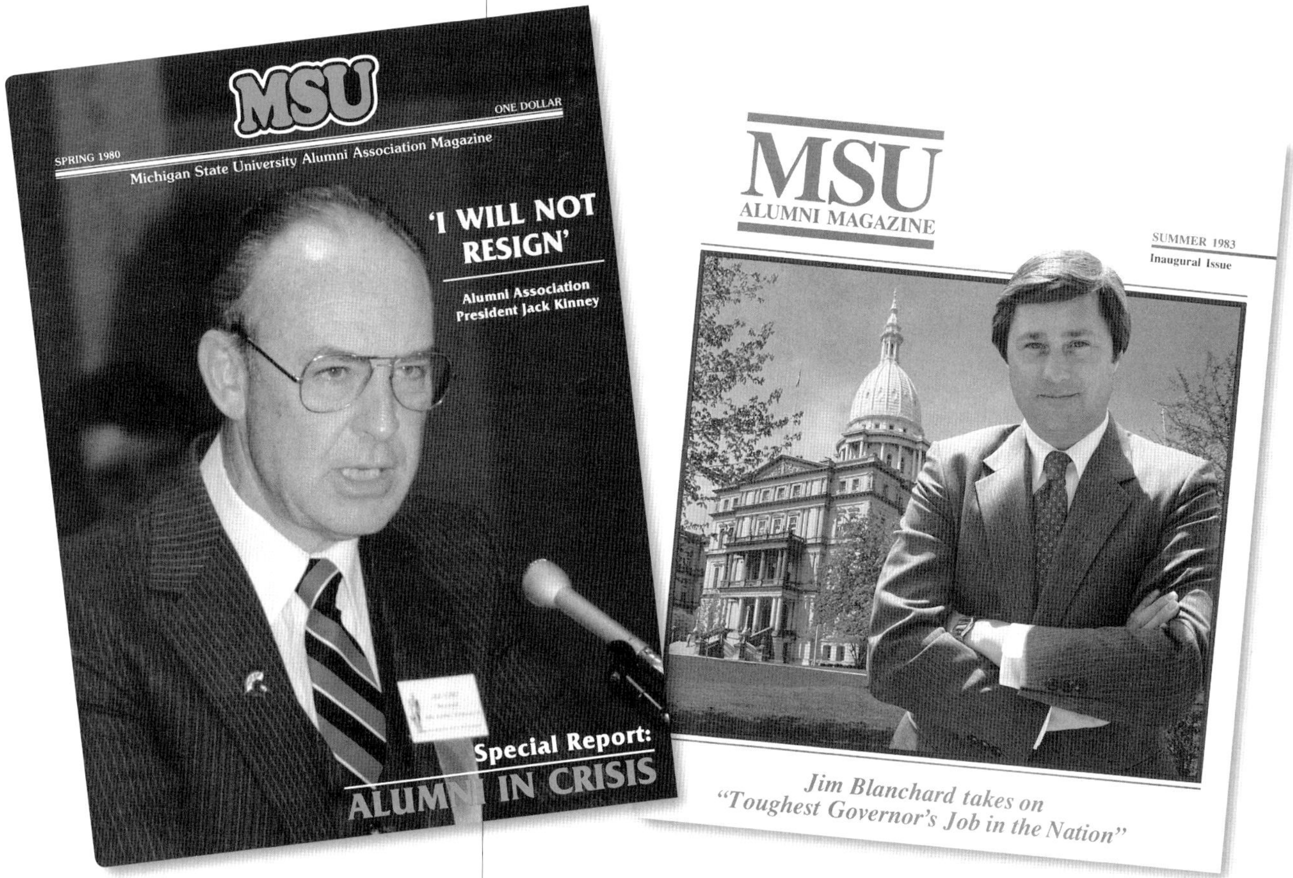

The cover of the *Michigan State University Alumni Association Magazine* for Spring 1980 featured a picture of a defiant Jack Kinney in an issue devoted to the "crisis" over control. By the summer of 1983 a new magazine in its "Inaugural Issue," edited by Robert Bao, shifted the focus to the recent election of an MSU graduate, James J. Blanchard, as Michigan's governor. He served from 1982 to 1990. Courtesy of Michigan State University Archives and Historical Collections.

any previous Board action or actions notwithstanding, the President is authorized and directed to take such actions as may be appropriate and necessary to assure that the University maintains effective direct relationships with its alumni apart from or in addition to any non-University organizations established for similar purposes" (Minutes, 29–30 November 1979).

In February 1980, Mackey asked for Jack Kinney's resignation, and Kinney refused then and later in a dramatic public way at an Alumni Association board meeting in April (Crawley 43). For those who sided with Kinney, who was a second-team All-American selection as an outfielder on the Spartan baseball team in 1949, and for those who were critical of Mackey's selection as president, there was plenty to talk about and exchange views on. Kinney added highly publicized comments to the media fire and accused Mackey of being "power hungry" with a need to control everything, as well as implying he was a bully who made threats. The feud took on something of the character of a local soap opera, but the fight was real and the stakes were high. At a budget meeting in the state legislature, State Senator Billy Huffman told Mackey directly to "call a halt to all this crap" with the Alumni Association and to stop hurting the university (Crawley 39–40).

At its meetings on 3–4 December 1981, on a 6 to 2 vote, the Board of Trustees took the next step when it withdrew "all authority from the Michigan State University Alumni Association, Inc. to represent the University in any capacity whatsoever," and when it gave President Mackey the authority and direction "to take all necessary action to implement these decisions and to plan and initiate a reorganized alumni program . . . which will emphasize and support college and school constituent groups, as well as regional clubs and a central alumni service."

John "Jack" Shingleton, appointed by Mackey as interim director of the Alumni Association, had the job of shutting down the old association and establishing the new. Shingleton had earlier served as interim athletic director when Burt Smith was dismissed from his position as athletic director by President Wharton. Courtesy of Michigan State University Archives and Historical Collections.

As the next step, Mackey appointed John "Jack" Shingleton as interim director. Shingleton's job was to close down the former alumni association and to see that the Alumni Executive Board terminated the corporation's operations. But beyond this, Shingleton responded to numerous invitations to speak to alumni clubs and to begin the process of their affiliation with, and membership in, the new organization. As the first line of contact and response from the university, Shingleton was an excellent choice as a recognizable and respected figure and as a person who understood the sensitivities involved.

Charles "Chuck" H. Webb was hired as executive director, and Mackey asked Clarence Underwood to serve as associate director. As Underwood describes it, he and Webb launched an ambitious and tireless campaign to renew the association and to overcome any of the bitterness or resentments that lingered. They both logged hours on the road to visit with alumni groups in their locations, and developed ways of connecting alumni to the university and their colleges or schools. The efforts at connection went beyond sports-related events or functions and included sponsoring alumni tours abroad or providing speakers from the university for meetings of local chapters (Underwood 145–47). Job assistance workshops were held. A new editor, Robert Bao, was brought in to publish the newly named *MSU Alumni Magazine*. By 24 June 1983, President Mackey could report that the first issue of the new magazine was in print and would be sent to all MSU Alumni Association members. Chuck Webb gave a report at the same meeting detailing all the progress that had

Charles "Chuck" H. Webb was President Mackey's choice as the new executive director of the reconstituted Alumni Association. Under Webb's leadership, the association emerged stronger and better connected to the missions and functions of MSU. Courtesy of Michigan State University Archives and Historical Collections.

been made in establishing the new alumni association. Shingleton, Webb, Underwood, and their staff accomplished an incredible task in a short period of time, launching and securing not just a different alumni association but one that was integrated into the university's mission and goals, one that stood within the structure and processes of the institution. These concerted efforts also helped turn the tide of negative talk and questioning of President Mackey's motives that had dominated the conflict. It was not just a different association, the one (as the talk went) Mackey wanted and was determined to have at all costs; it was a better association joined with the university in all areas of alumni relations.

The Budget Crisis of 1980–81 and Its Impact

The total operating budget for MSU in 1979–80 was $188.5 million, with a state appropriation of $120.3 million, $55.8 million from student fees, and $7 million from recovery on research contracts. In his discussion of the 1979–80 budget proposals at the Board of Trustees meeting of 26–27 July 1979, President Edgar L. Harden noted that the formulation of that budget had been "more difficult than ever before" because of the impinging factors of "shifting enrollments within severely limited resources, changing state budget priorities, the impact of the Headlee Amendment, and deteriorating economic conditions." The Headlee Amendment to the Michigan Constitution, passed by state voters in 1978, was a tax limitation device that established an overall limitation on total state spending each fiscal year. Harden noted that "the overall share of the state general fund budget going to higher education had decreased substantially" and that Michigan had dropped to "34th position among the 50 states in terms of relative support for higher education." He warned that the failing economic conditions "could lead to executive orders reducing 1979–80 appropriations by 1 percent or more." As a successful local businessman and former university president at Northern Michigan University, Harden saw the state budget picture clearly and understood that state funds were being diverted away from higher education to other state programs, and he estimated that amount to be $50 million, with $10 million that would have been directed to MSU. The total budget

Clarence Underwood (*left*) worked with Chuck Webb (*right*) to bring Alumni Association groups back into the fold and to create an organization that served the alumni as well as the university. Courtesy of Michigan State University Archives and Historical Collections.

of $188.5 million for 1979–80 was an increase from $173.6 million in 1978–79. The state appropriation to MSU was $109.6 million for 1978–79 and $120.2 million for 1979–80. The increases in state appropriations could not keep up with the operating costs increases, and as President Harden noted, student tuition and fees had "nearly doubled over the last several years."

The economic situation and conditions in Michigan worsened faster than analysts anticipated. In the period from 1979 to 1983, the state's population dropped 2.3 percent, unemployment levels reached 17 percent, and the state had a $1.7 billion deficit even

Before the Summer 1983 issue of the *MSU Alumni Magazine* appeared, the publication had featured stories about toxic waste on campus and the behind-the-scenes political turmoil of the MSU Board of Trustees. It appeared that the magazine was working against the university rather than for it, but that changed as the magazine found its balance and began a new era. Courtesy of Michigan State University Archives and Historical Collections.

with across-the-board spending cuts (Brace 55–57). For the 1980–81 year, Governor William Milliken had initially recommended an approximately $80 million increase to higher education, with $16.9 million that would come to MSU. However, what was a promising and much-needed increase of over 12 percent (later scaled down to 9 percent) actually turned out to be a budget adjustment plan cutting $10.2 million or 14 percent of the total budget, with those cuts having to be made in the last seven months of the 1980–81 fiscal year.

On 23 January 1981, the Board of Trustees met to discuss the budget crisis and to decide on a course of action. After reviewing the bleak budget picture (which included "a projected budget deficit of $27 million for 1981–82" to follow the revenue shortfall of $10 million in 1980–81), the board unanimously adopted the following resolution: "This Board hereby declares that Michigan State University is in a state of financial crisis which requires action on urgent financial and personnel matters in the best interest of the quality of this University. Consistent with this philosophy, the president is hereby directed to present to this Board recommendations for the resolution of this crisis commencing with its next meeting" (Minutes, 23 January 1981). At the next meeting, on 30 January 1981, eighteen deans, three vice presidents, and Provost Clarence L. Winder presented their preliminary budget proposals in a split session that totaled seven hours. On 6 February 1981, an opportunity was provided for public comments. Eighteen people made comments and statements. Some were concerned about the board's declaration of "financial crisis," fearing that such a declaration was premature, that it rushed the process of considering cuts, and that it might lead to the dismissal of tenured faculty and undermine the tenure system. At least nine of those speaking supported the view that a fiscal crisis or emergency existed, and that program reductions or eliminations were the only way to protect those programs that demonstrated academic excellence and high quality. Three of the people who spoke (Professors E. Fred Carlisle, Ruth Simms Hamilton, and Walter Adams) indicated that the members of the President's Select Advisory Committee, on which they served with Adams as chair, had advised President Mackey that in light of a "long-term financial crisis" the "University should continue to move systematically with the planning of long-range goals. . . , receiving as much input from the faculty and various groups on campus as necessary."

President Mackey then addressed the board and urged them to pass the resolution under their consideration. The resolution reaffirmed the existence and likely continuation of a serious fiscal crisis and endorsed "selected continuation and adequate funding of programs essential to the central role and mission of the University." After individual statements by each of the trustees, the board voted on the resolution and approved it 7 to 1, with trustee Blanche Martin voting no.

At the 3–4 April 1981 Board of Trustees meeting, the final acts of the budget reduction process were played out with the following results:

1. Personnel and support staff reductions in the Student Activities Office

2. Retention of the Department of Religious Studies, which had been recommended for elimination, as well as retention of the College of Nursing
3. Retention of James Madison College, with budget reductions of $70,480 recommended by the dean
4. Elimination of Lyman Briggs College, with the program retained as a school within the College of Natural Science, with reductions
5. Elimination of College of Urban Development, to be replaced by Urban Affairs Programs
6. Retention of four general education departments (American Thought and Language, Natural Science, Social Science, and Humanities), with the provision for a university-level assessment of general education in the 1980s
7. Retention of Community Development and the Highway Traffic Safety Center, with budget reduction in 1982–83 of $50,000.

Earlier in 1980, University College had been eliminated through action by Provost Clarence L. Winder, and the four general-education departments were sent to their new respective colleges. With regard to the College of Urban Development (CUD), Dean Robert L. Green had recommended a 21 percent cut for the college, but with additional graduate student support. At issue was whether college status would be maintained, and it was decided that it would not and that it should be reduced to program status.

Trustee Blanche Martin tried to save the CUD as a college, but his two motions to that effect failed for lack of a second to those motions. At the same meeting, Martin introduced a proposal that would have the university accept all the cuts proposed by the deans originally (at the 30 January 1981 Board of Trustees meeting) and that an all-university planning committee should "formulate a proposal whereby the university could live within its means without abandoning the land-grant philosophy, our commitment to affirmative action, or our unique ability to serve the people of this state in a variety of ways." Such a proposal would go through academic governance, be presented to the Board of Trustees, and be discussed in public hearings in a process that might take two to three years, according to Martin's proposal. This motion failed for lack of a second to the motion. The other seven trustees believed that the budget cuts had to be selective, even if it meant eliminating colleges and departments—which, of course, in the end it did. Certainly, the process was necessarily hurried because of the tight time frame established by the Board of Trustees. It was an uneasy period of time for everybody connected to MSU, with rumors and speculations circulating daily. However, the crisis was something that could not now be avoided. The 1959 *Report from the Committee on the Future of the University* had stated that the university should aspire to a future in which it "carefully selects the programs in which it will be distinguished and allocates its available resources in the fashion that will advance them" (5). In 1981–82 there was little time for "careful selection," but there were programs that were "distinguished" or in the process of becoming so.

The Board of Trustees took on the responsibility of protecting these programs as well as supporting the gains that affirmative action had produced. At the 3–4 April 1981 Board of Trustees meeting, President Mackey stated: "Throughout the budget process, we have kept the Board's commitment to affirmative action as a central part of our deliberations. We have worked with the deans to modify programs and personnel proposals to minimize the impact on minority and female students and faculty. While personnel decisions have not been made, we have tried to identify minorities and women who would be potentially affected by budget reduction plans." As part of the Board of Trustees' commitment to affirmative action, Lou Anna K. Simon, assistant to the president (later provost and president), prepared an impact statement that was presented at the first public hearing the board held. What was called the "Modified Coordinated Proposal" was analyzed, particularly with regard to the impact on minority and women faculty, and according to trustee John B. Bruff's statement at the 3–4 April 1981 meeting, there was impact on nonminority women holding temporary faculty positions. For example, in the Department of American Thought and Language, there were twenty-eight women faculty on the teaching roster for 1981–82 out of a department of seventy-four, with seven of them holding temporary appointments.

In their 1–2 April 1982 meeting, the Board of Trustees introduced a "Resolution of State Tax Increase," urging the state legislature and the governor "to develop and pass legislation instituting a necessary and effective tax increase." The preface to the resolution, which was unanimously approved, was written by trustee Peter B. Fletcher in the context of the "new federalism" that was returning tax revenues to the states as well as featuring an income tax cut. Fletcher argued that the tax increase in Michigan was bearable, and that in order for MSU to have "fiscal integrity" and to "remain competitive in the world of higher education," the state needed to return to its former levels of support before the 14 percent in cuts had been made.

In the 1982 state elections, James J. Blanchard, who received his BA in 1964 and an MBS in 1965 from MSU, was elected governor of Michigan. He was the first Democratic governor of the state in twenty years, and he was able to move a personal income tax increase through the Democrat-controlled legislature. With an economic recovery underway, he "restored public spending to its 1979 levels, targeting spending increases for public education, infrastructure, and economic development" (Brace 57). In 1979–80 the state appropriation to MSU had been $120.2 million, and in 1984–85 it was $151.9 million. Revenues from student tuition and fees were $55.8 million in 1979–80 and were $83.5 million in 1984–85. Another beneficial development was the authority for forward funding, which meant that the university books did not have to be closed fully at the end of the fiscal year. Funds could be held past the end of the fiscal year and moved into the next year's budget to cover ongoing projects or to serve as a "hedge" on increased costs. In the 1984–85 MSU budget there was a fund-forwarding factor of $15.1 million, or 10 percent of the total state appropriation. The forward-funding allowance encouraged efficiencies and economies and reduced rushed spending in the last quarter of the fiscal year. The full forward-funding authority offered to MSU by the Governor's Office in 1984 was in exchange for a commitment by the university not to raise resident undergraduate tuition. A new wrinkle had been introduced into the appropriations process, a quid pro quo that was as much a political bargain as an economic measure to help the university. The state personal income tax increase remained in place until early 1986, when Governor Blanchard rolled it back before the 1986 gubernatorial election, which saw him reelected and in office through 1990.

The fiscal crisis that spanned the administrations of Governors William Milliken and James Blanchard had another effect: that of bringing MSU into economic development policymaking. In 1981

Connie W. Stewart was the first female vice president at MSU, and in Mackey's administration she was responsible for relationships with the public and federal government. Her work carried over into the first two years of DiBiaggio's presidency and she left the university in 1987. Courtesy of Michigan State University Archives and Historical Collections.

Milliken created the High Technology Task Force, bringing together representatives from the financial, business, and academic communities with the goal of positioning Michigan in the "forefront of technologically oriented production" (Brace 56). President Mackey served as a member of this task force, and developments within the university and outside were reported on by Vice President John Cantlon to the trustees at the 22 October 1982 Board of Trustees meeting. The beginnings of a high-technology focus are evident with Cantlon's discussion of a developing network of interests and explorations of relationships (law, business, finance, government) needed to move into the high-technology area. Even with its downside, the fiscal crisis of 1981–82 brought about the beginnings of a greater connection of MSU (and the other research institutions) to the state's economy and its needs for future growth and health. The state's research universities were now seen as players in the active attempt to address the state's economic plight by "intervening and modifying the productive environment" (Brace 59). President Mackey served also on the Governor's Commission on Jobs and Economic Development, established by Governor Blanchard, and he was on the board of directors of the Michigan Biotechnology Institute.

In 1979 Moses Turner accompanied M. Cecil Mackey from Texas Tech University and became the first black vice president at MSU, handling student affairs and services. He served as vice president until 1992 and joined the Department of Educational Administration, helping to establish the Student Affairs Program as one of the highest-rated graduate programs in the country. He retired in 2004. Courtesy of Michigan State University Archives and Historical Collections.

President Mackey's close working relationship with the Board of Trustees was also reflected in their support for and endorsement of his selections of Connie W. Stewart as the first female vice president and Moses Turner as the first black vice president in the university's history. While there was some initial effort to raise the issue of faculty consultation and input on these key appointments, Stewart and Turner stepped into their positions easily and proved to be essential elements of Mackey's administration. These appointments signaled the beginning of the advancement of minorities and women, from the level of vice presidents down to the level of directors and chairs. Mackey and the Board of Trustees worked diligently to review, revise, and compile board policies as well as its bylaws. A regular, ongoing calendar was established for the board to review academic programs as well as to review all areas of policy.

Professor Lawrence Sommers, who was a major figure in academic governance as a faculty member and later as an administrator in President John DiBiaggio's presidency, observed in his Sesquicentennial Oral History Project interview that Mackey's "relationship with the board was, I think, better than it was with the faculty." Sommers believed that Mackey was "misunderstood" and not "appreciated by people, especially the faculty members" due to a personal style that some found "abrupt" and distant. Clarence L. Winder, who served as provost from 1977 to 1991 (two years under Wharton and the whole period of Mackey's six-year presidency), remembered Mackey as "open, direct, and organized" and found him "congenial" and easy to work with because he was "very orderly and organized in thinking about the institution" (SOHP interview, 20 September 2000). Sommers's evaluation was that Mackey "was one of the best presidents we had in terms of knowing the role of a university president" (SOHP interview, 24 July 2000).

What is important to note is that Mackey's presidency began with a crisis over the MSU Alumni Association and its status, and then with a fiscal crisis the likes of which the university had never faced. The showdown with Jack Kinney had its fallout in terms of producing critics of Mackey, and the feud spilled over into the state legislature, with vocal and harsh criticism of Mackey coming from prominent legislators (Crawley 39–42). A number of faculty believed that the declaration of "financial crisis" in early 1981 was premature and alarmist, and suspected that an underlying agenda of reshaping the university was driving developments. In both cases, the Alumni Association situation and the budget developments, sides were taken and factions emerged. Mackey had not been in East Lansing long enough to develop a loyal following, but he held the office of president by unanimous vote of the Board of Trustees. Many of those who did not know him still respected the office and recognized that the premature judgments and acceptance of gossip or rumors were unfair to a man doing a difficult job. Mackey's situation even became a ten-page story in *Change* magazine for November/December 1980, written by Nancy Crawley, a reporter and business editor for the *Lansing State Journal*.

Judgments or characterizations or assumptions about Mackey's motives were in the eye of the beholder and usually colored or slanted by the individual's relative relationship to developments. In whatever circumstance or under whatever pressures, Mackey maintained his poise and calm demeanor, was always well prepared to present and argue his positions, and was willing to pull back on issues (such as the switch to a semester system) if the timing was not right as indicated by opposition. As he moved into his third and fourth year, he became less the focus of controversy, settled into his role, and began to focus on further strengthening research and international connections. He was part of a three-week trip to the People's Republic of China in 1980, which established ties for research and exchanges following this official university mission. The year 1981–82 was proclaimed International Year as part of the 25th anniversary of MSU's International Programs (Smuckler 85–86, 151).

On 27 January 1984, President Mackey gave Board of Trustees chair Barbara J. Sawyer a memorandum proposing that the board and he "undertake the planning necessary to make it possible for me to leave the presidency of Michigan State not later than the end of the coming academic year" (Minutes, 14 February 1984). At the 14 February 1984 meeting, Mackey was ready for the entire board to learn that he believed a six-year term in office for him was an appropriate period and that he felt satisfied about the university's progress and accomplishments. Further, he stated his deep appreciation for the board's support and for their resolve during trying times: "I have appreciated personally the support from the Board, the direction it has given, and the Board's willingness to address major policy issues.

Clarence L. Winder served as provost from 1977 to 1991, two years with President Wharton and during all of Mackey's tenure as president. He saw the university through its first large-scale budget crisis and was responsible for the dissolution of University College and the relocation of its faculty. Courtesy of Michigan State University Archives and Historical Collections.

It is my judgment that there are very few Boards of other universities who could have done the things this Board did in 1980–81. It made and stuck by very difficult decisions. Those were vital to the quality of Michigan State University."

In response, and in regretful acceptance of Mackey's decision, chair Barbara J. Sawyer, speaking for the board, acknowledged the "most significant accomplishments" during his presidency, and just after that stated: "In light of these many accomplishments, the Board of Trustees deplores the recent media speculations regarding the Board's relationship with President Mackey. A careful review of the actual chronology of events will conform [*sic*] that Dr. Mackey formulated his plan prior to and independent of any of the recent media speculations. Reports and rumors to the contrary, the majority of the Board now wishes to express its continued support of Cecil Mackey as President of Michigan State University." What had once been a regular and solid unanimous support from the Board of Trustees for Mackey had now become a "majority of the Board." He still, of course, had over four months to continue to serve, but clearly politics and personalities had entered into his relationship with the board.

Lawrence Sommers came to MSC in 1950, and from 1955 to 1978 he served as the head of the Department of Geography. During four years of the DiBiaggio presidency he served as assistant provost. During his twenty-three years as department chair, Geography grew in size and prestige in terms of national ranking for its graduate program. He did the first atlas of Michigan by hand in 1977 and served as a consultant on the later CD-ROM version. He was involved in the development of the Asian Studies Center and African Studies Center, prominent in academic governance, and a major figure in international programs. Courtesy of Michigan State University Archives and Historical Collections.

Research Infrastructure and Facilities

The period from 1980 through 1984 featured the establishment and development of research facilities and resources that would substantially advance the university's reputation as a vital center for scientific, agricultural, and medical research. At the 22–23 October 1981 Board of Trustees meeting, John E. Cantlon (vice president for research and graduate studies and dean of the Graduate School) and Joseph E. Dickinson (vice president for university development and president of the MSU Foundation) reported that in 1980 gifts and grants to MSU were approximately $74.4 million, which was an increase of $26 million over the last five years and an annual increase of over 10 percent per year. Cantlon emphasized that the primary source was in the form of research-grant funds from the U.S. Government. In a time of economic downturn and resulting recession, this news of healthy and robust research, which the board heard about directly, certainly influenced or guided their decision to protect strong programs in the budget-cutting process. As Cantlon indicated in his report, the university had established an "area of strength in the biotechnology and bioresearch areas, which is demonstrated by the current activities in the medical and agricultural related programs."

On 26 September 1980, President Mackey announced to the Board of Trustees that Congress had provided $6.9 million in 1980–81 funding from the Department of Energy for the National Superconducting Cyclotron Laboratory (NSCL). A concerted and cooperative effort between MSU personnel and the Michigan congressional delegation was necessary to achieve this level of funding. By 1 November 1980, the Board of Trustees was ready to decide on the nine construction bids, with Foster Schermerhorn Barnes, Inc. getting the almost $5 million construction contract, and Commonwealth Associates, Inc. receiving the architecture contract. On 14 November 1981, the last part of the project was completed when $194,000 in two contracts was approved for the radiation-shielding doors.

Another important development was the approval by the Board of Trustees of a Continuing Faculty Appointment System for personnel hired into the Cyclotron Laboratory effective 1 January 1981. This allowed director Henry Blosser to develop continuity in his personnel and to identify promising individuals for possible appointment in the tenure system. Additionally, a department such as Physics and Astronomy could hire an individual in the tenure system with an assignment in the NSCL, as was the case with Hiroshi Toki in November 1981. David K. Scott came to MSU in 1979 as the John A. Hannah Distinguished Professor of Physics and Astronomy and of Chemistry, attracted to East Lansing by the construction of the Cyclotron Laboratory. In 1982–83 Scott served as associate director for nuclear research at the NSCL, then moved into upper administration, serving as associate provost and then provost and vice president for academic affairs at MSU from 1983 to 1992.

In 1981 the W. K. Kellogg Foundation provided a $10 million grant to support a five-year program in rural resource education at the Kellogg Biological Station (KBS) at Gull Lake. This grant, received exactly thirty years after the W. K. Kellogg Manor House and surrounding lands were transferred in 1951 to MSU, confirmed the critical role that the KBS had established for itself in the specialized areas of ecology, from microbial to plant and agriculture. After 1965, KBS became the

Provost David K. Scott came to MSU in 1979 as a John A. Hannah Distinguished Professor of Physics and Astronomy and of Chemistry and was connected to the Cyclotron. After serving as associate provost, he became provost and vice president for academic affairs from 1983 to 1992. In 1993 he became the chancellor of the University of Massachusetts Amherst. Courtesy of Michigan State University Archives and Historical Collections.

The Kellogg Biological Station (KBS) at Gull Lake has been part of MSU since 1951 and is the university's largest off-campus education complex as well as a center of specialized microbial and plant research. Its role and presence were substantially expanded in 1981 with a $10 million grant from the Kellogg Foundation. Courtesy of Michigan State University Archives and Historical Collections.

university's largest off-campus education complex as well as linked MSU to the National Science Foundation at this site. The project involved five new buildings that would create an educational complex.

On 22–23 October 1981, the Board of Trustees approved for a three-year trial period an Institute for Research and Advanced Study to be established in the College of Osteopathic Medicine effective 1 November 1981. The Institute would have seven components:

1. Carcinogenesis Laboratory
2. Neuroscience Program
3. Rehabilitation Engineering Services of the International Rehabilitation Center
4. General Research Support
5. General Advanced Study
6. Medical Training
7. Administration of Research and Advanced Study.

The goal was to combine a number of separate components into one unit and to emulate research development like that in the

Engineering Research Division, the Agricultural Experiment, and the Social Science Research Bureau.

This institute continues to function, with some modifications. The Carcinogenesis Laboratory, in its thirtieth year as of 2005, continues to specialize in research on the origin of human cancer in an effort to understand the biochemical mechanisms that can transform normal cells into tumor-producing cells. The laboratory has served as a research and training site for visiting scientists and postdoctoral research associates, graduate students, and undergraduate research assistants. The Neuroscience Program was transferred to the College of Natural Science as the lead program in the college. Rehabilitation Engineering was closed when the Department of Biomechanics in the College of Osteopathic Medicine was closed. The institute supports general research and advanced study, and is administered by an associate dean for research and graduate studies, who since 2000 has been University Distinguished Professor Justin McCormick, who also is director of the Carcinogenesis Laboratory. The history of the Institute for Research and Advanced Study Programs illustrates the process of right sizing and modifications due to program priority decisions, as well as a substantial commitment to the effective coordination of resources with a clear location of these in the institute.

In February 1982, the Board of Trustees approved the establishment of a university laboratory named the Analytical Electron Microscopy Laboratory in the Colleges of Natural Science and Engineering. The goal was to put MSU "in a competitive research position for chemistry, physics, and engineering in materials research." The laboratory would be equipped with a Field Emission Transmission Electron Microscope, an instrument that cost an estimated $468,000 in 1982.

In 1983 the Hancock Turfgrass Research Center (HTRC) was established on ten acres on the southeast corner of Mount Hope and Farm Lane. Turfgrass science became a notable research development area for the Department of Crop and Soil Sciences. With Mark Collins as its farm manager since 1983, the HTRC facility has grown to over 55 acres, with faculty from three different departments and graduate students doing research on soil fertility, feeding and pesticides, diseases, irrigation, maintenance methods, and so forth. What was unusual about the initial funding for this turf center is that golf

Professor Justin McCormick has served as associate dean for research and graduate studies in the College of Osteopathic Medicine since 2000, directing the Institute for Research and Advanced Study Programs as well as the Carcinogenesis Laboratory. Courtesy of Michigan State University Archives and Historical Collections.

The MSU–Department of Energy Plant Research Laboratory (PRL) is one of the crown jewels in university research facilities and came to MSU as a result of a nationally competitive research process. In 1984 the Board of Trustees committed $29 million to an addition. The PRL is recognized for the vitality and innovation of its research and graduate programs. Courtesy of Michigan State University Archives and Historical Collections.

course superintendents and turf contractors from Michigan helped fund its development. For one of the lowest initial investment and startup costs, the HTRC has produced substantial publicity for MSU, as well as had a positive impact on golf courses, athletic fields, and public parks and lawns all over the state.

In December 1983, President Mackey noted that the Board of Trustees "had placed as a high priority the construction of an addition to the Plant Research Laboratory" (Minutes, 1–2 December 1983). Efforts to secure matching funds from the state and federal government were not successful at that time, so alternative funding proposals were developed. By 20 October 1984, the Board of Trustees was ready to consider a bond authorization arrangement that would fund the laboratory addition as well as the Nuclear Magnetic Resonance Facility the board had approved at its 26–27 July 1984 meeting. The NMR Facility was budgeted at $2.7 million, and the Plant Research Facility at $29 million. The Plant Research Laboratory (PRL) was linked to the U.S. Department of Energy as an operating revenue source and was the locus of cooperative multidisciplinary research linking the College of Natural Science and the College of Agriculture and Natural Resources as well as the departments of Biochemistry and Molecular Biology, Crop and Soil Sciences, and Plant Biology. Like the Cyclotron, the PRL came to MSU as the result of success in intense national competition, and both facilities attracted highly talented directors and scientists: Anton Lang for the PRL and Henry Blosser for the NSCL. These two sites became venues of exciting, pioneering research and scientific innovation gained from the work of collaborative, multidisciplinary research teams.

In June and July of 1984, the Board of Trustees also approved the establishment of the Endocrine Research Center as a "formal entity" on the recommendation of two department chairs, Professor Robert G. Gast, director of the Agricultural Experiment Station, and Dean James H. Anderson of the College of Agriculture and Natural Resources. Again, this example of the joint administration of a research unit, focused on reproductive and developmental biology by two departments, illustrates the high value placed on multidisciplinary research and the university's long-standing commitment to research into the connections between animal and human health.

At its 26–27 July 1984 meeting, the Board of Trustees approved

Professors James Dye (*top*) and Anton Lang (*bottom right*) are the only MSU faculty members thus far to be elected to membership in the prestigious National Academy of Sciences and the American Academy of Arts and Sciences.
Courtesy of Michigan State University Archives and Historical Collections.

establishment of the Biotechnology Research Center, which would involve six different colleges and coordinate research efforts with the biotechnology efforts of the Agricultural Experiment Station. The goal of the center was to stimulate and increase faculty research by providing more time for research by relieving faculty of other duties, providing summer salaries, and providing support for postdoctoral fellows, as well as showcasing research in biotechnology. Earlier, the Michigan Biotechnology Institute, established in 1981 and initially supported by MSU as a private corporation, located its facilities and headquarters just off campus, establishing a close connection of a noncommercial research organization with the university.

In 1983 MSU professors Martin J. Bukovac (Horticulture) and Charles J. Arntzen (Plant Biology) were elected to membership in the prestigious National Academy of Sciences, as was Professor N. Edward Tolbert of Biochemistry in 1984. They joined Anton Lang, who had been elected to NAS in 1967, and in the same year to the American Academy of Arts and Sciences. The only other MSU faculty member thus far to be elected to both these organizations has been Professor James Dye of Chemistry.

Sports

In January 1980, athletic director Joseph "Joe" Kearney and head football coach Darryl Rogers left MSU as a team of two for Arizona State University, where Rogers would coach for four years before returning to Michigan to become head coach of the Detroit Lions from 1985 to 1988, and where Kearney would serve as athletic director for just one year before becoming commissioner of the Western Athletic Conference and staying fourteen years in that position. In 1979 President Mackey appointed Douglas "Doug" W. Weaver as athletic director, and Weaver had sole authority to appoint the next head football coach. On 31 January 1980, the Board of Trustees unanimously approved Frank D. "Muddy" Waters for a four-year contract at an initial annual salary of $47,000. In what turned out to be three seasons, Waters's teams compiled a record of 10-23, with half of those wins coming in 1981 when the team finished 5-6 with four Big Ten wins. When Waters was hired, Spartan fans wondered why a coach with

Frank D. "Muddy" Waters played fullback on the Spartan teams from 1946 to 1949 before membership in the Big Ten Conference and during the first three seasons (1947–49) of Clarence "Biggie" Munn's seven years as head coach. In Waters's seasons from 1980 to 1982 as MSU head coach, the Spartans won only 10 games and Waters was fired. He was a popular coach and remained a visible part of the MSU community for over twenty years after his firing. Courtesy of Michigan State University Archives and Historical Collections.

only small-college experience (albeit highly successful) was brought into a Big Ten program. The 2-9 season in 1982 sealed Waters's fate, although the team had been in fact competitive, losing a total of six games by seven points or less in each game. But in the end, Waters's teams lost to Michigan and Notre Dame all three seasons.

At its 2–3 December 1982 meeting, the Board of Trustees hired George J. Perles as coach on a five-year contract at a salary of $95,000 per year. The appointment was controversial because, as it turned out, it involved paying the Philadelphia Stars, a professional football team, $175,000 to buy Perles out of his contract, and because of the secret nature of the negotiations. Perles was to be paid a little more than twice the incoming salary Waters had received. Many fans said, "Why not earlier?" because rumors were that Perles had showed interest in the job after Rogers left. Others said it was about time that a "true green" Spartan had become head coach, and that the defensive prowess that the 1965–66 Spartans had featured would return, since Perles was a defensive specialist with nine years of professional coaching experience. What followed was twelve seasons for Perles at MSU before President M. Peter McPherson fired Perles in the midst of an NCAA investigation into the Athletic Department.

In his first four seasons as head coach, Perles's teams were 4-6, 6-6, 7-5, and 6-5, and Perles's record against Notre Dame was 2-2 and 1-3 against Michigan, with only six points scored in the three losses. But the next season, as every Spartan fan alive remembers fondly, was the 1987 season, with a 7-0-1 Big Ten record, an opening game win against Southern California, a Rose Bowl rematch against USC with a dramatic 20-17 win, and a final national UP/AP ranking of eighth with a 9-2-1 record. The 31-8 loss to Notre Dame and the 31-3 loss to Florida State in weeks two and three were all but forgotten as the team went undefeated (with one tie) thereafter. It was a memorable replay of the talented 1978 Spartans, who lost their first three games and then ran off eight consecutive wins to tie Michigan for the Big Ten championship.

In basketball, George Melvin "Jud" Heathcote's teams compiled a 63-26 record in his first three seasons, won two conference titles (the 1978–79 one being shared with two other teams), and captured the national championship in 1979. But the incredible combination of talent the 1977–78 and 1978–79 teams featured could not be maintained,

George J. Perles was head football coach for twelve years starting in 1983 and had his four best seasons from 1987 through 1990 with a 31-14-3 record, four consecutive bowl game appearances, and three bowl wins, including the Rose Bowl. He had a highly public conflict with President DiBiaggio over his wanting to be athletic director and head coach at the same time. Courtesy of Michigan State University Archives and Historical Collections (*Red Cedar Log* 1986).

and three losing seasons followed until the 1982–83 team went 17-13. In 1985–86 the Spartans, who were 12-6 for third place in the conference, ended up 23-8 overall and went to the NCAA Sweet Sixteen. The NCAA champion Spartans in 1978–79 had lost five conference games and finished 26-6 for the season. In 1989–90 the Spartans claimed another Big Ten Championship with a 15-3 record and made the NCAA Sweet Sixteen on the way to compiling a 28-6 overall record, the most wins for a Heathcote team in a season. In his nineteen seasons at MSU, Heathcote took his teams to nine NCAA tournaments. What he brought to the program was consistency, stability over almost two decades, and an ability to bounce back after losing seasons with strong teams. From 1986 through 1989 the Spartans posted a 39-50 record overall and 17-37 in the Big Ten. But in 1989–90 the team finished first in the Big Ten and compiled a 28-6 record, losing in the NCAA

George Melvin "Jud" Heathcote (*left front*) was hired as head basketball coach by athletic director Joe Kearney in 1976 and in nineteen years fashioned an MSU record of 339-221 with an NCAA championship in 1978–79, nine NCAA appearances, and six seasons with 22 or more wins. His teams were noted for fierce defensive play and discipline. Courtesy of Michigan State University Archives and Historical Collections (*Red Cedar Log* 1978).

regional semifinals 81-80 to Georgia Tech. Heathcote was a colorful sidelines personality, with a trademark gesture of slapping his palm to his forehead in frustration, and of course, he brought onto his staff a young assistant coach, Tom Izzo, who was destined to become the most successful basketball coach in MSU's history.

In hockey, the program benefited from the opening of Munn Ice Arena on 25 October 1974, and Amo Bessone coached his final four seasons (out of a total of twenty-seven) in this facility. In the 1975–76 season, the Spartans compiled their best record in the Western

Collegiate Hockey Association with a 20-12-0 record and lost to Minnesota 7-6 in a triple overtime WCHA playoff, undoubtedly the most dramatic and thrilling game in the history of the Munn Ice Arena. Bessone left a record of taking three teams to the NCAA championship game (1959 and 1966), with the 1966 team claiming a national championship by beating a 24-2 Clarkson team, 6-1. The 1965–66 team started the season 4-10 but fought their way to "underdog" glory.

Ron Mason succeeded Bessone in April 1979 and would spend twenty-three seasons as the head coach. When the Spartans shifted from the WCHA to the Central Collegiate Hockey Association in 1981, Mason's team won the CCHA playoff championships the first four consecutive seasons from 1982 through 1985. His teams made appearances in nineteen NCAA tournaments, and MSU claimed its second national title in 1986, defeating Harvard 6-5. Munn Ice Arena became a site for loud, enthusiastic fans in the 1980s, and tickets to games were hard to come by due to the team's consistent success. The MSU coaching careers of Heathcote and Mason overlapped for sixteen years, and both of their stays overlapped that of Perles, making this period one of the most stable in terms of the head coaches of major sports.

Ron Mason came to MSU in 1979 as head hockey coach with 289 wins and proceeded to amass 635 more for a national record 924 wins in thirty-six seasons at three schools. The success of his teams in the Central Collegiate Hockey Association helped establish the league as a national power, and he served as athletic director from 2002 to 2008 during the time of dramatic increases in revenues from sports. Courtesy of Michigan State University Archives and Historical Collections (*Red Cedar Log* 2003).

In women's sports, the 1970s and 1980s were a period of change and advancement. The passage of Title IX of the Educational Amendment of 1972 provided that neither men nor women could be "excluded from participation in, be denied the benefits of, or be subjected to discrimination under any educational program or activity receiving Federal financial assistance." While the legislation did not specifically mention sports or athletics, the Department of Health, Education, and Welfare (HEW) decided that athletic programs came under the scope of the law and that colleges had to provide equal athletic opportunities for men and women. The question, of course, was what constituted "equal," and where the funds would come from to run additional women's sports. Would this mean that certain men's sports would be eliminated or downgraded to club status in order that women's teams could be established? Was it reasonable to expect gender equity in sports by the HEW target of the 1978–79 academic year? With any pioneering national legislation comes the good and the bad, those who embrace and endorse it as progress and those who oppose it and are committed to obstructing it.

Douglas "Doug" W. Weaver was a starting center on the Michigan State football teams from 1950 to 1952, teams that went 26-1 and claimed the mythical national championship in 1952 under Coach Biggie Munn. In 1979 he became MSU's athletic director and served until his retirement in 1989. In Weaver's time as athletic director, the Spartans won national championships in hockey in 1986 and in basketball in 1978–79, as well as went to and won the Rose Bowl of 1 January 1988. Courtesy of Michigan State University Archives and Historical Collections.

Title IX implementation at MSU was overseen and administered by athletic directors Joseph "Joe" Kearney (1976–80) and Douglas "Doug" W. Weaver (1979–89), and of course involved coaches as well. The only men's sport that was eliminated was men's gymnastics, which had become a varsity sport in 1948, and in 1958 had shared an NCAA national team championship with Illinois. HEW regularly conducted audits of the Athletic Department to check for progress on implementation. Counterpart women's teams were established as well as teams in sports like gymnastics, field hockey, rowing, softball, and volleyball. The athletic picture gradually became more diverse and more representative of the skills and experience that women brought to athletic endeavors and competition. To say that Title IX implementation at MSU was smooth and untroubled would be a mischaracterization since there were points of conflict (such as quality of accommodations on the road or meal allowances); however, to say that there were those committed to Title IX as the law, and in terms of the opportunity and equity it required, would be a fair assessment. Professor Gwen Norrell, who served as the faculty athletic representative to the Big Ten Conference from 1979 through 1988 after serving in the MSU Athletic Council, and who served as vice president of the NCAA from 1983 to 1985, was a campus as well as national leader in integrating women's athletics into the Big Ten and the NCAA. Karen Langeland, who became the women's basketball coach in 1976 and who coached teams until 2000, was also an important part of this process. When the NCAA began to offer national championships for women's basketball in all divisions starting in 1982, and to invite sixty-four teams, women's programs now had their own "March Madness" and "Big Dance" on which to set their sights and dreams. When the Jack Breslin Student Events Center opened in 1989, the Lady Spartans shared a basketball showcase as their home court and had their platform on which to build ambitions.

Curriculum

With the dissolution of University College in 1980 came the end of a structure that connected back to the Basic College of 1944. When the four general-education departments were moved into three colleges, the visible and functional locus where students took their required core courses was gone. Under Dean Edward A. Carlin, University College published a quarterly journal from 1960 through 1980 featuring articles on the philosophy and pedagogy of general education. The college had proposed a general studies BA degree, and moved away from standard, uniform courses to a diversified curriculum, including the introduction of humanities courses focused on non-Western materials. The diversified curricular offerings gave students greater choices and fit individual faculty interests more closely.

A 1968 study conducted by Professor Sigmund Nosow and published in 1969 under the title *Professional Self-Images and Organizational Orientations of a General Education Faculty: A Case Study of the University College of Michigan State University* produced a wealth of data on faculty, students, and courses. One of the notable conclusions was that the more recently hired faculty felt some "status deprivation" and wanted opportunities to teach a wider range of courses and students (Nosow 135–37). The level of faculty satisfaction in teaching general-education courses was higher for those in the Humanities and the American Thought and Language departments. Many faculty felt the need for greater opportunities to pursue professional and research interests—in other words, the specializations for which they had been trained in graduate school. This case study was part of the work of the Ad Hoc Committee on the Future of University College established by Dean Edward A. Carlin, and represented one of the most thorough studies of a particular group ever done at MSU.

In the Provost's Office, Clarence L. Winder had a different perspective on University College. As he explained in his 20 September 2000 interview for the Sesquicentennial Oral History Project, Winder's "bias" was against "middle-level management" because he believed it was not cost-effective and because he favored a "very flat kind of organization" that would "minimize boundaries that limited interactions across the faculty or groups of faculty who wanted to engage in innovative associations." Distributing University College faculty to colleges with disciplinary departments would put them in more desirable circumstances, Winder argued. Because he had power and influence as the provost, and the support of President Mackey, Winder accomplished the dissolution of University College by administrative fiat and directive. College administrators were held to

Professor Gwen Norrell served on the MSU Athletic Council, as faculty athletic representative to the Big Ten Conference, and as vice president of the NCAA during the time of Title IX implementation. She worked effectively to bring women's sports into the NCAA. Courtesy of Michigan State University Archives and Historical Collections.

Edward A. Carlin served as the last dean of University College before its dissolution by Provost Clarence Winder. University College had become a national leader in general education but could not survive Winder's reorganization plan and determination. Courtesy of Michigan State University Archives and Historical Collections.

secrecy until Winder formally announced the College's disbandment at a meeting of the faculty. While many (if not perhaps a majority) of the faculty welcomed the change, in general, faculty were not pleased with the way in which it was handled or the demeaning characterizations of UC faculty by some as working in an "intellectual ghetto." This labeling of "ghettoized" faculty was galling to those who had heavier teaching loads in general-education courses.

In 1979 at its July 26–27 meeting, the Board of Trustees approved a revision to the *Bylaws for Academic Governance* that had been recommended by the Academic Council. The new section 4.9 established the University Committee on General Education (UCGE) and set its membership, purview, and functions. Seven members of other colleges with undergraduate degree programs (other than the three charged with teaching general-education courses) would sit on the committee, as would the provost or designee, a representative from the University Committee on Curriculum (UCC), and a representative from the University Committee on Academic Policy (UCAP). While some thought the size of the committee was unwieldy with nineteen members (including three students), what had been established was a university-wide forum for discussions about general education and decisions about "the acceptability of courses in fulfillment of the general education requirement." The UCGE could also review the "general education component of the academic program of the University and colleges" and recommend changes to UCAP. General education became part of the academic governance process, and a broad-based committee was charged with its maintenance. A large number of "substitute" courses were presented and approved, but only after review and discussion as well as by vote. The established colleges and departments offering general education did not have a majority on the UCGE. The salutary development was, of course, that a larger segment of the university was involved in the core curriculum, and that students now had a wider choice of courses and could take courses designed in their own colleges or departments.

In its initial consideration of the extensive budget cuts needed in 1981, the Board of Trustees had to consider the elimination of the four general-education departments as indicated in the "Modified Coordinated Proposal." Their unanimous decision was to "partially reinstate" the departments with the indicated budget cuts and position reductions (Minutes, 3–4 April 1981). This decision was most likely made on the basis of concerns for protecting gains from affirmative action, as well as the concern for a necessary capacity to provide full schedules for incoming students, and to move students ahead in terms of meeting basic requirements in the core curriculum. The Board of Trustees also endorsed a recommendation made by UCAP on 2 April 1981 that an assessment of general education be made by MSU in the 1980s, and that the study be guided by a commitment to sustaining and achieving excellence "by the appropriate cooperation and integration of the disciplinary and general education departments." That assessment came in the 1988 Report of the Council to Review Undergraduate Education (the CRUE Report) titled *Opportunities for Renewal*, which will be discussed in the next chapter.

Another major curricular development was the shift in student enrollments in the 1970s away from the humanities and liberal arts. As Professor Richard E. Sullivan reflected in his Sesquicentennial Oral History Project interview on 23 March 2000, from his vantage point as dean (from 1970 through 1979) of the College of Arts and Letters: "See, when I was dean, the College was hit hard financially because of the precipitous decline in student enrollment in the seventies, especially History and English. That was true all over the country, and so that meant resources were increasingly squeezed out of us." Sullivan noted that the university was becoming more "enrollment-driven than it had been in earlier days" and there was "heavy pressure from above to match resources with enrollments, primarily." The shift of undergraduates to majors in business, finance, and other professional areas reflected a concern for an education that would be more marketable in times of increased job competition and a shrinking job market. However, other factors were at work, such as a desire to maintain the level of income and lifestyle of parents or to keep up with one's ambitious peers. This was, no doubt, the beginning of what would become known as the national crisis in the humanities—that is, how did the humanities and the arts have value and contribute to society in ways that made a qualitative difference (intrinsic value) and that contributed to more general productivity, happiness, and well-being (an intrinsic-extrinsic value)? Graduate enrollments had also dropped by 20 percent in Arts and Letters when the job market sharply contracted in 1970–71 and thereafter. Before

After three years as chair of the Department of History, Richard E. Sullivan became dean of the College of Arts and Letters in 1970 and served until 1979; during his time as dean he was also director of the Humanities Research Center. He was part of the large group of World War II veterans hired into MSU after they had taken advantage of the GI Bill after their wartime service and obtained advanced degrees. A medieval historian, Sullivan published a Western civilization textbook that was widely used for thirty years. He was a part of the group that founded the Michigan Humanities Council and was active on the College of Arts and Letters Dean's Community Council after his retirement in 1988. Courtesy of Michigan State University Archives and Historical Collections.

December 1980, the college had an active and visible Humanities Research Center that provided summer research stipends for faculty, research grants for graduate students, and an agenda of lectures and visiting speakers. All this was lost with the budget cuts, as was an opportunity to vie for the National Humanities Center to be located in Michigan (Anderson).

Another curricular development was the first discussion of the shift to a semester system. With the permanent budget cuts under planning and discussion, the proposal for a new semester academic calendar came in April 1980 and stayed in play until November, when Academic Council action rejected the semester system. It would not be until 1992 that it came to a vote in an Academic Senate meeting and the semester system prevailed in what was a legendary one-vote win.

Developments on Campus

The "financial crisis" of 1980–82 brought with it some unexpected developments. In December 1980, all university personnel had to take a two-and-a-half-day furlough and thus had payless work days. At its 24 July 1981 meeting, the Board of Trustees "approved the use of up to $1.8 million in the first faculty incentive program designed to encourage early retirement and other options," and then in September 1981 authorized another $1.6 million "for the purpose of implementing additional incentive plans." This program was aimed at "reducing further the number of faculty and job security specialists at risk," but the so-called "buyout" was available generally. A number of faculty took advantage of the plan and accepted positions at other universities with MSU cash in hand.

The budget situation also resulted in often stark and startling statements that few thought they would ever hear in the relatively secure and stable world of the university. In a resolution the Board of Trustees passed at its 22 October 1982 meeting, they stated, "Our commitments and patience have been severely tested; our ability to provide the state, region, nation, world with Michigan State leadership has been threatened." Trustee Blanche Martin, in presenting his "Alternative Budget Reduction Proposal" (already discussed), put it

even more severely: "I feel we have already done enough damage to this University, which we all dearly love. We must act immediately to reverse the tide of hysteria, uncertainty and distrust that has permeated the University community." Seeing its way through and clear of this upsetting and often divisive period was perhaps the university's greatest accomplishment in the 1980s, as was doing this with a commitment to the affirmative action gains made earlier, ones that had resulted in a more diverse university. In his 14 February 1984 statement to the Board of Trustees announcing his intention of ending his presidency after six years, President Mackey cited the gains in affirmative action in his administration, which included the appointments of thirty-one minorities and women to administrative positions.

President Mackey also noted that in 1983 undergraduate minority-student enrollments "reached a record high of 8.5%" and that support programs had been introduced. Progress always seems to come with some backward steps, and President Mackey and the Board of Trustees had to address incidents of racism and racial insensitivity on campus. In one much publicized case, an advertising supplement

Established on 1 July 1955, the College of Communication Arts and Sciences celebrated its 50th anniversary in MSU's Sesquicentennial Year. Starting with a strong base in radio and television, the college added several degree programs bringing the total to sixteen and attracted large undergraduate and graduate enrollments. The college's alumni have distinguished themselves in business, advertising, television, film, journalism and media, public relations, and allied fields, and constitute a virtual who's who. Its national reputation and record for internships as well as the productive scholarship of its faculty have made it a leader and great success story. Photo by Thomas Kachadurian.

Invitation to the Dedication
of the
Duffy Daugherty Football Building
Saturday, October 4, 1980, 9:00 a.m.
Duffy Daugherty Football Building
Shaw Lane & Chestnut Road
Michigan State University

The Duffy Daugherty Football Building was opened in 1980 to provide facilities and practice fields, and for almost thirty years remained a functional and unimpressive site until it underwent a $15.5 million renovation and expansion of 25,000 square feet that provided state-of-the-art technology and training as well as instructional equipment. The transformation into a place of Spartan pride and history was made possible by generous gifts from Robert and Julie Skandalaris and the Demmer family of the Lansing-based Demmer Corporation. George and Sally Perles contributed to the construction of the plaza outside the building. Courtesy of Michigan State University Archives and Historical Collections.

in the *State News* showed a picture of a group of fraternity members gathered around a blackface statue. The fraternity was put on "investigatory probation" by its national headquarters, and the newspaper and the fraternity made public and private apologies. In addressing the situation, the Board of Trustees stated, "We emphasize that such apologies do not excuse the racial slur inherent in the photograph, nor do apologies erase the damage done to the entire University community" (Minutes, 25 June 1982). The lesson and the principle here were clearly stated. Racial slurs or racial actions are a serious matter in a community committed to a campus free of "discrimination or intimidation of any kind." Whatever lessens or undermines that commitment is of concern to each individual on campus. Hurtful actions cannot be excused by apologies.

The period of M. Cecil Mackey's presidency saw such buildings as the Wharton Center for the Performing Arts and the $21.5 million Communication Arts and Sciences Building open, as well as the Duffy Daugherty Football Building. The Cyclotron Laboratory, the building projects at the Kellogg Biological Station, and the Plant and Soil Sciences Laboratory provided a surge in research facilities. The university committed to $750,000 for accessibility and the removal of barriers for people with disabilities. What is remarkable and notable about this period is that even with the hammer blow of the budget reduction plan, progress was made on many fronts. There were losses, to be sure, but the gains and advances far outnumbered them.

4

A Steady State Period and Its Salutary Effects

During the search for President M. Cecil Mackey's successor, the Board of Trustees invited John DiBiaggio, then in his sixth year as president of the University of Connecticut, to an interview in Cleveland, with the board interviewing him in two groups of four. Previously, DiBiaggio had been a candidate for the presidency of the University of Florida, was selected as a finalist and made a campus visit, but was not offered the presidency. Back home in Connecticut, his loyalty to the institution was questioned, and the university had a president who did not meet the leadership requirements at another institution. In order to consider the MSU position, he required absolute confidentiality, off-campus interviews, and contacts only through a consultant (McLaughlin and Riesman 188–89). A second meeting, this time with four trustees in Boston, resulted in DiBiaggio agreeing to be the seventeenth president of MSU and to begin on 1 July 1985.

DiBiaggio's record as an administrator was impressive and by that point stretched across three institutions. After a brief period of dental practice and teaching part-time at the University of Detroit Dental School, from which he had graduated, he earned an MA degree in the Center for the Study of Higher and Postsecondary Education (CSHPE) of Rackham School of Graduate Studies at the University of Michigan. After that he accepted an assistant deanship at the University of Kentucky, where he spent three years, and then accepted a dental school deanship at the Medical College of Virginia, where he worked from 1971 to 1976. In 1976 the University of Connecticut offered him the position of vice president for health affairs and executive director for the medical center. In his Sesquicentennial Oral History Project interview of 12 July 2000, DiBiaggio noted that the position at Connecticut presented a serious challenge because of problems there,

As president, John DiBiaggio reaffirmed and revitalized MSU's land-grant mission and identity, headed a successful Capital Campaign, and developed a close relationship with John Hannah. He was an outgoing and engaging president who enjoyed representing MSU.
Courtesy of Michigan State University Archives and Historical Collections.

and that if he succeeded in addressing and resolving these, "then I would have a career before me in this area of the management of medical centers, not thinking beyond that at all" (SOHP interview, 12 July 2000). In 1979, three years later, the faculty at the University of Connecticut asked him to consider being president of the university, and he was the unanimous choice. In a period of about twenty years, DiBiaggio had gone from being a small-resort-town dentist in Michigan to the presidency of a university. In the process he had acquired a reputation for being a problem-solving administrator who could direct change, handle increasingly large-scale responsibilities and organizations, and do so with engaging personal skills.

From the Board of Trustees' point of view, DiBiaggio's administrative career curve pointed upward. While he did not have the scholarly or teaching credentials of Walter Adams, Clifton R. Wharton Jr., or M.

John and Carolyn DiBiaggio came to MSU as a team, and she was compensated for her work and contributions. Cowles House was an active and lively place where administrators, legislators, faculty, and locals mixed. Courtesy of Michigan State University Archives and Historical Collections.

Cecil Mackey, DiBiaggio had earned the trust and confidence of three universities, had experience with administering medical centers and health programs, had been involved in a successful capital campaign at Connecticut, and had been in a position as president where he reported directly to the governor and worked personally with the state legislature.

From DiBiaggio's point of view, he and his then-wife Carolyn were interested in returning home to the Midwest. His mother lived in Detroit, where he grew up, and his sister and her family lived in Michigan. There was also the challenge of taking on the administration of a larger and more complex institution that had, during M. Cecil Mackey's term, weathered the worst of the economic downturn and resulting deep budget cuts. As DiBiaggio indicated in his Sesquicentennial Oral History Project interview, he had hoped that starting as MSU president at age fifty-three in 1985, he would possibly stay in the position until retirement. He looked forward to getting to know John A. Hannah, which he did, as the two became close friends, and to guiding a great land-grant university in its mission. DiBiaggio came to East Lansing with a unanimous vote of the Board of Trustees. In fact, the DiBiaggios came as a team or partnership, as Carolyn was compensated for her responsibilities and activities in support of her husband as well as other campus initiatives she wanted to undertake. She would annually report directly to the Board

One of DiBiaggio's key appointments was moving Roger Wilkinson from acting vice president for financial administration to a permanent position. For over twenty-five years Wilkinson managed the finances of MSU with skill and resourcefulness and served as the chair of the search committee for a new athletic director in 1999. Courtesy of Michigan State University Archives and Historical Collections.

Mary Elizabeth Kurz became the first vice president for legal affairs and general counsel in 1987 when President DiBiaggio reorganized the legal structure and established a full-time legal office of three university lawyers. Kurz, Sally J. Harwood, and Michael J. Kiley constituted the first legal team. Courtesy of Michigan State University Archives and Historical Collections.

of Trustees. This arrangement raised some eyebrows of those who felt that the president's wife's role was to support him as a hostess at social and formal events even where planning and work on her part were required. Several key administrative changes came about in the initial years of DiBiaggio's presidency. After ten years in the position of provost under three presidents, Clarence L. Winder returned to the Department of Psychology to teach in 1986 and then officially retire in 1991. David K. Scott became provost and vice president for academic affairs and served until September 1992. Roger Wilkinson moved from acting vice president for financial administration into a permanent position. DiBiaggio noted in his 2000 interview that this "was one of the first times that the trustees intruded because they wanted me to appoint somebody from the state they had as a candidate. I said I didn't see any reason for doing that if there was somebody competent from the inside who had worked for the university for some years" (SOHP interview, 12 July 2000). Connie W. Stewart, vice president of university relations, left her position in September 1987, and President DiBiaggio commended her work at team-building and the establishment of a successful public relations program extending to the federal level, and her personal qualities of sensitivity and kindness (Minutes, 25 September 1987). Moses Turner, who had come from Texas Tech with Cecil Mackey in 1979, remained in his position as vice president of student affairs and services until 1992. After that he taught in the Department of Educational Administration until his retirement in 2004. From 1999 to 2002 Professor Turner served as the Peace Corps country director for South Africa. DiBiaggio was also fortunate to have John E. Cantlon in the position of vice president for research and graduate studies until his retirement in 1990. Cantlon had excellent connections in Washington, DC, and held presidential appointments on the Nuclear Waste Technical Review Board for ten years.

In 1987 DiBiaggio also significantly changed the structure of the university's legal team, moving from a single designated university attorney, Leland Carr (who also maintained a private practice), to a full-time legal office. Mary Elizabeth Kurz became vice president for legal affairs and general counsel, and Sally J. Harwood and Michael J. Kiley became associate general counsels. Many a university administrator would appreciate having legal counsel readily available when needed, and having lawyers who were full-time specialists.

Another key appointment came in October 1988 when Professor Gordon E. Guyer became vice president for governmental affairs as part of the reorganization of the office of senior consultant to the president for state, federal, and public affairs, a position held by Jacweir "Jack" Breslin, who had passed away on 2 August 1988. In announcing Guyer's appointment, DiBiaggio noted that he had extensive knowledge of the state, had served as a coordinator of state and federal relations, and was highly respected by both political parties (Minutes, 14 October 1988). At that time, probably no single individual represented the face and personality of MSU more than Gordon E. Guyer. DiBiaggio recognized that and persuaded Guyer to accept the position.

Guyer and Cantlon as well as others provided the connection back to the foundational period of MSC/MSU as a college emerging into a university and a land-grant leader. But the most direct connection was, of course, John A. Hannah himself, and DiBiaggio developed a close personal relationship and friendship with him. Hannah remained active after his return from his three years of work as head of the U.S. Agency for International Development (USAID), and as discussed earlier, he was asked to come in to assist in the stalled fundraising for the Wharton Center for the Performing Arts, an effort in which he was assisted by John "Jack" Shingleton. When DiBiaggio came, he quickly recognized that the university would need a capital campaign to generate needed revenues, since as he was soon to learn, funding equity from the legislature was not going to happen, and any efforts to generate additional revenues, such as the imposition of fees, were closely watched by the legislature and could be highly political. As DiBiaggio and Hannah met on various occasions and with various groups, DiBiaggio's admiration for Hannah increased, as did his understanding of Hannah's resolve and decisive actions to transform a small college into a nationally and internationally recognized university. Hannah would share all the classic inside stories about joining the Big Ten or being designated a university, tales that illustrated how obstacles were overcome even when they looked insurmountable.

DiBiaggio earned Hannah's friendship and respect by demonstrating that he understood the institution and its mission. First, he embraced the land-grant heritage and identity focused on service

Gordon E. Guyer became vice president for governmental affairs in 1988, succeeding Jacweir "Jack" Breslin, and represented MSU in all negotiations and discussions with state officials. When DiBiaggio left for Tufts University in 1992, Guyer was quickly named as the next president. Across the state Guyer was perhaps the most recognizable face of MSU. Courtesy of Michigan State University Archives and Historical Collections.

John DiBiaggio was the most well-traveled of any MSU president, making five major international trips and reaffirming and extending connections to universities and alumni all over the world. Two of the trips were to Africa. Courtesy of Michigan State University Archives and Historical Collections.

to various communities, rural and urban, and on social problem analysis. In 1987 he served as the head of the National Association of State Universities and Land-Grant Colleges during the centennial year of the organization, and he gave numerous speeches and presentations on the land-grant mission and contributions. As he frequently pointed out, the medical school at MSU was a "land-grant medical school" with its focus on family and community practice and service to rural areas. He was proud of this identity and tradition of community and social connectedness. This involvement distinguished MSU from the University of Michigan historically and contemporarily. DiBiaggio came to East Lansing believing that this institution suffered to some degree from a sense of inferiority when comparing itself to the Ann Arbor institution. He wanted to emphasize pride in the institution and its heritage, as well as pride in being different

David Wiley served as director of the African Studies Center at MSU for thirty years starting in 1978 and has been part of a distinguished and influential group of Africanists at MSU noted for their scholarship and professional leadership. Professor Wiley has been an effective promoter of the teaching of the Less Commonly Taught Languages (LCTLs) and was a cofounder of the Women and International Development (WID) Program. Courtesy of Michigan State University Archives and Historical Collections.

and not comparable to the University of Michigan, but rather being comparable to like institutions with similar histories and resources as well as missions. When President DiBiaggio visited Zimbabwe in January 1987, he spoke at the meeting of the African Association of Universities on the land-grant movement in the United States.

With different parties of MSU officials, DiBiaggio made five major international trips to renew working relationships with universities and make contact with MSU alumni. In late October and early November 1986, the MSU group visited five universities in Japan, including Shiga University, the University of Ryukyus on Okinawa, and Tokyo University. Included in the official party were Carolyn DiBiaggio, dean of International Programs Ralph H. Smuckler, and MSU trustee Thomas Reed and his wife. MSU had been involved in the establishment of the University of Ryukyus in 1950, and DiBiaggio, who was an avid photographer, brought pictures back for John Hannah showing the successful growth of the university. Contacts were made with many of the approximately one thousand graduates of MSU who lived in Japan. The Japan visit also had a commercial business purpose in terms of discussing linkages that could develop between Japan and the State of Michigan.

In January 1987, a delegation visited the African countries of Senegal, Republic of Kenya, Ethiopia, and Republic of Zimbabwe. Dean Smuckler, trustee Barbara J. Sawyer, and David Wiley of the African

Daniel Keathley became chair of the Department of Forestry in 1990, and during his first decade as chair the department received a no. 3 national ranking in 1992; received its first $1 million endowment, from alumnus Fred Arnold, in 2000; and celebrated its 100th anniversary. In 2005 a new curriculum for the future began, with five concentrations offered. Professor Keathley's research has focused on genetic engineering of woody plants. Courtesy of Michigan State University Archives and Historical Collections.

Studies Center and Donald Isleib of the Institute of International Agriculture accompanied the president. Smuckler and Wiley had a wide circle of contacts in these countries that made the meetings personal and individual. All of the efforts with the African universities focused on providing them with the research needed to address their national challenges, on providing exchanges that would enable their faculties to gain additional degrees and research experience in the United States, and on assisting the institutions in their growth and utilization of resources. The trip to the African countries came in the month following the divestiture of MSU Foundation funds in firms doing business in South Africa (Minutes, 12 December 1986). As President DiBiaggio stated in his report on the African trip, "It is time to move from divesting from those companies to investing in the development of Africa's human capital which is the greatest contribution that can be made" (Minutes, 6 February 1987).

These trips to Japan and Africa made the direct connection between DiBiaggio and Hannah and Michigan State with its international role and mission. The "service mandate" was, as DiBiaggio stated, "never forfeited . . . but, in fact, extended far beyond the borders of our own state and nation to the entire world" (Minutes, 6 February 1987). As Ralph H. Smuckler noted in his book *A University Turns to the World,* the visit to Zimbabwe came at a time when that country was emerging from an extended rebellion and United Nations sanctions but was now ready to seek U.S. cooperation and assistance. MSU's work with the University of Zimbabwe under an Agency for International Development contract resulted in "a broad pattern of cooperation in the medical and health fields, in education, and in agriculture [that] took shape and found support within MSU, the University of Zimbabwe, and foundation sources" (Smuckler 76–77). Michigan State faculty and program administrators were internationally recognized for their expertise with development aid programs, and that recognition expanded with the contacts, arrangements, and exchanges made on these two trips. President DiBiaggio took an active role in representing MSU in the International Association of Universities and became part of the IAU governing board at the 1990 meetings in Helsinki. He also regularly invited groups of state legislators to Cowles House, the MSU president's residence on campus, to hear faculty members discuss current international events and developments (157). In 1990 Dean Smuckler was asked by DiBiaggio to move into the President's Office as consultant to the president for special international projects, a position he held for a year until loaned to the Agency for International Development as deputy assistant administrator and director of USAID's University Center (175).

The debate about MSU's international reach and its tie to the land-grant mission has been prevalent on campus since the post–World War II period. In some ways it has been an academic version of engagement with the world vs. isolationism or neo-isolationism. Many believe the university works and contributes best when it focuses on its selected students and mission of educating them with life and occupational skills, when it focuses on basic research and basic problems and thus advances essential scientific and technological knowledge, when it preserves academic freedom, and when it addresses campus and community problems as well as provides knowledge to the state. For others, the question is why does a university draw to it all kinds and varieties of expertise and experts and then not give them a full field for their research and a full test of the application of their skills? Does the accumulation and concentration of knowledgeable people in a university not carry with it a responsibility to share with societies and nations less developed, less blessed with resources and stable, enduring institutions, or with nations that have been afflicted with strife or are emerging from a disastrous experience with war?

What President DiBiaggio sensed was that the land-grant mission that President Hannah had extended to Africa, South America, Japan, and other countries needed reaffirmation and revitalization. The university benefited from sending its people to work and assist in other countries, with the return benefit of those countries sending their researchers, faculty, and students to MSU. Exchange and mutual benefits were always at the heart of international programs. DiBiaggio also made visits to China and Korea in October 1988, a trip to the Republic of Indonesia with several trustees, and a 1992 trip to the Federal Republic of Nigeria, Ethiopia, and the Republic of Kenya in the company of trustee Melanie Rheinhold, the new dean of International Programs Gill-Chin Lim, Professors David Wiley and Margaret Aguwa, and the Midwest Universities Consortium for International Activities, Inc. (MUCIA) associate director Mary Joy

Robert L. Blomstrom served as director of Hotel, Restaurant and Institutional Management (HRIM) from 1969 through 1980 and was succeeded by Donald I. Smith. HRIM benefited from strong leadership, with an emphasis on research and publication that advanced the field and the commercial success of the related industries. Courtesy of Michigan State University Archives and Historical Collections.

DiBiaggio enjoyed the formalities and traditions of MSU celebrations and brought back former trustees and presidents to be recognized and honored. He is seen here with Edgar L. Harden, John Hannah, Clifton Wharton Jr., and M. Cecil Mackey. Courtesy of Michigan State University Archives and Historical Collections.

Pigozzi. While some characterized DiBiaggio as a "globe-trotting" president, each of these trips had a strategic purpose and was aimed at achieving or furthering identifiable goals. He included trustees on each of these visits so they could see personally the impact of the university's international programs and gauge their impact. He took along university experts who had scholarly stature and personal contacts in the countries visited. This was an ambitious international agenda that also included a major conference on campus: the Conference on United States Initiatives for Education and Training of South Africans and Namibians in November 1986, another indication of the strong reputation of the African Studies Center.

DiBiaggio was also deeply committed to continuing the traditions of MSU. In June 1987 he announced that the painting of presidential portraits starting with John Hannah was in the process of being commissioned, and by the 1 December 1989 Board of Trustees meeting he announced that these portraits had been completed and now were displayed in the Board Room. He took a special interest in the portrait of John Hannah, which was completed and placed in a location of honor in the Board Room by November 1990, just two months before Hannah's death on 23 February 1991. DiBiaggio also brought former trustees back to campus and recognized their contributions. He would, and did, talk to any groups across the state about the traditions and heritage of the institution. In his July 1990 interview, DiBiaggio spoke movingly and proudly about how John Hannah recognized and appreciated DiBiaggio's work. He recalled one particular moment:

> One night at a foundation dinner I was talking gifts for the university. John wasn't like this; this was not his nature. If you know the man, he's quiet. He got up and he walked over and put his hand on my shoulder, and he said, "This is the greatest gift to Michigan State University." And I was just stunned, you know. But it was the highest praise that I could imagine, because what I wanted to do was to remind people what Michigan State was about. I wanted them to feel really, really, proud, and I think maybe that's what I did when I was there. I think maybe people felt good. With all the problems, people felt good about being associated with Michigan State. The students felt proud to be there, proud to be associated with an institution that cared a lot, that reached out to people. (SOHP interview, 12 July 2000)

The Capital Campaign and the Campaign for Resources

One of John DiBiaggio's concerns about the university when he became president in July 1985 was the fact that MSU was lacking an endowment and had a limited formal fundraising organization. The challenges of fundraising became apparent when the contributions for the building of the Wharton Center stalled, and President Emeritus John A. Hannah was brought in to address the situation and use his presence and reputation to raise funds. The Capital Campaign or "MSU 2000," which was launched in 1986, received substantial early gifts from General Motors, Ford, and the Chrysler Corporation, and a leadership team was formed to provide a stronger concentrated push to the goal of $100 million (later changed to $160 million). At its 6

Malcolm G. Dade Jr. served on the MSU Board of Trustees from 1983 to 1991, joining the board the same year as Bobby D. Crim and Patrick J. Wilson. The board was rapidly changing at this point, with Elizabeth P. Howe resigning in 1983 after just two years of her term, John B. Bruff resigning after his service from 1975 to 1983, and then Bobby Crim resigning in 1984 after only one year and replaced by Lawrence "Larry" D. Owen. Trustee Dade's daughter graduated from MSU in 1986, and as chair of the Board of Trustees at that time, he signed her degree. Courtesy of Michigan State University Archives and Historical Collections.

February 1987 meeting, the Board of Trustees approved an executive management position titled Director of Annual Giving Programs. By 14 October 1988, Board of Trustees chair Malcolm G. Dade Jr. announced that the halfway mark had been reached, and by 3 February 1989, President DiBiaggio announced that the university expected to exceed $100 million in commitments. The overall goal was reset to $160, with the $130 million mark reached by April 1990.

Several factors contributed to the outstanding success of the Capital Campaign. DiBiaggio's popularity as president and his tireless commitment to meeting with alumni and supporters across the state, no matter what the size of the gathering, was one factor. A committed leadership team with broad campus involvement also was essential, as was the employment of sound fundraising strategies and tactics. The Spartan football team won the 1988 Rose Bowl at the end of the 1987 season with a 9-2-1 record, the Aloha Bowl in 1989 as part of an 8-4 season record, and the John Hancock Bowl as part of an 8-3-1 season for 1990. In 1988, the Spartans, who had a 6-1-1 Big Ten record to finish second, played in the Gator Bowl and lost to Georgia 34-27. The Perles-coached Spartans had their best four seasons at MSU and three bowl wins. From 1989–90 to 1991–92, Jud Heathcote's teams went to the NCAA basketball tournament, won a Big Ten championship in 1989–90 and went to the Sweet Sixteen, and won first-round games in other appearances. Coach Ron Mason's hockey team won a national championship in 1986, won regular-season conference championships in 1985, 1986, 1989, and 1990, and regularly made the NCAA playoffs. In 1990–91 women's basketball coach Karen Langeland's team finished 13-5 in the Big Ten for second place, had a 21-8 final record, and advanced to the second round in their first NCAA appearance. The overall success of Spartan sports teams no doubt created a positive mood in alumni and an overall feeling that the university had reclaimed some lost glory.

The high point of the Capital Campaign was the acceptance of a gift of $20 million from Mr. Eli Broad and Edythe Broad with the stipulation that the money be used "to achieve excellence in graduate business studies" (Minutes, 23 June 1991). The university agreed to change the name of the College of Business and the Graduate School of Business Administration to the Eli Broad College of Business and the Eli Broad Graduate School of Management and to use the names "in perpetuity." With the generous donation of the Broads, the Capital Campaign's goal was increased to $210 million and extended to 1993. It was a grand moment for the university when an alumnus stepped forward as a generous donor and benefactor and focused the gift on educational excellence and prominence.

As president, DiBiaggio believed that the state higher-education appropriations were not equitable or always distributed fairly in recognition of the university's mission and level of educating the state's students. As he indicated in his 12 July 2000 Sesquicentennial Oral History Project interview, he soon realized how political the budget was and how the institution's autonomy was, in reality, limited. "The reality is that the autonomy didn't truly exist, because, as I said, the concept was that you would manage your own affairs, but if you did something that the legislature or the governor disagreed with, they'd penalize you the following year by decreasing your budget by not providing funds for a facility you wanted to build or whatever. There was always that threat." Early in his presidency, DiBiaggio was attempting to find funds to improve faculty salaries, which lagged behind those of other Big Ten institutions. When he was told by Governor James J. Blanchard he could not raise tuition, he explored the possibilities of raising student fees and the governor approved. However, after raising fees, he was called before the legislature and harshly reprimanded for making a deal in an area the legislature believed to be their territory.

The best budget year in the DiBiaggio presidency came in 1990–91, when the University General Fund operating budget was $375,898,000, up from $354,286,000 in 1988–89. Even when the Michigan legislature was generous in its appropriations to higher education, and it certainly was when it had the resources, a 5 percent or 7 percent increase actually provided already limited funds since operating expenses and materials or supplies increased in cost. In order to keep incoming revenues up, MSU had to maintain a high enrollment level of nearly 43,000 as well as raise tuition and housing costs. The challenge for the administration and the Board of Trustees was to find a way to keep tuition and board increases at a reasonable rate while demonstrating at the same time containment of costs and reduction of expenses and a commitment to high-quality undergraduate education.

With his wife Edythe, Eli Broad, who graduated from Michigan State in 1954, has been a generous benefactor and distinguished alumnus. In 1991 Broad endowed the Eli Broad College of Business. The extensive philanthropy of the Broads includes the arts, education, and biomedical research at the national level. Courtesy of Michigan State University Archives and Historical Collections.

John E. Cantlon came to Michigan State in 1954 from George Washington University and was a distinguished researcher of plant life in the Arctic and in Michigan, serving as president of the Ecological Society of America. At MSU he served consecutively as provost and then vice president for research and graduate studies, and his extensive Washington, DC, connections were immensely valuable. Courtesy of Michigan State University Archives and Historical Collections.

DiBiaggio did not manage to make any substantial progress on the issue of funding equity over his seven years as president, but he was fortunate to have experienced and effective individuals such as vice president of university relations Connie W. Stewart, and then Gordon E. Guyer, handling relationships and discussions with the legislature. DiBiaggio learned that too much direct exposure to the legislature was not beneficial for a president, and that his time was more profitably spent on other matters such as public relations and fundraising. He accepted the fact that tuition increases were necessary in order to improve faculty salary levels at an even more incremental level.

Research and Research Facilities

At the 12 June 1987 Board of Trustees meeting, President DiBiaggio reported that "for the first time, a plateau has been reached of gifts, grants and contracts to the university which exceeds $100 million [for the year]." He attributed this increase to the "increasing competitiveness of the faculty" and to the leadership provided by John E. Cantlon as vice president for research and graduate studies. For eight years until Professor Percy Pierre replaced him in 1990, Cantlon provided stellar and consistent leadership, and his work in the DiBiaggio period saw the establishment of new research facilities that would become a permanent part of MSU and achieve national distinction.

At its 2 December 1988 meeting, the Board of Trustees voted to "approve a recommendation that the Composite Materials and Structures Center be established in the College of Engineering on a permanent basis." The center, which had been conditionally established in 1986, was to become a site of substantial contractual research for private firms as well as for state and federal agencies.

In January 1992 a major gift of $5 million came to the College of Engineering from the Herbert H. and Grace A. Dow Foundation in Midland, Michigan. It was the largest gift ever received by the college and one of the largest ever given by the foundation. The money was designated to provide construction of a new wing of the Engineering Building. That addition would house the Composite Materials and Structures Center (CMSC), related research laboratories, and faculty offices. As John E. Cantlon explained, the $5 million Dow gift came about in part because MSU had supported the location of a material science institute in Midland in order to build a broader base in this field and put a science footprint down in mid-Michigan (SOHP interview, 27 March 2000). As a result of its growing materials research capacity, MSU found itself networked with the Michigan Materials and Processing Institute, a consortium of corporations involved in polymer composites, and with the Composites Automation Consortium, a network of interests that cut across industry, independent research labs, and traditional research university giants Stanford University and the Massachusetts Institute of Technology (McVey).

The marvelous end result had its beginning when Cantlon was provost and decided that a science development program should focus on the material science contributions of chemistry, physics, and mathematics. Cantlon and Professor Jack B. Kinsinger went to Washington, DC, to get support for this concentrated and interdisciplinary emphasis focused on material science (SOHP interview, 27 March 2000). What followed eventually was MSU's designation as the state center for material science. A particular institutional strength had been identified, with support and resources located and a vital research center secured for the future. When the CMSC was fully developed, it would feature eight laboratories totaling nearly 20,000 square feet with high-tech equipment, and would become nationally and internationally known for its work in analyzing and testing polymer composites.

In June 1989 the Board of Trustees appointed an architect and engineer for the proposed Food Toxicology Center, which became known as the National Food Safety and Toxicology Center (NFSTC) and would bring together toxicologists, microbiologists, epidemiologists, and social scientists from nineteen departments and seven colleges. One of the most interdisciplinary research centers on campus, the NFSTC partners with government, industry, and consumer groups on food safety and toxicology. An adjunct to the center is the Food Safety Policy Center at MSU, which conducts surveys. The connection between research and public health, rural or urban, is one of the longest-standing commitments of the institution, fostered and advanced in earlier years by such pioneer and iconic professors as Henrik Joakim Stafseth and G. Malcolm Trout.

Percy Pierre came to the College of Engineering as a professor of electrical and computer engineering in 1990, after serving as president of Prairie View A&M University for six years and before that four years with the Department of the Army managing the development of a billion-dollar weapons system. He came in as the vice president for research and graduate studies at MSU and served until 1995. His work in promoting the recruitment of minority and underrepresented students in the field of engineering has been dedicated, and as the first African American to earn a PhD in electrical engineering, he has mentored and guided close to 40 minority doctoral graduates. Courtesy of Michigan State University Archives and Historical Collections.

The National Food Safety and Toxicology Center houses the Center for Integrative Toxicology, which has had continuous funding since 1988 from the National Institute of Environmental Health Sciences Superfund Basic Research Program. This has been one of a number of continuing links between federal agencies and MSU where focused research on national-scale problems is a collaborative partnership between the federal government and the university.
Courtesy of Michigan State University Photography Services.

Also, in July 1989 the university established the University Corporate Research Park, but it was not until February 1991 that the first occupant moved into the park. The North American Business and Technical Center of Himont Advanced Materials, a molded fluoropolymers business, established its offices, and in 2007 a production plant was built. The effort to create a corporate research park was hindered by the fact that in 1990–91 the state experienced another serious economic downturn. Occupancy grew slowly in the first phase and came to include MBI International, the MSU Composite Vehicle Research Center, the Michigan Virtual University, the MDOT Lansing Transportation Center, and nine commercial and corporate entities.

On 7 February 1992, President DiBiaggio announced that MSU had received a $6 million grant from the U.S. Agency for International Development to focus on plant biotechnology that would increase crop production in developing nations. The connection with USAID reached back to President Hannah, who left MSU to become the head of USAID in 1979, and to M. Peter McPherson, a 1963 MSU alumnus, who was head of USAID from 1981 to 1987 and who would become president of the university in 1993. The teamwork that put together the successful grant proposal and its focus on the world's food needs signaled in many ways the success that DiBiaggio had in reaffirming the "service mandate" of the land-grant mission and its world reach. This Hannah legacy had found an articulate and passionate voice in John DiBiaggio, as well as in the presidents who followed.

Developments in National Rankings

In 1968 the National Science Foundation published a list ranking of the universities and colleges that had the largest federal research and development awards, and in this listing MSU was ranked twenty-fifth with $13.4 million, while in the 1970 Roose-Andersen rankings (previously discussed) MSU was ranked twenty-fourth nationally (Graham and Diamond 59–60, 212). In 1986 MSU was ranked ninth in federally financed research and development (R&D) expenditures in the social sciences at $2,620,000, with the University of Michigan ranked first at $14,757,000 and Wisconsin second at $7,846,000 (Graham and Diamond 137).

These 1968 and 1970 figures indicate a high-water mark for MSU in terms of reputation and national rankings, due to several factors. First, the surge in doctoral studies and PhDs produced at MSU brought national attention to its emergence as a graduate studies institution. Second, budgeting practices that allowed a department to retain funds gained from instructional efficiency and economy measures meant that units had flexibility in terms of providing faculty with research time or leaves, assigning faculty to research-only positions, being more competitive nationally with salaries and job conditions favoring research, and developing research infrastructure in terms of labs and equipment. Third, the establishment of the Cyclotron Laboratory in 1963 and the Plant Research Laboratory in 1965 gave MSU two "signature" research facilities and significant national visibility. In scientific research, MSU was solidly on the map, with talented researchers like Henry Blosser and Anton Lang serving as the faces of these sites. Fourth, a number of individuals in the sciences had experience with assignments in national agencies, as well as spent time seeking federal funds with direct contact in Washington, DC. Last, and certainly not least, was the substantial flow of federal grants and contracts into universities paired with a healthy state economy.

The 1960s boom was followed, as Graham and Diamond note, by an "age of adjustment" from 1968 to 1978, as there was a decline in federal funding for academic research and as a new group of research-intensive universities vied for the same funds. After MSU became a member of the Association of American Universities in 1964, another twenty-two universities were admitted to membership, with seven added between 1966 and 1974. The rising institutions, both public and private, sought to attract federal funding and contracts, and with their advancing and fresh reputations could attract top researchers.

National Research Council rankings of graduate programs came out in 1982 and again in 1990, but the 1982 NRC report did not, in fact, provide rankings as such. In the title instead was the term "An Assessment of Research-Doctorate Programs," and the introductory material stated that "No attempt has been made to establish a composite ranking of programs in a discipline. Indeed, the committee is convinced that no single measure adequately reflects the quality of a research-doctorate program and wishes to emphasize the importance of viewing individual programs from the perspective of multiple indices or dimensions" (Jones, Lindzey, and Coggeshall, 29). Institutions and programs were listed alphabetically with the set of data for each one, which included program size, characteristics of program graduates, reputational survey results, university library, along with a complicated system for valuing each measure. The reporting format, of course, did not lend itself to quick or easy judgments or comparisons, or to press releases touting how many places a department or graduate program had moved up in seven years. Botany at MSU could not say, "We've moved from a tie for ninth to sixth." Or Entomology could not say, "We've moved from a tie for twelfth to ninth." Any rankings departments created or established for themselves, they would have to claim on their own and base it on their own comparison and evaluation of the data. The straightforward simplicity of the American Council on Education 1970 Roose-Andersen *Rating of Graduate Programs* was gone (at least until the 1995 NRC reports, when actual rankings came back into view).

In a 1992 nationwide survey conducted by Penn State, the MSU Department of Forestry was ranked third in the country ("Historical Timeline"). The School of Hospitality Business in 1992 began a remarkable annual record of scholarly publications that would by 2001 make it distinguished for the highest mean publication productivity of any hospitality school in the world (*Hospitality Business Leader* 1, 3).

One study, that of Hugh Davis Graham and Nancy Diamond titled *The Rise of American Research Universities: Elites and Challengers in the Postwar Era* (1997), looks at research productivity over the period from 1965 through 1990 by using the following measures: (1) federal R&D support obligated to the institution, (2) number of journal articles produced, (3) articles in top-rated science journals, (4) articles in top-rated social science journals, and (5) fellowships and grants in the arts and humanities. The number of full-time faculty heads each set of numbers. In the per capita scores for 203 research universities (that is, all five measures figured on a faculty per capita basis from 1980 to 1990), MSU is ranked fifteenth out of twenty-six Research II public institutions. The reason MSU is not grouped with Research I public institutions is because its per capita R&D index was $23,940, and the cutoff for inclusion in Research I was $28,000. Research I and Research II categories were used by the Carnegie Classification of Institutions of Higher Education, but in 2000 the Carnegie Foundation ceased using this classification.

Several underlying factors explain or account for what has happened to MSU in terms of national rankings. The maintenance of a large undergraduate enrollment necessitates, of course, a large faculty complement, so per capita numbers (whether on the measure of federal R&D support or the faculty's scholarly productivity) are spread over a larger number. Heavy undergraduate enrollment means that fewer graduate students are available to assist professors at some point in their studies or to take on teaching their own courses. Another factor was the rise of the National Institutes of Health (NIH) and the shift in national emphasis to biomedical research. By 1994 the NIH share of all federal R&D funding to universities was 52 percent, a development favoring institutions with an emphasis on medical research (Graham and Diamond 202). MSU's medical and

Construction on the Jack Breslin Student Events Center, with groundbreaking on 24 July 1986 and the arena opening on 9 November 1989. Basketball coach Jud Heathcote is shown shaking hands with Breslin, surrounded by his four assistants and his team. In the inaugural season at Breslin, Heathcote's Spartans had a 28-6 season record, won the Big Ten, and went to the NCAA Sweet Sixteen. Breslin did not live to see the facility opened and dedicated. Courtesy of Michigan State University Archives and Historical Collections.

osteopathic schools were developed with a land-grant philosophy that emphasized family and community practice. Lastly, there were the periodic budget crises in Michigan, with the resulting decreases in higher education appropriation that limited efforts to improve faculty salaries and to be competitive in terms of attracting or retaining top researchers.

Campus Developments

The national drought of 1988, covering about 45 percent of the United States, hit Michigan and the MSU campus hardest during that summer. As the awaited rains never came and the 90+ degree days multiplied, on campus a drought-management team established priorities for watering and caring for special commemorative plantings and trees that had teaching/research value or would be difficult to replace. In response to the state's needs, the MSU Cooperative Extension Service initiated special publications and laboratory testing programs as well as provided assistance in the field to help farmers deal with the stress of excessive heat on livestock and farm animals and with the loss of income from withered crops. This was a situation where the land-grant service mission was put in full motion to address the needs of Michigan agriculture and forestry, and where the extension agents made an invaluable contribution in a time of stress as well as distress.

On 18 February 1988, an accident occurred during the construction of the Jack Breslin Student Events Center. The accident involved cranes that were putting the roof trusses into position, with the cascading collapse of trusses already put in place. One construction worker was killed, and the accident was a somber reminder of the risks workers take in order to make a living. After a study of the mishap was conducted, the construction work moved ahead and was back on schedule. The first commencement was held at the Breslin Center on 2 December 1989 with singer/artist Stevie Wonder as the commencement speaker, less than a month after the building officially opened.

Student concerns and activism in the period of DiBiaggio's presidency reflected a wider awareness than the usual and necessary ones of getting needed courses and a decent class schedule, achieving a good grade-point average, and having good roommates or housemates. For the 1985–86 academic year, Governor James Blanchard (now in the third year of his first term) requested that the Board of Trustees freeze tuition for in-state students as well as forego the use of forward funding, a practice that had been made available earlier in return for a hold on tuition increases. What became evident is that tuition rates and increases were becoming increasingly more politically sensitive issues as well as a matter of public and legislative discussion. This would become a permanent feature of the higher education landscape, especially during the twenty years that Blanchard and John Engler, both graduates of MSU, served as governor.

"Tent City" sprang up in May 1970 in what became known as People's Park, near the International Center and Wells Hall. It featured a hippie counterculture and war protesters as well as peace activists. Twenty years later, shanties were erected in this same area to express different student discontents. Courtesy of Michigan State University Archives and Historical Collections (*Wolverine* 1971).

Groups like Associated Students of Michigan State University (ASMSU), black student groups and the MSU Black Alumni, the Office of Black Affairs, the South African Liberation Committee, MSU and United Ministries in Higher Education, and professors like Kenneth W. Harrow and William Derman combined efforts to focus on the divestiture of MSU Foundation funds from corporations operating in South Africa. This divestiture took place before President DiBiaggio's January 1987 trip to Africa. ASMSU also sponsored a forum on racism on 20 April 1987 in response to incidents on campus. The campus visit and speech of Louis Farrakhan Sr., head of the Nation of Islam organization, in 1990 created controversy and debate over his appearance on campus and the university's funding of his speech. Concerns focused on Farrakhan's alleged anti-Semitism and his sharp criticism of white America and the U.S. government. Ten individuals addressed the Board of Trustees meeting of 2 February 1990 on the scheduled Farrakhan visit, and the debate circulated widely and passionately for those opposed. It was a good test of the university's openness to speakers with controversial views and positions, especially when these connected to the racial history of the United States. Farrakhan's appearance went on as scheduled.

Also, in the fall of 1990 the issue of shanties in People's Park emerged. This area, located in between Wells Hall, the International

The shanties that sprang up in People's Park in the Fall semester of 1990 recalled the earlier Tent City of 1970 in the same area. The subject of a great deal of media attention and curiosity, the shanties also got the attention of university officials and the Board of Trustees, which prohibited the shanties and provided them with a one-month lease on existence. The Department of Public Safety demolished them and hauled away the remains. Courtesy of Michigan State University Archives and Historical Collections (*Red Cedar Log* 1991).

Center, and Erickson Hall had been an active scene of antiwar protestors and peace proponents during the Vietnam War and the site of "Tent City," which virtually sprang up overnight in the spring of 1970 and caused administrators consternation. Concerns about Tent City had to do with safety and sanitation as well as the fact that police could not see or control what was going on inside the tents. It became a big headache for President Wharton and the Board of Trustees because of all the heavy media coverage it received and because it was another open act of students' defiance and opposition.

The shanties students erected in 1990 were another expression of students' issues and concerns—temporary structures that called attention to dilapidated housing that poor and dispossessed people had to live in all over the world. The social-cause groups that put up the shanties were informed by the Office of Student Affairs and Services that they were not registered organizations and that their structures would have to come down soon. In response, the diverse groups formed an umbrella organization and sought a faculty adviser to make them "legitimate," and Professor Roger Bresnahan agreed to serve in this capacity. One of the shanty groups was the Young Republicans, whose conservatism did not fit the radical nature of the other groups but who wanted a presence in the mix.

The student shanties were visible reminders of a part of the world not represented on campus, but were also a place to meet and discuss issues of poverty and inequality, as well as campus issues like free speech and recognition of sexual preference. From the administration's perspective the shanties presented concerns about safety, just as the earlier tents did. Another concern was that students would live and sleep in these shanties. From the students' viewpoint a proposed ordinance to ban shanties infringed on freedom of speech and expression and represented the repression of students' conscious and deliberate expression of concerns about radical issues. At its 12 October 1990 meeting, the Board of Trustees heard fourteen individuals address the issue of the Shanty Ordinance, but at the end of that meeting a new Ordinance on the Erection/Maintenance of Structures was passed and made effective 12 November 1990. An amendment "effective immediately" was made to the Camping Ordinance, and camping now meant "the erecting of a tent or a shelter of natural or synthetic material" (Minutes, 12 October 1990). The shanties could remain only for another month, but no one could occupy them overnight. In the end, the Department of Public Safety (DPS) came in to tear down the shanties, but not without a scuffle from those defending them. People's Park would, however, retain its focus as a place for advocate groups to put up tables or booths along the sidewalks and pass out literature, and the spot near Wells Hall became the expected location for the itinerant preachers to denounce students for their "sinful" and "dissolute" lifestyle and urge them to "repent."

Early 1989 saw the appearance of recycling as a movement on campus. At the 3 February 1989 Board of Trustees meeting, Carl Brach and James Garland, students and members of Project Recycle, presented a petition signed by students, faculty, and staff urging the establishment of a campus-wide recycling program. With the statewide passage of Proposal C and the bottle deposit law, the state made available funds that would support recycling programs. As a result of the petition, an administrative task force focused on the development of a comprehensive plan for recycling, and the first phase focused on office paper, with collection containers for white paper distributed across campus in 1991 by the newly formed Office of Recycling and Waste Reduction. Returnable bottles left by students in classrooms or other places were often collected by some recognizable and colorful local individuals who scoured the buildings daily in order to earn money from the refunds.

ASMSU also promoted the national "Into the Streets" volunteer program in 1991, and thirty MSU student organizations linked together in an effort to address needs, issues, and problems in the greater Lansing community by direct personal involvement. At their 11 October 1991 meeting, the Board of Trustees approved a resolution supporting this program and commending students for their involvement. At the 9 October 1992 Board of Trustees meeting, Sam Singh, an MSU student and local co-coordinator of the "Into the Streets" national initiative, reported to the Board of Trustees the success of the 1991 program and previewed the activities that would occur in November 1992. At the age of 24, Sam Singh was elected to the East Lansing City Council, serving ten years and also being elected mayor in 2005. As chief of staff of ASMSU, Singh also was involved in starting the MSU Alternative Spring Break Program, and after graduation became president and CEO of the Michigan Nonprofit Association.

The "Into the Streets" programs came about when a group of campus leaders created the MSU Campus Outreach and Opportunity League (COOL) with the goal of extending the students' field of vision to the nearby community and beyond, and to give them a positive first experience with volunteering as well as first-hand experience with an existing set of social conditions. Volunteering has been a very prevalent activity on MSU's campus since the establishment of the Office of Volunteer Programs in 1968, which would later become the Center for Service-Learning and Civic Engagement.

Two major changes were coming in the campus lives of students, the first being major changes in the core curriculum. The general-education philosophy that had guided the university for almost fifty years disappeared, and the academic calendar moved from the quarter system to semesters, with the 1991–92 academic year being the last academic year of the quarter system. The director of the Semester Transition Team was Professor Bruce Miller, and this team provided a critical service to the entire university and its students with a smooth and efficient changeover that had more potential hang-ups and challenges than most could imagine. The overall cost of conversion was just over $1 million, a reasonable amount in terms of what had to be done.

Bruce Miller, professor of philosophy and logic and chair of the department, served as chair of the Semester Conversion Committee in 1990, a task of gigantic proportions and implications. Known for his sound judgment and ability to see the big picture, Professor Miller was involved in the development of the Medical Humanities Program and became the university's mediation services coordinator, offering courses on inclusion and diversity as part of the Human Resources Development program. Courtesy of Michigan State University Archives and Historical Collections.

The vote on the semester conversion came at a rare meeting of the Faculty Senate in the MSU Auditorium. After considerable debate and discussion, the question was called by Professor Walter Adams and a secret ballot agreed to by those present. When the ballots were counted, the semester system passed on a vote of 400 to 399, with the matter decided by only one vote. Now the university would be on the same calendar as the other state research-intensive schools, and MSU students could hit the summer job market at the same time as others. No longer would young people flock to East Lansing on the weekends for rites of spring parties that used to go on into early June, but by the same token MSU students now left campus before its annual transformation into glorious natural beauty.

Another transformation of the campus was occurring, one less visible but no less important to the future. At its 6 April 1990, 1 February 1991, and 11 October 1991 meetings, the Board of Trustees approved contracts and budgets totaling $1,294,000 for broadband distribution in fourteen residence halls. At the 1 February 1991 meeting, the board approved the position of vice provost for computing and technology, and heard from President DiBiaggio that starting with Spring term 1991 students would be able to enroll through an experimental computer program that promised fully computerized registration in the near future. The campus Fiber Optics Phase I Project was approved on 5 April 1991 with a budget of $790,000. With the development of computer registration, a rite of passage for all students would eventually disappear, the ritual of registering and securing the needed class cards at the Intramural (IM) Sports West Building. Almost every student had stories about the frustrations, heat and humidity, bureaucracy, heartbreak, and challenges of facing the maze of successive stations that constituted "The Pit." The computer cards that signaled success in getting into a class were the prizes sought, and many a schedule was torn up or extensively revised, with the pieces scattered on the floor of the IM Building. Computer registration would systematize and rationalize what to many students seemed an irrational or capricious registration system. The horror stories and tales of "The Pit" became part of the many legends and lore of MSU.

The "wiring" of campus, of course, was part of a larger transformation taking place within a developing revolution in information

Before the Men's IM Sports West Building became the location of "The Pit" for registration, the process was held in the Auditorium; but the experience of trying to put together a class schedule was essentially the same as securing coveted class cards.
Courtesy of Michigan State University Archives and Historical Collections (*Wolverine* 1958).

technology. At its most visible, the revolution could be noted in the transfer of the Main Library's card catalog to electronic form. Many preferred the long pull-out drawers found in solid wooden files, and the task of going through each section of a file card by card. It was part of the ritual of learning to do research and was a physical and tactile experience. The acquisition of a faculty member's first desktop computer and its first uses signaled the beginning of a change of patterns of work and creation of texts, one that accelerated with new generations of computers with increased memory and speed and connection to e-mail and the Internet. Faculty who were "early adapters" moved faster and more readily into the computer age, and those in science, engineering, and medicine saw new applications and uses faster than faculty in the humanities. The Internet boom of the early 1990s, as the number of host sites numbered close to four million, with a million added each quarter, produced widespread interest, and starting in 1995 Microsoft provided the software that made the personal computer usable for access to the Internet (Campbell-Kelly and Aspray 299). It would not be long until the first computer-generation students arrived on campus.

In the area of the core curriculum, a major change came about with action on the part of the Board of Trustees that discontinued the departments of Humanities, Natural Science, and Social Science, three of the four units from University College. Except for the Department of Thought and Language, the last vestiges of the Basic College/University College were now erased, and faculty from three units moved into disciplinary departments. Under Provost David K. Scott, the shift was on to Integrative Studies as General Education disappeared from the curricular lexicon.

The driving force behind this shift was the 1988 Report of the Council to Review Undergraduate Education, titled *Opportunities for Renewal*. That committee, with thirty-four members including one graduate and two undergraduate students as well as five consultants, produced a remarkably thorough and comprehensive study with 72 recommendations and 16 "Items for Further Study." With regard to the core program, the CRUE Report recommended "that the Core Program will consist of courses whose subject matter areas and themes are chosen from the knowledge and skills areas of language, arts, and humanities; the physical and biological sciences; and the social, economic, and behavioral sciences; and the emphasis areas of international and multicultural experience, national diversity, historical consciousness, and values and ethical judgments. The emphasis area modes of inquiry and critical analysis will be present in all core courses" (*Opportunities for Renewal* 34). The key here was the six "emphasis areas" that put the design of core program courses into different contexts and frameworks. In traditional general-education courses, the subject was presented and treated generally—that is, it was an overview or general introduction providing a survey that familiarized students with the accumulated knowledge of a subject or field. This would provide a base level of knowledge or familiarity and ensure some level of recognition acceptable for university-level students.

Integrative Studies was aimed at a change in the course content and a change in the priorities of the knowledge, skill, and emphasis areas (*Opportunities for Renewal* 46). The goal was that "integrated studies," i.e., the core courses, no matter what the knowledge area, would have repeated common emphasis areas as well as featuring inquiry and critical analysis experiences in each and every course. Integrative Studies, then, would involve exploring specific knowledge and skill areas by the active process of investigative learning, with a focus on an emphasis area or areas such as international and multicultural experience, national diversity, historical consciousness, and values and ethical judgments. The desired integrations would be interdisciplinary and multidisciplinary and grounded in the experiences of diverse national and international groups at all levels, collective and individual. Knowledge became important for how its content was reached, established, understood, used or applied, and valued.

The story about how Integrative Studies as the core curriculum was developed and deployed is, of course, too lengthy and detailed for this book's purposes. Like the implementation of any curricular goals and guidelines, Integrative Studies depended on tangible and instrumental incorporation into syllabi and teaching and learning practices. Certain of the monitoring and incorporation mechanisms, such as the School of Integrative Studies in each college responsible for core curricula and a University Center for Integrative Studies that would oversee all courses, were not implemented due to financial constraints and opposition from the involved colleges. The work of teaching these new courses still fell on former general-education faculty who had to retool their pedagogy and philosophy. Faculty from within the disciplinary departments were hard to recruit for core courses because the rewards system did not value this kind of commitment, at least not at first. In spite of these limitations, many of the goals of Integrative Studies were advanced in new courses with a different philosophy and pedagogy. However, the anticipated revolution and reinvigoration of the core curriculum did not come about on a broad, sweeping scale across the university. The University Committee on General Education (UCGE) had served as a monitoring agent, even when disciplinary departments began offering substitute or alternative courses. Integrative Studies lacked an oversight committee or a center of its identity. The Integrative Studies core curriculum did not become what the CRUE Committee envisioned it could be, but it was a grand vision and "opportunity for renewal" that was unable to put down deep roots.

One program from the period of DiBiaggio's presidency that did put down deep and lasting roots was the MSU IDEA, which stood for "Institutional Diversity: Excellence in Action." This plan was put forward by the Office of the Provost in 1989 in response to MSU trustee Malcolm G. Dade Jr.'s suggestion that the "University's ideas should match its concerns" (Minutes, 13 October 1989). The "Executive Summary" in part read:

> The MSU IDEA is a plan for achieving a new level of diversity and excellence at Michigan State University to meet the needs of a changing America. It calls for renewed sensitivity to issues of race, handicap, and gender. . . . Diversity and pluralism are essential for MSU's continuing world-class distinction as a progressive land-grant/AAU institution committed to excellence and equity. . . . Racism, sexism, denigration of the worth or abilities of handicappers or other painful manifestations of inequity cannot be tolerated at Michigan State University.

The initial document was followed by MSU IDEA II in 1992, which contained "50 initiatives in the areas of leadership and administration; recruitment and retention of faculty, students, and staff;

instruction, research, and outreach; and climate." This comprehensive plan set forth the goals and ideals of a "truly multicultural community" where "diversity is woven into the fabric of daily activity." No other document has described so thoroughly and eloquently the "new community" to which MSU aspired and to which it was committed. Diversity was directly linked to excellence, and the university began to track data that would provide benchmarks for its progress. For a university that had few people of color (students, faculty, or staff) or of diverse ethnic and national backgrounds until small beginnings in the 1960s, MSU IDEA took the institution and put it on the threshold of its future as a rich and vibrant multicultural community that "demonstrates the University's social, economic, and moral reason for being." A few points in time signal the maturation of an institution and its community. This was one of them (Executive Summary, MSU IDEA II, 1992).

The President, the Board of Trustees, and the Coach

The 5 February 1988 Board of Trustees meeting featured President DiBiaggio's report on the trip to the Rose Bowl, with more than 4,500 MSU alumni and fans traveling to Pasadena to see the Spartans defeat the University of Southern California 20-17 and, after the final polls, earn an eighth-place standing in the United Press and Associated Press polls, the school's highest ranking since 1965 and 1966. A Board of Trustees resolution was presented to Coach Perles, the football staff, the team, and athletic director Douglas "Doug" Weaver offering "commendation and congratulations for the historic football season that resulted in a Big Ten title and the Rose Bowl championship." Perles's contract was extended from 3 December 1987 through 2 December 1997. President DiBiaggio "commented that the contract extension . . . is the University's commitment to Coach Perles recognizing that his personal values are consistent with the value system advocated at this University" (Minutes, 5 February 1988). It was a moment of celebratory unanimity that was, however, not destined to last.

The contract extension with an accompanying $45,000 annuity came about in the wake of a coaching offer from the Green Bay Packers that would have paid Perles $2.4 million over five years with

An MSU alumnus, Lawrence "Larry" D. Owen joined the Board of Trustees in October 1984 when Bobby Crim resigned, and Owen served through 1990. He was the major player in the maneuverings to keep George Perles at MSU when he was courted by the Green Bay Packers and later by the New York Jets, and was a supporter of Perles's appointment as athletic director while being head football coach, as was trustee Joel Ferguson. Courtesy of Michigan State University Archives and Historical Collections.

substantial retirement benefits. Perles's supporters wanted him to stay at MSU and desired some degree of security for him, and state attorney general Frank J. Kelly called Lawrence "Larry" D. Owen, chairman of the MSU Board of Trustees, to line up the majority of votes for the retention package. President DiBiaggio was in the Republic of Indonesia at the time that bargaining took place and had talked to Perles long-distance, assuring him of a long-term contract and other "things that would be helpful to [him]" (SOHP interview, 12 July 2000). When DiBiaggio returned, he was informed of the total package that had been offered and that Perles had accepted. The president had been presented with a fait accompli, and as he said in his SOHP interview, he "swallowed" the fact that the head coach had been given special considerations that professors would not receive as part of retention efforts. In his 1995 autobiography, Perles stated that "Whatever went on, this really was pretty much the end of my relationship with DiBiaggio. The funny thing was I wasn't really aware of it then. I mean, he said nice things after I got the extension" (Perles 137).

In December 1989, athletic director Doug Weaver announced he would retire in July 1989. With this opening, Perles became interested in the athletic director's position, feeling confident he could "honor Doug by continuing his good work" and admitting that he "didn't like the idea of working as football coach for somebody who didn't hire me" (Perles 144). DiBiaggio tried to convince Weaver to stay in the position he had held for ten years, but Weaver could not be persuaded.

When Perles made it known to DiBiaggio that he was interested in holding both the athletic director and head coach positions, the president made it clear that his position was that Perles could not hold both, and that if he wanted to be athletic director he would have to be a candidate in a national search conducted under affirmative action rules. Some of the trustees wondered why DiBiaggio was unwilling to take this action of dual appointment on his own the way that interim president Robben W. Fleming had done at the University of Michigan in 1988 when he appointed football coach Glenn Edward "Bo" Schembechler Jr. athletic director. Under pressure, DiBiaggio stood his ground on the principle of upholding an open search under affirmative action guidelines, the principle that expediency does not produce the best results, and the principle that the bylaws of the Board of Trustees did not allow them to make this kind of appointment without a recommendation from the university president.

The matter assumed a greater sense of urgency when before the 25 December 1989 Aloha Bowl, won by MSU over the University of Hawaii, Perles was being courted by the NFL's New York Jets. In the heat of contract negotiations and under acceptable terms, Perles accepted the position and the Jets called a press conference to announce their new coach. In response the wheels began to turn in East Lansing to deliver something that would keep Perles at MSU; that something was enough votes on the Board of Trustees to make Perles athletic director. At the 23 January 1990 special meeting, which was televised locally, the board of the Downtown Coaches Club had a resolution presented supporting the recommendation to make Perles athletic director effective 1 July 1990 at no additional salary, with the arrangement "subject to a one-year review based on criteria to be developed by the administration in consultation with the Athletic Council and approved by the Board of Trustees." Fourteen of the fifteen individuals who addressed the Board of Trustees spoke in opposition to the action. Trustees explained their positions on the matter, and trustee Barbara J. Sawyer, opposed to the resolution, had her complete comments, over two full pages, included verbatim in the meeting's minutes. Kathleen M. "Kathy" Wilbur, who would cast the deciding yes vote, did not comment before the vote. After the resolution was approved on a 5-3 vote, DiBiaggio repeated his commitment to fair and equal opportunity in searches and stated he was disappointed that "equal opportunity was denied rather than encouraged" (Minutes, 23 January 1990). He stated further "that he is philosophically opposed to a Head Coach assuming simultaneous duties as Director of Athletics as there is an inherent need for a formal system of checks and balances in all administrative areas."

This Board of Trustees meeting was indeed high public drama. The meeting ended with the president saying he did not "consider this action as a personal affront but as one that could hurt the University" and that he was "disappointed that perceived pressures of the moment were elevated over long-term benefits to the University." For a second time, chair Larry Owen had delivered the votes needed to provide Coach Perles with what he wanted to continue at MSU. For

Kathleen M. "Kathy" Wilbur was elected to the Board of Trustees in 1984 and served from 1985 to 1991, when she resigned with two years remaining in her term. On 23 January 1990 at the locally televised meeting of the board held in the Lincoln Room of the Kellogg Center, Wilbur cast the fifth and deciding yes vote for George Perles to hold the athletic director position while serving as head coach. She found herself under intense pressure from both sides of the issue. Courtesy of Michigan State University Archives and Historical Collections.

a second time, the retention package extended to Perles had been put together quickly in order to respond to his having been offered a head coach position in the NFL, and President DiBiaggio was outside the process and not in agreement with the results. To most observers it appeared that the football coach was pitted against the president and that Perles had more supporters on the Board of Trustees and behind the scenes. In his autobiography Perles stated: "The sentiment I could understand was about how DiBiaggio was being mistreated, and I had compassion for him. That put him in a bind. In a way, the vote for me was the same as a vote of no confidence in him. After that, he had to ask himself whether he was only a lame duck. Still, I don't think he had to be the bad sport about it that he was. He seemed determined not to let it work" (Perles 155).

What was operating here was larger than two individuals. It was the clash of two cultures within the university, and in actuality, it only involved one area of the university, that of athletics. The culture that Coach Perles came from was one dominated by and predicated on strong loyalties and close personal friendships that stretched over periods of time. It was a culture based on a shared love of institutional rivalries through competition on the football field, with outcomes measured in wins and losses and special distinctions like All-American players, bowl games, and awards to coaches. In many ways this culture operated on its own within the university on its own budget and by an outside set of rules, those of the National Collegiate Athletic Association (NCAA). But at the same time, this culture was vulnerable and uncertain because the coach could be fired for his team's unsatisfactory performance record. The way for a coach to reduce the uncertainty and to gain some level of security was to cultivate influential and well-placed friends, to develop a loyal following of alumni and fans, to get the best contract terms possible, and to demonstrate loyalty to the institution and its traditions. Perles was particularly good at doing all of these things and consciously connecting his football program back to his mentor and hero, Hugh "Duffy" Daugherty.

DiBiaggio was a product of a different culture, that of institutional administration—and specifically, medical and health services, where vigilant oversight and regular reviews were necessary to ensure quality and to measure efficiency. He believed in processes and administrative structures and tried to improve their functioning. As university president, he was the spokesperson for the institution's commitment to affirmative action, diversity, and multiculturalism as well as to all the processes that upheld or advanced these goals. Further, as DiBiaggio informed the Board of Trustees at the 5 April 1991 meeting, he had been tapped to serve as a presidential representative on the Knight Foundation Commission on Intercollegiate Athletics, which had recently released a report on student-athletes and defined the principles the commission believed should guide intercollegiate sports. He asked the board to consider endorsing the report. At that same meeting, trustees Barbara J. Sawyer and Dolores "Dee" Cook did just that, with Cook stating that she believed MSU "is now in a unique position to move ahead and be a front-runner in supporting the work of this Commission." Trustee Sawyer "asked the administration to provide the [Board of Trustees] Finance Committee with more specific details of athletic department financial operations" (Minutes, 5 April 1991).

At its 11 October 1991 meeting, the Board of Trustees passed a resolution regarding the Knight Foundation Commission on Intercollegiate Athletics Report that stated: "To assert unequivocally Michigan State University's participation and leadership in the national reform movement, be it resolved that the Board of Trustees commit the University to the philosophy stated by the Knight Foundation Commission of firm institutional control of athletics, to the highest standards of academic and financial integrity of the intercollegiate athletic program and to the full accountability of the Department of Intercollegiate Athletics to the values, goals, policies and procedures required of a distinguished land-grant university." This resolution, introduced by trustee Thomas Reed, was certainly the kind of endorsement DiBiaggio had sought, and it confirmed the importance of his position on the Knight Commission. In fall 1990 the Board of Trustees had established the Spartan Athletics Review Committee "to conduct a comprehensive review" of all issues related to intercollegiate athletics.

At the same time it was moving toward this resolution, the Board of Trustees at its 7 June 1991 meeting approved the evaluation criteria for the position of athletic director. The matter of Perles's dual position was to come to a head. After evaluating Perles's review as

Merrily Dean Baker became athletic director in April 1992 and stepped into a difficult situation where her every move was scrutinized and discussed. She focused on what she could accomplish and increased student-athlete support services and a community outreach program to give student-athletes a mentoring experience. She left in 1995 and Ron Mason became AD. Courtesy of Michigan State University Archives and Historical Collections.

athletic director, Provost David K. Scott recommended separation of the positions, and President DiBiaggio concurred and made a formal offer of the athletic director position; but Perles rejected the offer. The provost then recommended that Perles give up his duties as athletic director with full assurance that his contract as head coach would be honored. The board voted 6 to 2 to support this action, which would keep Perles as the coach and athletic director "on an interim basis, effective 1 December 1991, until such time as a new Director of Intercollegiate Athletics is appointed." On resolutions to delegate to the president authority for all personnel decisions regarding the athletic director, head men's basketball coach, head football coach, and head hockey coach, the board vote was 4 to 4, as was the vote to separate the athletic director position from the three head coaching positions (Minutes, 6 December 1991).

What had been definitely decided was that Perles would not continue as both head coach and athletic director for any lengthy period of time, but that he would continue as athletic director only until his successor was appointed. The proposal that the president be empowered to hire, terminate, and determine raises for the athletic director and the three head coaches was met with a 4 to 4 vote stalemate and thus defeated. On the first issue the president was supported on the separation of the two positions, but enough members of the board believed that they needed to remain involved in all personnel matters related to athletics. When Merrily Dean Baker was appointed athletic director on 3 April 1992 at the recommendation of Provost David K. Scott, the matter was finally settled, and Perles coached the Spartans in the 1992, 1993, and part of the 1994 seasons.

In his Sesquicentennial Oral History Project interview of 7 February 2001, Perles stated that "the Green Bay thing really wrecked our [Perles and DiBiaggio's] relationship. We were decent friends before that, but he was tee'd off at that." In DiBiaggio's 12 July 2000 SOHP interview, he stated that "the conflict was really with the Board of Trustees and it superseding the authority of the president." When DiBiaggio asked a board member for a public statement from the Board of Trustees that his performance was acceptable and that he would be reappointed for a period of time, he was told that the board could not do that. Without a vote of confidence from the Board of Trustees, DiBiaggio felt he was a weakened president. He had had many expressions of interest from other institutions who wanted him as their leader, and he decided to move on to Tufts University. DiBiaggio clearly envisioned finishing his administrative career at MSU and retiring from the presidency. He was a popular and successful president who accomplished a great deal and who revived and brought new energy to the land-grant identity and to the international mission of the university. Like M. Cecil Mackey, he came with the unanimous endorsement of the Board of Trustees, and then due to difficulties with the board, decided to end his presidency. Mackey moved into the Department of Economics and resumed a faculty position, but lacking an academic appointment, DiBiaggio had to leave. Perles stayed on as coach until he was fired by President M. Peter McPherson before the end of the 1994 season, and would later return to serve MSU as an elected member of the Board of Trustees.

5

Growth, Expansion, and Distinction

During the period of John A. DiBiaggio's and Gordon E. Guyer's presidencies, four iconic university figures passed away: Hugh "Duffy" Daugherty on 25 September 1987 (the exact date of the first game he coached for MSC in 1954); Jacweir "Jack" Breslin on 2 August 1988; President John A. Hannah on 23 February 1991; and Professor Russel B. Nye on 2 September 1993. Each one of these individuals had left a distinctive imprint and signature in the areas of athletics, administration, academics, and scholarship. While President DiBiaggio was working hard to connect to and revitalize their legacy, these touchstones, exemplified in such remarkable individuals, were passing from the scene. Others were nearing the end of productive careers and reaching retirement. Every large educational institution has to face the challenge of replacing individuals whose work and contributions were marked by excellence and who led with balanced judgment and a vision for the larger welfare of the university. Michigan State College underwent a period of dramatic growth into a complex and diversified institution that became a megaversity as well as an AAU research-intensive university by the mid-1960s. Those who were part of that surge, and who contributed to and directed it, came to East Lansing in the period from 1946 through 1965, and a large number of them stayed for personal, professional, and family reasons.

As an indication of the transitions underway, John E. Cantlon and Clarence L. Winder retired in 1990 and 1991 respectively. Besides establishing themselves as experts in their fields, they had served as provosts from 1969 through 1986: Cantlon from 1969 through 1976 and Winder (after serving three years from 1974 to 1977 as associate provost under Cantlon) from 1977 through 1986. Cantlon then went on to serve as vice president for research and graduate studies from

In 1993 Dean Carole Ames (*back center*) of the College of Education succeeded Judith Lanier and brought a research orientation to the college, which under Lanier had a community outreach and service orientation. Dean Ames is shown here with Provost Kim Wilcox (*left*) and President Lou Anna K. Simon (*left center*), who is shaking hands with Xu Lin, director general of the China National Office for Teaching Chinese as a Foreign Language. The college soon became a national leader in literacy studies, curriculum, international education, teacher development, and instructional technology and achieved top national rankings for its departments. Courtesy of Michigan State University Photography Services.

1977 through 1988. Cantlon had come to MSC in 1954 as an associate professor in Botany and Plant Pathology, and Winder joined the university in 1961 as the director of the psychological clinic and as program director for the doctoral program in clinical psychology. Ralph H. Smuckler, who served as dean of International Programs from 1969 to 1991 and who was probably the most readily recognized representative of MSU in the most places in the world, retired in 1993. In 1989 Henry Blosser retired as codirector of the National Superconducting Cyclotron Laboratory (after serving as director from 1958 to 1986 and then with Sam Austin and Konrad Gelbke as codirectors). Gwen Norrell, who came to MSC in 1945 and who made landmark contributions to student recruitment and athletics, retired in 1988. The foundational generation of the transition from agricultural college to modern university was taking its honored place in MSU's history.

The next generation of leadership came to the forefront in this period of transition and change. Carole Ames became dean of the

College of Education in 1993 and quickly positioned the college's departments for number-one national rankings year after year, making the college a leader in literacy studies, curriculum, teacher development, and instructional technology. Kenneth Keegstra became director of the Plant Research Laboratory after it had four different directors between 1978 and 1992, and Keegstra would provide leadership and direction for thirteen years until 2005. Konrad Gelbke's directorship of the National Superconducting Cyclotron Laboratory starting in 1992 provided continuity and leadership in the post-Blosser era.

When John DiBiaggio decided it was time for him to leave MSU and move on to the presidency at Tufts University, the Board of Trustees acted quickly to name Gordon Guyer the next president. As Guyer related the story in his Sesquicentennial Oral History Project interview of 6 April 2000, he found out that he was the new president on an outside public phone along Highway 2 near Manistique in Michigan's Upper Peninsula while he and his wife Norma were driving to their cabin. The chair of the Board of Trustees said, "Mr. President, can you come back tomorrow?" Guyer drove to Escanaba and flew back to Lansing for the formal introduction.

For the Board of Trustees there was no question that Guyer was the right person for the vacated presidency. He had his BS, MA, and PhD degrees from MSC and began his teaching career in entomology, becoming department chair in 1963, only ten years after receiving his doctorate. In 1974 he became an associate dean and took over as the director of the Cooperative Extension Service. He was part of the generation of World War II veterans who came to campus on the GI Bill, and as a graduate student had done summer entomology fieldwork in Menominee County, Michigan, and at Lake City. Guyer was a link back to John A. Hannah as well as to Jack Breslin, since he worked with Breslin while he was ill and then became vice president for governmental affairs for three years under DiBiaggio. Guyer also was involved in the state's problems with the pesticides DDT and PVB, and as department chair of Entomology he secured the federal funds to build the Pesticide Research Center.

Guyer's presidency officially began with his presiding over the 9 October 1992 Board of Trustees meeting. Just ten days later, on 19 October 1992, the third and last U.S. presidential debate took place

Kenneth Keegstra became director of the Plant Research Laboratory (PRL) in 1992 and provided leadership and direction until 2005. A University Distinguished Professor, Keegstra's research focuses on plant cell walls and the import process of proteins. Work in the PRL is done in a cross-groups approach in a system developed by Anton Lang, PRL's first director. Courtesy of Michigan State University Archives and Historical Collections.

Konrad Gelbke came to MSU in 1977, and after serving as associate director for nuclear science in the National Superconducting Cyclotron Laboratory for three years, he became the director in 1992 upon Henry Blosser's retirement. He is the director of the Facility for Rare Isotope Beams (FRIB), which when completed will be a premier world-class research center. Courtesy of Michigan State University Archives and Historical Collections.

at the Wharton Center with an estimated television audience of 91 million people. The university took center stage as the only campus to host a debate, and President Guyer took a very public position that more students beyond those ushering should be admitted to the debate. He was able to get seats for one hundred students, including students with disabilities. MSU's organization of the event, especially the smooth handling of security, received high praise, and President Guyer hosted a post-debate reception for candidates George H. W. Bush, Bill Clinton, and H. Ross Perot. On 27 April 1993, University Relations and MSU's Institute for Public Policy and Research sponsored "The Debate Revisited at Wharton Center," an event focused on President Bill Clinton's first one hundred days in office. The event featured two of the moderators—Susan Rook from CNN's *Prime News* and Gene Gibbons, chief White House correspondent from Reuters—from the original debate panel. Candidate and then President Clinton

took a personal liking to MSU's campus and made stops here in his initial campaign and second campaign for the presidency, as well as visited the campus during his national farewell tour as he concluded two terms in office.

The Guyers moved into Cowles House, and he began a year of extraordinary activity and commitments. In every detail Guyer was a full-time president who had the same level of energy and visibility that DiBiaggio had. He visited local high schools to meet with prospective students and their guidance counselors and visited Cass Technical and Renaissance High Schools in Detroit. He and Norma made it a priority to interact with people through events at Cowles House, and, as the class gift, he worked with representatives of MSU's 1993 senior class to make Cowles House accessible for persons with disabilities.

With trustees John "Jack" Shingleton and Dorothy Gonzales, as well as Dean Gill-Chin Lim of International Programs and other MSU

After participating in the third presidential debate in October 1992, hosted by MSU at the Wharton Center, and becoming president, Bill Clinton made campaign stops on campus and gave the convocation address in Spring 1995 to 6,500 graduating seniors and 50,000 parents and friends. Clinton became an honorary Spartan and delighted crowds with his accessibility and enjoyment of the events. Courtesy of Michigan State University Archives and Historical Collections.

The presidential debate held at the Wharton Center on 19 October 1992 was the third meeting featuring candidates President George H. W. Bush, Bill Clinton, and H. Ross Perot. MSU received high marks and plaudits for its staging of the debate and its security, and President Gordon Guyer hosted the three in a reception following the debate. Courtesy of Michigan State University Archives and Historical Collections.

representatives, Guyer made a trip to Costa Rica, the Dominican Republic, and Mexico for the purpose of renewing or establishing relationships with universities that could lead to exchanges or Study Abroad programs. The contingent observed the dedicated work of the W. K. Kellogg Foundation programs in Costa Rica and the Dominican Republic. In April 1993 the Board of Trustees approved a $7.5 million budget for the Food Safety/Toxicology Center. The total of the gifts, grants, and contracts for 1992–93 was over $168 million, which was an increase of 16.59 percent over 1991–92.

Guyer's year as president had its difficulties and rough spots. At the end of the fall semester, on Thursday, 10 December 1992, the "great snowball fight" erupted in the area of the Brody Complex and the parking garage adjacent to the Kellogg Center. Letting off end-of-semester steam, students engaged in a pitched battle with hand-packed snowballs or iceballs. Several students were injured. When President Guyer read that some students claimed "such an event has become a tradition," he responded by stating at the 11 December 1992 Board of

Trustees meeting: "I want to make one thing clear—this is a tradition that is over. This activity was not typical of MSU student behavior. We will not tolerate any activities that put student safety at risk and reflects negatively on the positive image of our quality student body. I assure everyone we will respond quickly and firmly to any attempts to stage such unacceptable fights in the future."

Guyer was also president during the time of the investigation into the arson committed on a university faculty member's office, destroying thirty-two years of research records, and a raid on an MSU mink research farm as cages were opened, animals released, and equipment destroyed. What followed was an uneasy time, as the MSU Police had to increase protection for research facilities and faculty offices. An indictment was made on 16 July 1993, but it was not until 1995 that the individual responsible for the attack was convicted and sentenced to 57 months in prison. What the university learned was that certain kinds of research could be a "lightning rod" for radical groups protesting for animal rights or other causes, and that these groups were capable of taking extreme measures against university research facilities.

Other important developments in 1992–93 included a dismissal of a tenured faculty member for cause and a dismissal for scientific misconduct; the institution of new training sessions related to the Americans with Disabilities Act, as well as a university-wide sexual-harassment awareness program; and the discontinuation of a requirement of health assessments for everyone prior to beginning work at MSU. For those hired before 1993, the physical examination had been part of the ritual of being hired and certified to work. The Board of Trustees also adopted a smoke-free policy for university classrooms and public spaces to be implemented by 1 January 1994.

Gordon E. Guyer's presidency was in many respects like that of Professor Walter Adams. Both were immensely popular with students and highly visible. The energetic commitment of both to guiding the university through a period of transition to the next president was greatly appreciated, and neither had ambitions beyond the administrative work they were asked to perform, although both would have made excellent presidents and many wanted them to continue in the position. A highly public effort was made to draft Walter Adams to continue as president, but he resisted the effort. Both had a distinctive

A resident of East Lansing, Dorothy Gonzales was elected to the Board of Trustees in 1992 and reelected in 2000, serving until 2008. Her connections and involvement in MSU included serving as a guidance counselor in the Office of Supportive Services and work with the School of Social Work, College of Nursing, School of Criminal Justice, and College of Human Medicine. She also had strong connections with state government for twenty-four years, serving as an educational policy adviser to Governor James "Jim" Blanchard. She gained a well-deserved reputation on the Board of Trustees as an advocate for accessibility and for the needs of first-generation students and students of color. No other trustee has had such deep working connections with MSU. Courtesy of Michigan State University Archives and Historical Collections.

personal style that was outgoing and engaging, and most of all, they had a deep identification with the university, a history with it that was long and meaningful and that translated into personal character. On 16 July 1993 the presidential portrait of President Guyer was unveiled in the Board Room.

During Guyer's presidency, the search for the next president began on 11 November 1992 with the appointment of an international consultant service firm named Heidrick and Struggles, Inc., and the second part of that name would characterize the search struggle that ensued. The original search committee was to include the eight members of the Board of Trustees, one dean, two faculty from the Executive Committee of the Academic Council (ECAC), one undergraduate and one graduate student, one alumnus or alumna, and one nonacademic administrator for a total of fifteen members (Minutes, 11 November 1992). In November, Dorothy Gonzales and J. Bob Traxler were elected to the Board of Trustees; Russell G. Mawby had joined the board in January 1992, appointed by the governor to replace Thomas Reed, who had resigned. Joel Ferguson was selected as chairman of the board at their 9 January 1993 meeting.

On 18 March 1993, the Board of Trustees met to discuss the process to be conducted by what had now became a seventeen-member search committee, with eight trustees and nine non-trustees. However, by the first week in April a hitch developed when the list of prospective applicants was disclosed to the press and made public. At this point the board decided at its 9 April 1993 meeting to disband the current Presidential Search Committee and reconvene a committee with only four trustees as members. These were Joel Ferguson, Dolores Cook, Dorothy Gonzales, and Robert E. Weiss. The nine non-trustee members of the search committee would continue. This reconstituted committee would submit a slate of candidates for the Board of Trustees to consider. At the same time the board affirmed the following proviso: "Any Trustee may, at any time, add any applicant(s) or nominee(s) to the slate of final candidates recommended to the Board of Trustees by the Presidential Search Committee" (Minutes, 9 April 1993).

On 16 July 1993, the names of four recommended candidates were revealed, and on 22 July 1993 the Board of Trustees interviewed three of them. One of the candidates had withdrawn before the interviews, and another encountered difficulties related to problematic statements he had previously made about African American athletes, which effectively disqualified him from consideration. The two remaining candidates were Lou Anna K. Simon, MSU interim provost and vice president for academic affairs, and Henry T. Yang, dean of Engineering at Purdue. At a Board of Trustees meeting on July 27, twenty-five individuals appeared to make statements regarding the presidential search, including two students who were on the search committee. All the speakers were there to speak for the selection of Lou Anna K. Simon as president (McConeghy).

Behind the scenes, however, developments were taking place that pointed in another direction. Trustees Joel Ferguson and Jack Shingleton were interested in M. Peter McPherson, who had contacted trustee Mawby early in the process and indicated his possible interest in being a candidate. Mawby advised McPherson as to where the process was and how he should make contact to express his interest (SOHP interview, 17 May 2001). At the 17 August 1993 Board of Trustees meeting, M. Peter McPherson was introduced as a candidate for president and asked questions by the trustees. At the same meeting, Shingleton moved to appoint McPherson as the nineteenth president "effective at an agreed upon open date but no later than 1 January 1994" (Minutes, 17 August 1993). The initial vote was 6 to 2 with trustees Traxler and Weiss voting no, and under a recommendation made by Traxler to make the vote unanimous, Traxler voted yes and Weiss abstained. The trustees had exercised their control over the search and selection process by adding McPherson's name to the slate of final candidates, according to the rights established in their 9 April 1993 resolution. A difficult and somewhat troubled search had come to an end with the appointment of an individual who did not have a traditional or standard dossier as a university president.

Appointed MSU's president ten days before his fifty-third birthday, McPherson brought to the position a rich and powerful combination of experience. As an MSU undergraduate from 1959 to 1963, he discovered his politics and was a member of the Young Americans for Freedom conservative student organization. After receiving his undergraduate degree in 1963, he volunteered for the Peace Corps and served in Peru for a year and a half, beginning a lifelong interest in South America and a commitment to doing

Joel Ferguson worked his way through MSU, spending days on campus in classes and working nights at the Oldsmobile plant in Lansing. He graduated with a BA in elementary education, taught for two years, and then began a highly successful company that develops residential complexes and manages rental properties. He also founded two local television stations. An active and influential Democrat, he served his first term on the Board of Trustees from 1987 to 1994 and began a second period of service in 1997. As a successful and savvy businessman, Ferguson has brought budget and investment management skills to the board and consistently focused on the university's accessibility and accountability. Courtesy of Michigan State University Photography Services.

Lou Anna K. Simon served as a faculty member after earning her PhD in administration and higher education from MSU in 1974, and then moved through a series of administrative appointments, eventually becoming provost and vice president for academic affairs from 1993 to 2004, the entire period of McPherson's presidency. She served as interim president during the year of his service in Iraq and guided the university though its second worst budget crisis in its history. Courtesy of Michigan State University Archives and Historical Collections.

constructive work to deal with hunger and poverty. After returning from Peru, he attended Western Michigan University, took a master's degree in business administration in 1967, and then went directly to American University in Washington, DC, and received a law degree in 1969. He remained in the nation's capital working from 1969 to 1975 for the Internal Revenue Service as an international tax law specialist, and after Gerald R. Ford assumed the presidency due to Richard Nixon's resignation, McPherson moved to the position of White House Staff special assistant, serving to the end of Ford's term on 20 January 1977.

From 1977 through 1980 he was a managing partner of a private law firm in Washington, DC, and with Ronald Reagan's election in 1980, he was named the general counsel to the Reagan-Bush transition team. From 1981 to 1987 he was head of the U.S. Agency for International Development (USAID) and then served as deputy secretary for the U.S. Treasury Department from 1987 to 1989. When he expressed interest in the presidency of MSU, he was executive vice president for the Bank of America, having worked there since 1989. At this point in a now twenty-four-year professional career, McPherson had served as an appointee of two U.S. presidents, worked for three federal agencies, practiced private law, and become a finance and banking executive. He had spent twenty-two years in Washington, DC, and had many powerful connections throughout the capital as well as internationally due to his direction of USAID. In some respects his qualifications and experience were like those of M. Cecil Mackey, since they both had law degrees and administrative experience in Washington, DC. The difference, of course, was that McPherson's numerous administrative positions were more diverse and lasted longer, involved serving personally for presidents, and were focused, to a large degree, on managing large agencies and their personnel and budgets. McPherson's identity as a conservative Republican was also widely and generally known.

Looking back, it is hard to understand why out of the almost two hundred publicly identified candidates McPherson did not make the list of four finalists recommended to the Board of Trustees. This can be partially explained by the fact that he had not served as a university president, which many viewed as substantially different from managing a government agency or a bank. While his politics certainly

M. Peter McPherson came to MSU's presidency in 1993 from government service, presidential appointments, and finance, as well as from a distinguished family of Spartans. The hallmarks of his administration were the MSU Promise and the Tuition Guarantee, as well as the expansion of Study Abroad programs, with MSU becoming the national leader. Courtesy of Michigan State University Archives and Historical Collections.

fit those of the State of Michigan since John Engler, a conservative Republican, had become governor in 1991, McPherson's conservative Republicanism was not an identity that most university presidents had, at least in a highly public way. Further, the other final candidates had credentials that placed them in the framework and organization of the university, and they had demonstrated some scholarship in a field. McPherson's profile was harder to read or to see its connections to the university setting and culture, and he seemed better suited to the realms where he had been, and was being, immensely successful.

McPherson had roots and connections to MSU that went back to his grandfather, Melville B. McPherson, who had served on the Board of Agriculture from 1922 to 1933, and again from 1940 to 1946 during John A. Hannah's tenure as president of MSC. Peter's mother and father had both graduated from Michigan State, and of course, McPherson had served as head of USAID, as Hannah had earlier from

1969 to 1973. Russell G. Mawby, an MSU trustee, knew the McPhersons as a "well-respected family over by Lowell" and knew Peter and his brothers and sisters through Kent County 4-H fairs, where the McPherson children showed their Shorthorn cattle. Mawby also knew Peter's sisters during the time they attended Michigan State (SOHP interview, 17 May 2001).

What the Board of Trustees saw in McPherson was an individual who had top-level administrative experience in large-scale organizations, who could make strategic and tough decisions, and who had a well-developed knowledge of finance and budgets. History had shown that state appropriations for higher education were subject to variations due to economic downturns or legislative changes in the appropriation formula. The per-student funding gap that left MSU significantly behind the University of Michigan and Wayne State University remained a continuing reality, and operating MSU at a high level of enrollment increased revenues while at the same time increasing operating costs. What was needed was a president who could manage prudently the ups and downs of state appropriations as well as maximize returns from the university's investment portfolios while protecting them. In Michigan, economic storm clouds were always on the horizon; it was just a matter of time and conditions until the storm hit. For these reasons and others, McPherson was thought to be an excellent choice.

At his first Board of Trustees meeting as president, McPherson announced to the board that he planned to consult with groups across the university "to determine guiding principles which will be used to make important decisions related to financial allocations and other types of decisions." He believed that a formulation of these principles should not be made during a crisis but in advance of one (Minutes, 8 October 1993). By the end of March 1994, the Board of Trustees endorsed the concept of six Guiding Principles:

1. Improve access to QUALITY education and expert knowledge
2. Achieve more ACTIVE LEARNING
3. Generate new KNOWLEDGE and SCHOLARSHIP across the mission
4. Promote PROBLEM SOLVING to address society's needs
5. Advance DIVERSITY WITHIN COMMUNITY
6. Make PEOPLE MATTER

These six Guiding Principles represented a reaffirmation of the land-grant philosophy and identity with its extension to the state, nation, and the world; a statement of the Association of American Universities (AAU) goals on the thirtieth anniversary of MSU's attainment of that status; and a confirmation of the university's commitment to diversity and the enhancement of the potential and importance of each individual within the university's community. For 1993–94 $2 million were budgeted for implementation. Charles Greenleaf, who was appointed as vice president for university projects on 9 December 1994, became the point person for the implementation and regularly reported to the Board of Trustees on the progress of the Guiding Principles. These became connected to progress on Study Abroad programs, retention, and strengthening of the academic environment and advising.

The value and utility of the Guiding Principles cannot be underestimated. They were an invaluable way of framing and focusing progress on a set of values and goals, and conveying reports on their implementation to the Board of Trustees and the public outside. Other than the initial commitment of $2 million they did not require further investments, since they incorporated or captured activities and initiatives already operating within the university but now guided by an articulated set of principles. While the Guiding Principles certainly served as good public relations, internally they served as a guide to charting and benchmarking progress on almost every major front of the university's operations.

The Guiding Principles were then extended into the MSU Promise, which the Board of Trustees adopted by resolution at its 10 December 1999 meeting. The Promise articulated five goals that the university hoped to achieve by its 150th anniversary celebration in 2005. The goals had been vetted and discussed in more than fifty meetings by representative students, staff, and administration, and by more than three hundred faculty members across all the colleges ("MSU Board Formally Endorses"). The goals in the Promise were:

- MSU will offer one of the best undergraduate educations available by providing the advantages of intellectual inquiry at a major research university and practical learning in the land-grant tradition.

Starting in late 1994, Charles Greenleaf was vice president for university projects under President McPherson and was the individual responsible for directing the implementation and diffusion of the six Guiding Principles. Greenleaf regularly reported on progress to the Board of Trustees and was an effective communicator. Courtesy of Michigan State University Archives and Historical Collections.

The Tuition Guarantee program lasted from 1994 through 2001, providing students with the guarantee that tuition would be held to the projected rate of inflation unless state appropriations decreased to make this impossible. It was an effort to make MSU accessible and allowed students and parents to anticipate costs better. Courtesy of Michigan State University Archives and Historical Collections.

- MSU will extend its national and international prominence in research, creative arts, and graduate professional education, through selective investment in programs of distinction and unusual promise.
- MSU will be a great global university serving Michigan and the world.
- MSU will be an exemplary "engaged university," transforming and strengthening outreach partnerships to address key Michigan needs and developing broadly applicable models.
- MSU will be a more diverse and connected community.

The provisions of the Promise expressed in more detail and elaboration the six Guiding Principles and introduced an important caveat, which was "through selective investment in programs of distinction and unusual promise." Those who had written the 1959 document *A*

Report to the President of Michigan State University from the Committee on the Future of the University (discussed in chapter 1) had stated that MSU should aspire to a future in which the university "carefully selects the programs in which it will be distinguished and allocates its available resources in a fashion that will best achieve them" (*Report* 5). This report also had as one of its "six broad principles or guides" the following: "The necessity of selectivity among programs to insure distinctiveness and quality" (*Report* 6).

Another "signature" program during President McPherson's administration was the commitment to keeping tuition costs down through what became the Tuition Guarantee. At the 14 December 1994 Board of Trustees meeting, MSU made a public commitment to holding tuition rate increases in 1995–96, 1996–97, and 1997–98 to the projected rate of national inflation, and gave assurance to the entering Fall 1995 class that this would be extended to them for a fourth year in 1998–99. The only proviso was that state appropriations for MSU's general fund had to be "at least the rate of inflation" (Minutes, 14 December 1994). At the 9 July 1998 Board of Trustees meeting, the Tuition Guarantee was extended for fiscal years 1998–99, 1999–2000, and 2000–2001, with the assurance to the entering class of Fall 1998 that the rate would be extended to them in 2001–02.

The Tuition Guarantee had the purpose of attempting to maintain accessibility to MSU (Guiding Principle 1) by providing a way that students and parents could calculate more exactly their costs over the time of their education, especially where unknown increases could be a factor in a student's attending or not. It also encouraged students to finish their studies in four years if possible. As long as inflation stayed low, the students could depend on about a 3 percent tuition increase each year. The Guarantee was also a demonstration that the university would and could manage its funds prudently, with an emphasis on finding cost savings and areas of reduction and efficiencies. What it meant was that the university would forego any revenues from tuition increases that it might have made or found necessary in the stipulated years. Of course, if inflation suddenly rose or if state appropriation increases did not meet the rate of inflation, or if the state did not "provide at least cost of living increases, it [was] anticipated that the tuition decision [would] be considered by the committee [the Board of Trustees Finance Committee] accordingly in order to sustain quality" (Minutes, 9 July 1998). The Tuition Guarantee received wide national media attention and plaudits for its college costs containment program, and it certainly garnered the appreciation of Spartan students and families. It has been widely debated among faculty as to whether it was the best decision for the time or if it benefited the university in any substantial or strategic way. Some faculty felt that salaries suffered and ended up lagging further behind their Big Ten counterparts.

It was, of course, an experiment that could have failed and been rescinded if economic conditions had developed otherwise. What was remarkable is the fact that the Tuition Guarantee lasted seven years and benefited as many students as it did. But in early 2001 the question was raised about the difficulty of maintaining it, and by July 2001 it was clear that it could not be offered for 2001–02. The 1999–2000 state appropriation for MSU had been $303,826,465, a 5 percent increase from 1998–99. The appropriation for 2000–2001 was $321,161,401, and the appropriation for 2001–02 was $325,982,300, which was a 1.5 percent increase. In 2003–04 the operating budget took a 5 percent hit under a governor's emergency budget order, and for 2004–05 the change from the previous year was nil. As the university neared its Sesquicentennial Celebration in 2005, it was experiencing a budget situation of unrelieved bad news. Thus, for 2002–03 the university was facing the absolute necessity of an 8.5 percent tuition increase after a seven-year average tuition increase of only 2.8 percent, and with the tuition increase would come budget cuts. President McPherson had said it was important that guiding principles should not be made during a crisis but in advance of one (Minutes, 8 October 1993). The beginning of that crisis, which would be a prolonged one, came in 2001–02 when the storm clouds on the economic horizon began to gather ominously.

Another hallmark of the McPherson era was the focus on the Study Abroad program and its expansion. McPherson had developed expertise in South America and Africa, and his years in directing USAID focused on the acute problems of starvation and food scarcity in Africa. As a Peace Corps volunteer, he had seen poverty in Peru and been involved in a food distribution program. He knew the experiential value of being put into a culture where one had to observe, learn, and adjust as well as adapt to other ways of living. In December

1999 he announced to the Board of Trustees a goal of doubling the number of participating students by 2005, and by December 2002 the MSU Study Abroad Program was ranked number one nationally in terms of the number of students participating. In 1995 the Overseas Study Action Task Force had set a goal of 40 percent of graduating seniors participating in a Study Abroad program by 2006. By 2004 MSU's Study Abroad programs had grown from 800 students to more than 2,200, from sixty available programs to more than two hundred. The growth of this program was accompanied by careful assessment of risks and concerns for student safety as well as attention to cost containment achieved through central planning. What secured the successful expansion of Study Abroad was the commitment of the MSU Federal Credit Union to establish $2.5 million in endowed scholarships for students in the program. In June 2003, MSUFCU issued a check for $500,000 as the first part. In every way it was not a program set on rapid growth to achieve numbers; it was focused on a quality learning experience and security, as well as expectations regarding student conduct.

Challenges and Issues

During his eleven years as president, Peter McPherson enjoyed a positive and supportive relationship with the Board of Trustees, which annually gave him evaluations of "impressive" or "outstanding" and awarded him raises of 3 percent, which was the limit he would accept. In 2000 the Board of Trustees gave him an additional increment of $25,000, which he donated back to plant trees on south campus. He declined a raise in 2003 and returned his raise for 2004–05 to the General Fund. No previous president had such a continuously compatible relationship with the Board of Trustees or earned such strong accolades from them. Much of the respect and support he enjoyed had to do with his strong sense of fiscal responsibility and his thorough knowledge of budgets. In many ways the Tuition Guarantee complemented his fiscal conservatism, since the Guarantee's limiting factor meant that new programs or initiatives had to be carefully selected and limited, and every possible economy or efficiency had to be pursued. However, the sheer scale of budget cuts necessitated

Before becoming vice president for finance and operations for MSU in 1999, Fred L. Poston served as dean of the College of Agriculture and Natural Resources and guided the $74.2 million Revitalization of Michigan Animal Agriculture project through its phases and to completion. With his graduate degrees in entomology, Poston is another in a line of scientists who have moved into key administrative positions and provided leadership in challenging times. Courtesy of Michigan State University Archives and Historical Collections.

program eliminations and moratoriums, such as the program to train teachers of the visually impaired, and elimination of departments such as the Department of Material Science and Mechanics in 2001, with reassignment of its faculty and programs. In all, eight programs were discontinued and moratoriums put on sixteen programs, with program cuts in sixteen others. All Urban Affairs programs were eliminated as of 1 July 2003. This time also saw the beginning of cuts to the Agricultural Experiment Station and Agricultural Extension, a downward spiral of lessening support that would continue unabated. McPherson was fortunate to have Provost and Vice President for Academic Affairs Lou Anna K. Simon as the guide through these troubled waters. Her calmness, ability to assess curricular and programmatic areas of strength and promise, and her toughness but fairness in making difficult decisions helped the university see its way through its most perilous financial crisis in twenty years.

Another reason McPherson enjoyed such a strong relationship with the Board of Trustees was the trustees' awareness of how much he was involved with the oversight and review of the university's trusts and its portfolio of investments. Because of his knowledge of financial and investment markets and the reputations of firms in 2004, MSU was in the top 2 percent nationally in terms of returns and endowments. The Board of Trustees, which oversees all the university's assets, was fortunate also to have highly successful businessmen as trustees—individuals like Randall L. Pittman (elected in 2002) and Joel Ferguson (1987–94 and again starting in 1997). Behind McPherson and the Board of Trustees were excellent financial officers, such as Vice President and Treasurer Fred L. Poston and Controller David B. Brower.

There were a few bumps along the road for McPherson in the form of issues, unwelcomed developments, or questioning of his decisions. For example, the decision in 1994 to privatize the MSU Bookstore in the International Center was opposed by the Clerical-Technical Union (CTU) of MSU on the grounds that it was a hasty decision, and many of the faculty were concerned as well, believing that the bookstore was an institution that should not be run by an outside corporation. From the administration's point of view, the bookstore had been badly managed and was losing money when it should be able to produce revenues and be more competitive with local bookstores.

McPherson also had to deal with student disturbances that were connected to sports. The first incident had to do with a ban placed on alcohol consumed at tailgate parties on the Intramural Athletic Field (Munn Field) before and after home football games. Urged on by an e-mail call to action, students gathered on 1 May 1998 to protest not only the alcohol ban, but a ban on gathering at Munn Field to protest, with the stipulated punishment of arrest if they trespassed. It was a confrontation that the students won due to numbers, as more than half of the estimated three thousand of them climbed the fence around Munn Field and played games until they were tear-gassed and driven away to Grand River Avenue, where tear-gas was again used.

However, the most serious incident occurred the evening of 27 March 1999, after the MSU Spartans basketball team lost to Duke 68-62 in the NCAA National Semifinals in a game played in St. Petersburg, Florida. It was the first Tom Izzo–coached team to make the Final Four. Large crowds of gathering and roaming students hit the streets just off campus, and whatever disappointment they might have felt in the loss turned to throwing projectiles at police, smashing and overturning vehicles, setting couches on fire, and resisting efforts to control or disperse them. Of the 132 people arrested, about half were students. Property damage estimates ranged from $250,000 to $500,000. Some attributed the riot to poor relations between police and students, and what students saw as heavy-handed police stifling of student recreation where large numbers gathered, drank, and partied. Other rumors and stories claimed that certain individuals and groups planned to riot and had prepared in advance for it. When the Ingham County Prosecuting Attorney's Office subpoenaed visual evidence of the rioters taken by news media reporters, eleven different news organizations refused to turn over their footage, and the case went all the way to the Michigan Supreme Court, which upheld the right of the news organizations to withhold whatever they had recorded. Thus, the only ones who suffered liability due to their actions were those arrested. A smaller-scale outbreak took place on Saturday, 2 April 2005 after Michigan State had lost a Final Four semifinal game to North Carolina 87-71. The number of students involved was small by comparison with 1999, and property damages were estimated at less than $10,000.

In response to the surprising and disappointing event on 27 March 1999, the Board of Trustees passed an Interim Student Conduct Policy at its 9 April 1999 meeting that prohibited students from engaging "in disorderly conduct at or in connection with a riot" and provided for temporary suspension "pending final determination of whether the student has violated this Policy." The policy covered "disorderly conduct" on the campus, all areas adjacent to the campus, and any other campus or community. On 8 December 2000, the Board of Trustees made the policy permanent and framed the document within the context of relevant university documents governing students, as well as enumerated more descriptively the kinds of actions covered. Concerns were raised about due process, students' right to assemble and protest, and First Amendment rights. However, the policy had wide support from faculty and student groups. What had happened was that whatever liberality and latitude had been extended regarding student behavior on and off campus was now definitely restricted, and the consequences (prosecutions and fines in addition to suspensions) for dangerous and unacceptable behavior had been clearly defined. MSU had received a great deal of negative publicity in national media coverage from the riots or disturbances, perpetuating its image as a "party school" of hard-drinking and unruly students who could get out of control. Internally, however, this slanted reputation was unacceptable to the administration, faculty, staff, and to the great majority of students. Out of concern for the university's good name and public safety, the campus community came together through open forums and discussions to set clear and reasonable limits on student behavior, and to make it clear that definite consequences would result from actions that were proven to be unreasonable and irresponsible.

Another shocking development came on 31 December 1999 with an act of arson at Agriculture Hall. The fire, which caused an estimated $1 million in damage, affected offices involved in research on the enhanced use of crop biotechnology in developing countries. Those responsible for igniting the fire bomb somehow believed that the research project involved genetically modified organisms. It was not until 2008, eight years later, that four members of the Earth Liberation Front were charged with the crime identified as an "act of domestic terrorism" ("Four Charged"). Fortunately the fire was

The arson fire at Agriculture Hall on 31 December 1999 was fortunately contained to the fourth floor, but it shocked the campus community and reminded everyone of the challenges involved in protecting university research facilities on a large, sprawling campus. The perpetrators were not identified and charged with the "act of domestic terrorism" until 2008. Courtesy of Michigan State University Archives and Historical Collections (*Red Cedar Log* 2000).

contained, but the blackened scar on the north side of the fourth floor of Agriculture Hall was a reminder of the fact that extremist groups could target university research programs and facilities for the purpose of making symbolic statements through destructive acts. It was a painful reminder of how science and scientific research can be misunderstood and even demonized.

New Buildings and Research Facilities

Even with the restricted budgets that were part of President McPherson's administration, this was a remarkable period of new buildings and specialized facilities as well as additions. The gem of the new construction was the $93 million, 360,000 square-foot Biomedical and Physical Sciences Building, which opened in February 2002 and was dedicated on 12 April 2002. In 1999, after the project had been approved, the Ford Motor Company contributed $5 million to its

ABOVE AND OPPOSITE: The Biomedical and Physical Sciences Building opened in February 2002, providing more than 360,000 square feet of space in seven stories and a new home for three departments and other interdisciplinary centers and projects. The State of Michigan funded three-fourths of the $93 million cost, and several generous private donations were made. The building represents and provides for an interdisciplinary science center where collaborative and interconnected scientific research can flourish, and where the facility serves as a magnet attracting top-flight researchers and graduate students. Courtesy of Michigan State University Photography Services.

construction. Shared by the Physics and Astronomy, Physiology, and Microbiology and Molecular Genetics departments, this building is located at the heart of what is becoming the physical and geographical center of campus, and it anchors what is a remarkable series of research buildings and facilities extending from the Engineering complex east to the Cyclotron, and then from the Veterinary Medical Center complex back west to the Communication Arts and Sciences Building. And south of the Vet Med Center is another cluster of buildings located around the Clinical Center. Two other major additions to this were the National Food Safety and Toxicology Center, built at a cost of over $24 million, and the Radiology Building housing the Department of Radiology, a unit that represented a new investment in 1997, when it was established, and that quickly became a major provider of health services and National Institutes of Health–funded research, with a special focus on sports medicine.

The Veterinary Medical Center added the Mary Anne McPhail

Equine Performance Center, which opened in June 2000, and earlier established the Horse Teaching and Research Center in 1994. Combined, these centers cost almost $4 million. The Pavilion for Agriculture and Livestock Education (or "the Pavilion" for short) cost $14 million. The MSU Center for Comparative Oncology addition to the Veterinary Medical Center was budgeted at $12.7 million, and now provided treatment for domestic pets diagnosed with cancer, as well as focusing on research. During this eleven-year period, $15.9 million was budgeted for the "Revitalization of Michigan Animal Agriculture Project," and every research center (cattle, poultry, swine, equine) was renovated or entirely new facilities were built. This level of commitment, established in a brick row of buildings built in the 1890s, signaled that the health of the animal population and humans, and their complex relationships and interdependencies were a central focus of a land-grant institution.

National Rankings

In 1995 the National Research Council published its 740-page study *Research-Doctorate Programs in the United States: Continuity and Change,* an updating of the 1982 NRC study examining programs in forty-one fields. The key difference between these two studies was that the 1995 one provided relative rankings of programs from top to bottom. Another difference was that the two top-ranked programs at MSU in the 1970 Roose-Anderson ratings (Botany ranked ninth and Entomology was tied for twelfth) were now no longer separate identifiable fields in the 1995 report.

The MSU programs ranked in the top quarter of their fields were:

- Cell and Developmental Biology .... 40th of 179
- Chemistry .... 39th of 168
- Mathematics .... 45th of 135
- Physics .... 32nd of 147
- Psychology .... 46th of 185

Additional programs that ranked in the top third of their fields were:

- Biochemistry/Molecular Biology .... tied for 51st of 194
- Ecology, Evolution, and Behavior .... tied for 34th of 129
- Economics .... 27th of 108
- Pharmacology .... 36th of 127
- Political Science .... 27th of 98

Additional programs that ranked in the top half of their fields were:

- Chemical Engineering .... 45th of 93
- Civil Engineering .... 41st of 86
- Computer Science .... 52nd of 107
- Electrical Engineering .... 44th of 126
- English .... 60th of 127
- History .... 48th of 111
- Mechanical Engineering .... 43rd of 110
- Molecular and General Genetics .... tied for 36th of 103
- Physiology .... 47th of 135
- Sociology .... 42nd of 95
- Statistics and Biostatistics .... 30th of 65

In each of the five fields where in 1995 MSU programs ranked in the top quarter, at least five (in the case of Physics) or six (in the case of Cell and Developmental Biology) Big Ten schools were ranked ahead of MSU, and in the other three fields eight or nine were ranked ahead of MSU. This certainly indicates the overall strength of the Big Ten in national rankings, and their longstanding identities as research-oriented institutions with AAU membership and funding connections to the federal government and its agencies. A quick look at the rankings might lead one to the conclusion that most of the top-ranked departments or programs slipped between 1970 and 1995, and in terms of placement that is true. But the impression obscures some significant progress evident here. Graduate faculty whose quality was rated second-tier and whose rated effectiveness of the graduate program was third-tier in the Roose-Anderson 1970 report moved their programs ahead and received improved ratings. The group in 1970 with a second-tier rated faculty and third-tier program included Political Science, Economics, History, and English. The first two

In 1980 Judith E. Lanier became the first woman named dean of the College of Education. As a faculty member she helped establish the Institute for Research on Teaching (IRT), which was funded from 1976 to 1986 by the National Institute of Education. The IRT focused on interdisciplinary research that connected the college with public school teachers in a collaborative effort to improve classroom teaching overall and the instruction of specific subjects. Courtesy of Michigan State University Archives and Historical Collections.

moved into a top-third ranking in 1995, and the two from the College of Arts and Letters moved into the top half. Each of the four engineering programs (Chemical, Civil, Electrical, and Mechanical) were ranked in the top half of their fields. Each of these eight programs made substantial gains and progress. Overall, of course, MSU doctoral programs had been hurt by a decline in graduate school enrollments that began in the mid-1970s, and by the later impact of a series of budget crises in Michigan that resulted in more limited funding for graduate student support. MSU programs granted 3,710 doctoral degrees in the 1960s; 5,642 in the 1970s; and 4,375 in the 1980s. The need to increase undergraduate enrollments in order to offset lower state budget appropriations meant having to staff the basic courses, with departments having more limited flexibility in terms of assigning faculty to research. The demand for master's degrees continued strong, with resources needed to provide courses and seminars and to supervise theses. The number of master's degrees granted from 1960 to 1970 was 17,745, with 19,232 granted from 1970 to 1980, and 18,227 granted in the 1980s. The production of master's degrees does not count in the National Research Council ratings.

In 1980 Judith E. Lanier became the first woman dean of the College of Education (which in 1955 succeeded the School of Education established in 1952). The college had won a national competition in 1976 and established the Institute for Research on Teaching (IRT) on the basis of a $3.6 million grant from the National Institute of Education. Lanier had played a major role in securing the IRT grant; she contributed two significant papers to the institute's growing list of publications: "Research and Development Needs for the Advancement of Teacher Education" (with Professor Robert E. Floden) and "Research on Teaching: A Dynamic Area of Inquiry" (both in 1978, and both distributed nationally by the Educational Resources Information Center [ERIC]).

The IRT received funding for another five years in 1981, and in 1985 the college established the National Center for Research on Teacher Education with a grant from the U.S. Department of Education. The center was renamed in 1991 as the National Center for Research on Teacher Learning when its funding was renewed, and its work ended in 1995, two years after Carole Ames was appointed dean to succeed Lanier.

The IRT emphasized collaboration and teamwork to address the problems and challenges of American education. Four teams of researchers were organized around the teacher, the learner, the subject matter, and the setting ("The 1970s: IRT Helps Shape Direction"). In 1980–81 there were thirty-five individuals listed in the IRT, including teaching collaborators, graduate assistants, and support personnel. The research projects conducted were wide-ranging and inclusive, with a focus on the teacher as the professional who planned, executed, managed, monitored, and evaluated the learning process. K–12 teachers worked in the IRT, spending half days teaching in public schools and half days working at the Institute. The project stimulated group and individual research and publications, which had not previously been a priority or practice among the education faculty. The College of Education became a hub of research on how classroom teachers learn to teach and become more effective managers and directors of complex learning activities. One of the highlights of Dean Lanier's twelve-year tenure was the 1983 visit of U.S. Secretary of Education Terrel H. Bell to Erickson Hall to honor the Institute for Research on Teaching and to use the occasion to release the important *A Nation at Risk* report.

The IRT had succeeded in prompting and supporting faculty research, given the college's national visibility, and helped establish a new research agenda in education. These salutary developments attracted even more highly qualified graduate and undergraduate students and made the college a center of spirited critical discussions about teaching education in all its phases. The research emphasis was on service to the profession and to education. Including public school teachers who worked half-time in the IRT was an innovative feature, and the institute's publication *Communication Quarterly* reached twelve thousand teachers at one point.

In 1993 Carole Ames was brought in from the outside as the college's next dean. The contract funds supporting the IRT had ended in 1986, and the funding for the National Center for Research on Teacher Learning would end in 1995. A number of the faculty were near retirement or moving into their last few years. For a new dean, it was a promising situation and a challenging one. Certainly, momentum had been gained and the reputation of the college was on the upswing on and off campus. From Ames's perspective, the education faculty needed to be more productive in the form of publications that counted: articles in professionally refereed journals and books. The scholarly fields needed to be more diverse and distinctive and to take in the full range of developing scholarship. Faculty needed to understand and embrace the reality that regular, consistent published scholarship was expected for tenure and promotion. The dependence on a large grant that could support faculty activity needed to be replaced by aggressive grant-seeking by individuals and groups and aimed at a wider range of funding sources. Dynamic work and activity needed to be demonstrated by everybody.

Certainly, one could say that Dean Ames found herself in the best possible situation in only her second year at MSU when in 1994 *U.S. News and World Report* ranked several of the college's graduate programs in the nation's top ten and gave the elementary- and secondary-education programs number-one rankings. Over the eighteen-year period she guided the college, four institutes and five centers were established, each with its own agenda for research and outreach. The Institute for Research in Teaching and Learning (IRTL) works with faculty on research funding opportunities and provides in-house seed grants, and is very different in scope and purpose from the IRT established in 1976. Some of the centers have very specific focuses, such as the Center for Teaching and Technology or the Center for Physical Activity and Health, while others, such the Literacy Achievement Research Center or the Center for the Scholarship of Teaching, take on broader areas. This organization has served the college well and earned it increased recognition. In Dean Ames's tenth year, MSU became one of the first four institutions in the "Teachers for a New Era" initiative, as well as received a $6 million grant from the Broad Foundation to establish the Broad Partnership between MSU and the Detroit Public Schools with the goal of providing support for future teachers in Detroit.

MSU programs outside the NRC rankings also were recognized for their strong reputations. In 1992 the Department of Forestry was ranked number three in the country in a national survey. In the *Farm Futures* magazine for mid-March 1993, the College of Agriculture was cited as one of the "10 schools that stand out for their general excellence" and was noted for its specialization in "livestock and subjects other than the traditional grain crops of many Midwestern states" as well as for its involvement "with Third World development projects" (Jacobitz 12). In 1995 MSU's Graduate School of Music was named one of the top twenty-five graduate programs nationally (Minutes, 13 October 1995). In 1998 the doctoral program in industrial and organizational psychology would become the top-ranked program in the country and remain as such year after year. In 2002 the *Wall Street Journal* rankings of full-time MBA programs put MSU thirteenth nationally and fifth among public institutions (Minutes, 13 September 2002).

The lessons MSU has learned from its history with national rankings have been illuminating. In the 1960s, when federal funds were flowing generously to higher education and when MSU was growing rapidly into a "megaversity," departments were able to build graduate programs and move students through to degree completion. The institution was seen as an up-and-coming one that was energetic, ambitious, and resourceful. In its rapid growth, it was guided by individuals in key positions who had good connections nationally and internationally, and who knew how to direct grants and funds that strengthened the infrastructure for research. Internally, departments were encouraged to innovate and experiment with some large-scale instructional models, and were allowed to retain the savings from their economies for program expansion if it was well planned and articulated. The university had established a good base for doctoral programs in the 1950s, when 1,245 PhDs were granted, and the influx of new appointments, often at the rank of full professor or advanced associate professor, established departments attractive to graduate students. The high point in terms of doctorates awarded was 1969–70 and 1970–71, when 1,407 degrees were conferred. Of the 5,642 doctorates awarded in the 1970s, there were 4,257 (an average of 608 per year) in the period from 1970 to 1977. The number of PhDs awarded slipped below 500 in 1977–78, and it would be thirty-two years before more than 500 doctorates were again granted in a single year.

With the surge that was evident starting as early as 1963–64, but especially evident in 1968–69, came good national rankings of departments in 1970 that had expanded graduate programs and faculty and were moving students to degrees, while other programs in the Roose-Anderson ratings had well-rated faculty but their doctoral programs were not highly rated for effectiveness. In a rating system that was based on the number of degrees granted and on the number of graduate students supported (in addition to faculty publication productivity and reputation in their fields), MSU was fated to suffer a decline in ratings when its production of doctoral degrees declined and when its resources became more constrained. As time would show, setting one's heart or goal on a high national ranking was not realistic, but relative position in a field comparable to similar institutions with like resources could be improved. Research affecting and improving lives, or providing possible solutions to problems or conditions could be valued as part of a mission. Specialization programs or discrete fields, such as nuclear physics (developed in connection with the Cyclotron), could provide a nationally high-ranked program, as was the case with the MSU unit that moved into the second spot behind MIT (and eventually became the top-ranked program). The eleven programs rated in the top half or top third in the 1995 NRC rankings reflect a process of selective investment made by MSU as well as historical strengths demonstrated by these units. The number-one ranking of the MSU industrial and organizational psychology program in 1998 also indicates how a specialized field can move ahead, while rankings in discrete fields or subfields can vary more from year to year.

The Arts and Culture

In 1962 the large single School of Science and Arts founded in 1944 was broken up into three colleges: Natural Science, Social Science, and Arts and Letters. Journalism became a school and was transferred to the College of Communication Arts. In 1985 Provost Clarence L. Winder formed the Consolidation Evaluation Committee to look at the possibility of creating a unified college of liberal arts and sciences, but that possibility was roundly rejected. In 2004 Provost Lou Anna K. Simon set up the Committee on College Reorganization after proposing a consideration of a new College of Communication, Arts, Literature and Media. That proposal was met with stiff resistance, so the committee was charged with looking at options and making a recommendation. The door was thus opened to talk of alternative organizational structures or new affiliations. In this context the Department of History negotiated a move to the College of Social

Science and thus left Arts and Letters. The School of Music wanted to report directly to the provost and not to the CAL dean, and it left Arts and Letters and became its own college under Dean James Forger. The Committee on College Reorganization recommended the improvement of the "liberal arts and sciences education of MSU without significant college reorganization now." Part of the improvement would be the establishment of the Residential College in the Arts and Humanities, a recommendation that found favor and support.

In the single School of Science and Arts (1944–62), those departments and faculties in the fine and performing arts, language and literature, and social science divisions were part of a large college organized into six divisions, each with a director. The pressures of increasing enrollments and the growth of majors pointed to a simpler organizational structure where departments became more important and distinct. The umbrella School of Science and Arts, which lasted just eighteen years, gave way to a more traditional and conventional organization of the three colleges, which has continued since then.

Three of the first four deans of Arts and Letters were historians. Paul A. Varg (dean from 1962 to 1970) and Richard E. Sullivan (dean from 1970 to 1979) came from the MSU Department of History, and John W. Eadie (dean from 1987 to 1997) came from the Department of History at the University of Michigan. In between Sullivan and Eadie, Alan M. Hollingsworth, who had been chair of the Department of English, served as dean from 1979 to 1987. Professor Gordon Stewart of the MSU Department of History served as interim dean in 1997–98 until the college had its first woman dean appointed, Wendy K. Wilkins, who served from 1998 to 2004.

The challenges the deans of Arts and Letters have faced involved building strong disciplinary departments, fostering the fine and performing arts, and making the case for the liberal arts and humanities as a vital part of a university education. As a university education has become more professionalized with a focus on careers and job placement, the case for the desirability of studying literature and experiencing culture of a wide variety and types is increasingly more challenging to assert. Previous generations of students came to the university with a goal of becoming more culturally sophisticated and more knowledgeable about literature, history, music, drama, and the arts. The goal included a freedom of inquiry and exploration as

Dean James Forger was appointed director of the School of Music in 1990, and under his leadership the school became its own college, experienced a 70 percent growth in enrollments, and developed a nationally ranked graduate program. He is an accomplished saxophonist and recording artist and has been a regularly invited guest artist at summer festivals in Mexico and the United States, as well as performing as a soloist with five symphony orchestras, including ones in Poland and Colombia. He founded the Community Music School in 1994 and brought the vibrant Jazz Studies program into the curriculum. Courtesy of Michigan State University College of Music.

Dean John W. Eadie assumed leadership of the College of Arts and Letters in 1987, and while serving for ten years, he established the highly successful Celebrity Lecture Series, which brought distinguished writers and performing artists to campus and put the college in the limelight. He also established the Dean's Community Council to provide local support for the arts. Courtesy of Michigan State University Archives and Historical Collections.

well as the development of tastes that would enrich and enhance one's life during college and long after. College offered a wealth of riches in terms of the kinds of courses and professors available over a broad spectrum of fields, and the core curriculum offered this to all students. The university also offered occasions to see and hear great writers, artists, philosophers, musicians, thinkers, and others invited to campus. One never knew when a cultural encounter or experience would turn one in an unanticipated, exciting direction or prompt a change in one's major.

During John W. Eadie's tenure as dean of the College of Arts and Letters, he established the Dean's Community Council in 1998, which included such individuals as local businessman Alan Suits and former CAL dean Richard E. Sullivan. Out of this productive partnership of the college and community came the Celebrity Lecture Series, which ran from 1988 through 1999. In each of the first eight years, the series featured the appearance of two or three prominent individuals (four in 1991). The first three lectures in 1989 were attended by over six thousand people (Jones). A total of thirty-one writers, poets, playwrights, and dancers appeared in the series, including Pulitzer Prize winners, National Book Award winners, and a Nobel Prize in Literature winner, poet and playwright Derek Walcott. International figures included Isabel Allende of Chile, Margaret Atwood of Canada, Carlos Fuentes of Mexico, and Walcott of Saint Lucia. For those who followed major American writers, the appearances of Arthur Miller, Joseph Heller, Philip Roth, Norman Mailer, John Updike, Kurt Vonnegut Jr., Edward Albee, Susan Sontag, and Joyce Carol Oates were special. African American writers included Maya Angelou, Terry McMillan, and August Wilson (Celebrity Lecture Series). The series brought additional excitement about the written and performing arts to the campus and gave high visibility to the College of Arts and Letters for a decade. Dean Wendy K. Wilkins created Fora: Lectures in the Arts and Humanities Series, which connected the lectures to programs in the college and featured the lecturers meeting with students in classroom settings or colloquiums.

The Department of English developed and fostered an emphasis on creative writing taught and practiced by talented faculty. Virgil Scott joined the faculty in 1947 and published six major novels with top-rank publishers between 1947 and 1976. He retired in 1977 after teaching creative writing for thirty years. Glendon Swarthout (PhD in English from MSU in 1955), professor of communication skills, published *Where the Boys Are* (1960), a seriocomic novel about six Michigan State students who go to Ft. Lauderdale, Florida, for spring break in 1958. The novel was quickly adapted into a major Hollywood film in the same year and is credited with the phenomenon of the mass migration of U.S. college students to Florida for their spring breaks (Castanier). In 1958 Swarthout published *They Came to Cordura*, a Western novel set in Mexico during the time of the U.S. expedition to capture Pancho Villa, and it was produced as a film in 1959. Swarthout took a leave without pay for the Fall quarter of 1958 to be part of the filming. Although the rest of his novels were published after his move to Arizona, Swarthout brought national media attention to East Lansing through his skill in writing best-selling novels that quickly became popular and successful films. Another talented creative writer later joined the English department faculty in 1966 and taught creative writing until his retirement in 1991. Albert Drake was a multigenre writer who published poetry, fiction, and nonfiction, both with small presses and in the prominent literary magazines and journals. Other creative writers who have been or are English faculty include poet-in-residence Diane Wakoski, fiction and nonfiction writer Marcia Aldrich, and fiction writers Gordon Henry Jr. and William S. Penn.

The *Red Cedar Review*, a journal of literature and art, was founded in 1963 and is the longest continuously published undergraduate-run journal of its kind in the United States. It publishes original prose, poetry, and visual art of undergraduates all over the country. The *Centennial Review* began in 1957 as the *Centennial Review of Arts & Science*, a publication within the School of Science and Arts. It has been published continuously, beginning as a quarterly and then becoming a triquarterly. Beginning in 2001 the Michigan State University Press began publishing the journal (renamed the *New Centennial Review*), and in 2003 the *Red Cedar Review*. An important part of the literary culture at Michigan State has been the presence of noted national journals and editors, which have been strongly supported by Lou Anna K. Simon as provost and as president, and by the deans of the College of Arts and Letters as well as the MSU Press. *Fourth Genre: Explorations in Nonfiction*, founded in 1999 by

Samuel "Sam" Raimi and his brother Ivan, along with Robert "Rob" Tapert, made a film titled *The Happy Valley Kid* that became an on-campus sensation and launched Sam Raimi and Tapert into careers as independent filmmakers. Rami has achieved phenomenal success in Hollywood, directing all three Spider-Man films, which together have grossed well over $2 billion. Courtesy of Michigan State University Archives and Historical Collections (*Red Cedar Log* 1978).

Professor Michael Steinberg of the Department of American Thought and Language, has become one of the top two publications nationally for creative nonfiction, and its featured authors have won many national prizes for their pieces in the journal.

The cultural ferment of the 1960s and early 1970s on campus produced several generations of students with creative and experimental temperaments. Part of that can be attributed to the university's aggressive and successful recruitment of National Merit Scholars, the rapidly expanding enrollment and growth of dorms that brought an increasingly diverse mix of students to campus, the presence of liberal and radical professors who encouraged independent thinking and questioning, the upsetting effects of the Vietnam War and the draft with the resulting protests and radical organizations, and the development of a visible counterculture and hippie lifestyle. The size and complexity of Michigan State and its necessarily bureaucratic organization gave the students something to push back against, confront, or subvert. At the same time, the university provided a field of open play and exploration for creative students. Clubs were easy to organize, and with a faculty sponsor they gained recognition and status from the university. Equipment for making films could be checked out for no fee, and ASMSU had funds to support student projects. A liberal and flexible atmosphere up through the Spring quarter of 1971 allowed eight radical and activist student movement groups to have offices in the Student Services Building. One of the groups was the staff of *Joint Issue*, an underground publication presented as the alternative to the *State News* (Wachsberger 218).

In the wake of all this student ferment, Samuel "Sam" Raimi came to MSU, as did Robert "Rob" Tapert, joining Ivan Raimi, Sam's older brother, in creating a campus organization called the Society for Creative Filmmaking. Together, they made a film called *The Happy Valley Kid*, an offbeat fantasy comedy about a young man who is met with rejection everywhere at college, has a breakdown, and then dresses up as a cowboy and guns down all his tormentors. The film was screened on campus for fourteen weekends and proved to be so popular that Raimi and Tapert made a profit on the film ("Sam Raimi"). After three semesters, the two left MSU and launched a career as independent filmmakers. Raimi would go on to direct all three Spider-Man films, which collectively have grossed well over $2 billion.

Another MSU student, Jack Epps Jr., made a documentary film called *Pigs vs. Freaks*, based on the series of challenge football games between counterculture young men and the police. Epps was able to sell the concept to NBC, and it became a 1984 made-for-television film. But the most important connection Epps made was with Jim Cash, who had received a BA in English from MSU in 1970 and an MA in Television and Radio in 1972, and who began teaching creative screenplay writing and film history. Epps and Cash teamed up after Epps enrolled in Cash's screenplay writing course, and they wrote several unproduced screenplays before their incredible success with *Top Gun* in 1986 and six more that followed between 1987 and 2000. It was an amazing creative and productive partnership and friendship that ended only with Cash's early death at age 59. Cash was a dynamic

Jack Epps Jr. (*right*) connected with his MSU professor Jim Cash (*left*), and the two wrote the screenplay for *Top Gun* and other successful commercial films. Their creative partnership and friendship ended only because of Cash's early death at age 59. © 1987 Douglas Elbinger.

presence on campus, accessible and personable, and his "History of the Motion Picture" course in the Department of Television and Radio was probably the most popular large-enrollment course on campus. The parties he threw and hosted often were populated with guests from Hollywood. His breakthrough success and fame shared with Jack Epps was the stuff of legend and pride. Not since Glendon Swarthout's earlier success with *They Came to Cordura* and *Where the Boys Are* had an individual gained as much publicity as Cash and Epps did, and they stayed in the spotlight for over a decade.

The story of Spartans in Hollywood, both in film and television, has been told in detail in a 1999 and 2000 series of articles in the *MSU Alumni Magazine*, and a rich story it has been, which reaches back to individuals like Edward S. Feldman (class of 1950) and Frank Price (class of 1951), who have become highly successful film and television producers as well as executives with careers that have each lasted

The Verdehr Trio—featuring music professor Walter Verdehr (violinist), Elsa Ludewig-Verdehr (clarinetist), and Professor Silvia Roederer of Western Michigan University—is a well-traveled performing group highly sought after in venues across the United States and internationally. Courtesy of Michigan State University College of Music.

for over fifty years (Lunde and Hoppenstand). At last estimate there have been close to thirty individuals from MSU who have fashioned successful careers as film executives, producers, directors, writers, and actors. California has proven to be a "land of opportunity" for many MSU graduates in the arts and entertainment industry with an active alumni group resulting. Because of the university's size and the variety of its programs and degrees, MSU graduates are located all over the world, and the group in Hollywood has carried with them a passion and excitement about film that, in many if not most cases, had its origin on campus.

The School of Music (before its becoming the College of Music) has been a focal point for culture on campus, with a long history of accomplished musicians who have become nationally and internationally known and loved. Ralph Votapek, professor of piano and artist-in-residence, has played with almost every major American city orchestra, made tours of Latin American countries every other year for over forty years, and appeared in concerts and as a solo recitalist on four continents. His stature and reputation in his field exceeds that

Ralph Votapek, professor of piano and artist-in-residence, became a nationally and internationally known pianist who has performed on four continents and has gained true stardom in his field. Courtesy of Michigan State University College of Music.

For forty-seven years, Professor Frank Rutledge directed, produced, and wrote plays for the Department of Theatre, and with his wife, Gretel Geist Rutledge, established the Summer Circle Theatre in 1961, which has been part of the summer entertainment scene in East Lansing ever since. Private collection.

of anyone in any field who has been a faculty member at Michigan State. The Verdehr Trio, featuring violinist Walter Verdehr and clarinetist Elsa Ludewig-Verdehr (joined by Professor Silvia Roederer of Western Michigan University), plays in major U.S. cities and throughout the country and has done tours in Europe, South America, and the Far East. Both professors of music, Walter Verdehr and Elsa Ludewig-Verdehr appear on their own as soloists with orchestras and enjoy their own notable reputations. The College of Music also features a growing Jazz Studies program that began with the appointment of Rodney T. Whitaker as professor of double bass and director of the program and has grown to eight faculty. An interesting feature of the music program overall is that many of its faculty spend their summers in residence as performers in music festival orchestras

Summer Circle Theatre stage sets were necessarily minimal, and plays were subject to the weather. Private collection.

located in places like Aspen, Colorado, or other vacation sites. In this way they keep their playing skills sharp and enjoy the company of other accomplished musicians before returning to campus for an academic year of demanding individual lessons.

As part of the College of Arts and Letters, the Department of Theatre and Department of Art and Art History have been a vital cultural presence on campus. Frank Rutledge joined the faculty in 1959 and brought with him a passionate commitment to theatrical performances, and a directorial intensity that pushed actors to develop their full potential, bringing characters alive in plays that moved audiences emotionally. In his forty-seven years at Michigan State, he produced and directed over 150 plays, with a special skill for staging Shakespeare's works as well as plays dealing with social issues. He was equally adept as a technical director and scene designer, creating evocative and expressionistic sets that were visually stunning.

The Jazz Studies program in the College of Music started with the appointment of Rodney T. Whitaker as professor of double bass and director of Jazz Studies. After his appointment, six other performing jazz faculty joined the program: Etienne Charles (trumpet), Michael Dease (trombone), Randy Gelispie (drums), Perry Hughes (guitar), Diego Rivera (saxophone), and Reginald Thomas (piano). They perform as a jazz ensemble, doing concerts, workshops, and master classes for audiences of all levels. Kenneth Prouty is the faculty member in jazz musicology. Courtesy of Michigan State University College of Music.

For the production of *A Tale of Two Cities,* done in connection with the French Revolution Bicentennial, Rutledge both wrote the script and directed. His wife, Gretel Geist Rutledge, designed costumes and sets for over one hundred Department of Theatre productions, winning awards for her costume designs. Together, Frank and Gretel founded the Summer Circle Theatre, an outdoor theater located on the banks of the Red Cedar River just south of the Auditorium. The theater's original location, from 1961 to 1969, was in Demonstration Hall. Every summer, four or five plays were presented (and still are), with standard favorites, Shakespeare, historical plays, and new plays by relatively unknown playwrights. Public school students come to campus for special matinee performances or the MSU high school touring company originally named "Simply Shakespeare" and later "Shakespeare Tour" performs at schools. Another important part of the Department of Theatre team was Joyce Ramsay, who was trained at the Pasadena Playhouse acting school and who appeared in Hollywood film productions before joining the MSU faculty in 1979. She was a skilled professor of acting and directing, with a marvelous, rich voice that inspired performance. Dixie Durr, who came to Michigan State originally with an appointment in athletics, was a skilled choreographer and served as artistic director for the Repertory Dance Concert performances.

One of the great contributions was the diffusion of the culture of theatre and dance throughout the community, state, and nation. This was accomplished through the Summer Circle Theatre, the Simply Shakespeare touring company, or faculty sharing their talents in summer stock theatre. Most importantly, this diffusion came through the department's graduates, who acted, directed, and produced plays wherever they went, or who became drama or dance teachers or organized new amateur production companies. The same can be said for the graduates of the College of Music and the Department of Art and Art History. Those with developed artistic skills and knowledge and a passion for performance of all kinds and forms bring culture to local audiences. Some of those graduates gain national recognition and fame, but the majority are locally recognized and appreciated for their dedication to the arts and their contributions to the quality of life.

The Department of Art and Art History has also had an illustrious history on campus since its establishment in 1931. Two faculty left works that are part of the university's heritage. Leonard D. Jungwirth, who taught at Michigan State from 1940 until his death in 1963, created *The Spartan* terra-cotta sculpture in 1945 and a campus icon was born. In the previous year Charles C. Pollock, who taught art here from 1942 to 1965 and was the brother of famed abstract expressionist Jackson Pollock, completed a three-panel casein on canvas mural for installation in the foyer of the MSU Auditorium (opened in 1940). The three scenes were titled *We Assure Freedom to the Free*, *Proclamation of Emancipation*, and *The Modern Man I Sing*. This paean to the central role of freedom in American history is expressed as a historical, social, and economic struggle, and the work was executed during the great struggle for freedom during World War II when students, faculty, and staff went to participate in a global war against tyranny.

The gift of $1.5 million from the Kresge Foundation for a new building for the Department of Art (dedicated in May 1959) signaled the beginning of a new era, as did the rapid growth of art faculty and students, and in 1964 the building was expanded (Word 25). A cultural center was created where excitement and passion for the visual and plastic arts found expression. Art theory and history found their place in the practice and execution of painting, sculpture, ceramics, poetry, photography, printmaking, all forms of design, typography, and so forth. The art culture revolved around faculty and student exhibitions, the excitement of visiting artists-in-residence and speakers, and the anticipation of critiques. Creativity and innovation were valued, as were discipline and critical intelligence. This central core of activity is a common denominator regardless of which generation of students or faculty has passed through the halls of art. Faculty practiced and developed their art in their studios, often at home, and sought to be exhibited in prestigious or "name" galleries or museums in order to gain outside recognition. The term "show" had more meaning to art faculty than anyone could imagine, except for theatre people.

In her excellent essay "The Humanities in the 1990s," Alberta Arthurs points out that a "new positioning of the humanities disciplines" was taking place that pointed to a greater engagement with critical issues and questions of a global nature and that connected specialties in the humanities to other specialties and fields (Arthurs 263–64). The need for humanists to connect with non-humanists was becoming increasingly more important as issues of human rights and justice, the effects of rapid changes in science and medicine, and clashes of ideological and belief systems became greater in scope and scale. Evidence of movement in this direction at MSU can be seen in the establishment in 1977 of the Medical Humanities Program, which connected faculty from the Department of Philosophy with the College of Human Medicine and developed into the Center for Ethics and Humanities in the Life Sciences, involving six different colleges. MATRIX: Center for Digital Humanities and Social Sciences became nationally and internationally recognized for digital archives, as well as applications and programs aiding digital research and instruction. The challenge for those in the arts and humanities has been to find the points of connection across the university and outside the university where profitable conversations and exchanges can take place that will have an ongoing impact, while at the same time maintaining the vitality of the liberal and performing arts in their traditional and original contexts and in terms meaningful to those who select them as their primary activity.

The Michigan State University Press and Its Development

Founded in 1947, in a decade where fourteen university presses were established, the Michigan State College Press, most significantly under the leadership of Lyle Blair, forged a solid reputation for publishing high-quality scholarly works across a broad field of subjects. From 1951 through 1979, Blair ran the press on a modest annual subsidy from the university, soldiered on with a small staff, and managed to keep income ahead of revenues in most years. However, rising costs for clerical and technical personnel, the additional competition from other university presses (thirty of them opened in the 1950s and 1960s), increased production costs, and the university budget cuts in the early 1970s all served to put the MSU Press in dire straits. The four volumes of President James A. Garfield's personal writings, edited by Department of History professors Frederick Williams (all four volumes) and Harry J. Brown (the last three volumes), were published between 1964 and 1981 and were a major achievement and contribution to American history.

During Jean W. Busfield's time as director, from 1980 to 1986, the Press published notable books (such as Dorothy McMeekin's *Diego Rivera: Science and Creativity in the Detroit Murals,* Clarence Underwood's *Student Athlete: Eligibility and Academic Integrity,* and Rollin H. Baker's *Michigan Mammals*), but few of them, and had to discontinue the acceptance of manuscripts (Hungiville). In 1986 Richard Chapin became the part-time director of the Press, devoting half of his time there while continuing to be director of the MSU Libraries. As director, Chapin brought a different perspective and background to the Press, just as he had done when he came earlier to the Library. With Chapin's eye to the popular market and a wider readership, the Press in 1987–88 published *Leadership Is An Art* by Max De Pree (CEO of Herman Miller), *Three Bullets Sealed His Lips* by Bruce A. Rubenstein and Lawrence E. Ziewacz (on the sensational 1945 ambush assassination of Michigan State Senator Warren

As director, Lyle Blair established the MSU Press as an up-and-coming publisher of books by nationally as well as internationally recognized authors, and for wider audiences beyond academia. Blair brilliantly managed a press that was underfunded and always having to manage from book to book. Courtesy of Michigan State University Archives and Historical Collections.

Frederic Bohm (*left*) was hired in 1990 as a full-time director to revive the MSU Press. From 1990 to 2007 Bohm kept the Press in the news with such books as *Letters from Robben Island: A Selection of Ahmed Kathrada's Prison Correspondence, 1964–1989* and Harriet Simpson Arnow's unpublished novel *Between the Flowers*. The MSU Press under Bohm also began the publication of a series of remarkable books on African American history and established its journals program, which became one of its signature strengths. Shown in the photograph are South African activist and author Ahmed Kathrada (*far right*) during his book tour of the United States and his public appearance translator (*center*). Courtesy of Michigan State University Press.

G. Hooper), *Feeding a Billion: Frontiers of Chinese Agriculture* by Sylvan H. Wittwer, Yu Youtai, Sun Han, and Wang Lianzheng (on revolutionary agricultural practices in China aimed at maximum food production), and *The Grain Traders: The Story of the Chicago Board of Trade* by William G. Ferris. These four books were part of the economic turnaround for the Press as it veered in new directions while maintaining its commitment to publishing MSU scholars such as Carl S. Taylor, whose important sociological study of urban violence titled *Dangerous Society* was published in 1990.

Chapin's years of directing the Press put it in a position of strength and allowed it to search for a full-time director with credentials and experience in the field. For several months after Chapin stepped down, assistant director and editor-in-chief Julie L. Loehr served as interim director of the Press. Frederic Bohm, with a doctorate in history and seven years of university press experience, was appointed in 1990. Two critical developments during Bohm's directorship deserve attention. In the period from 1992 to 1996, the Press began to publish scholarly journals, and Laura Luptowski was hired to guide this development. The *Journal of International Marketing* was first published in 1993 with MSU's Center for International Business Education and Research as the originator, and the journal continued to be published by the Press through 1997, when the American Marketing Association began to publish it. *Northeast African Studies* began in 1979 as a journal published by the African Studies Center under the leadership of MSU Ethiopian scholar Harold G. Marcus and ceased publication in 1991. The Press began a new series in 1994, and the journal became one of the three crown jewels in the Press's developing journals program. In 1994 the international journal titled *Contagion: Journal of Violence, Mimesis, and Culture* became another jewel in the crown as MSU English professor William A. Johnsen became its editor. In 1995 *Real Analysis Exchange*, a biannual mathematics journal, became part of the Press's stable of publications, and for six years (1995–2001) the Press was home to *The Historian*. In 1998 a quarterly titled *Rhetoric & Public Affairs* debuted, an interdisciplinary journal on all forms and venues of public rhetoric and discourse. The MSU Press became the home of the Karlyn Kohrs-Campbell Prize in Rhetorical Criticism, a biannual prize of $10,000 to reward original research and scholarship. One of the nation's most prominent scholars in political rhetoric, Professor Karlyn Kohrs-Campbell of the University of Minnesota and her husband Paul Newell Campbell established and funded this prestigious award. Other publications joined the journals program: *Fourth Genre: Explorations in Nonfiction* in 1999 and *French Colonial History* in 2001. As mentioned earlier, the Press also published *CR: The New Centennial Review*, a continuation of the *Centennial Review* founded at MSU in 1957, and from 2003 *Red Cedar Review*, a literary journal founded in 1963 and undergraduate-managed since its founding.

When it coalesced and stabilized, the MSU Press journals program became a valuable asset for a number of reasons. First, the articles and scholars would be cited in other scholarship, bringing recognition and currency to the names of the journals. Second, the frequency of the publication of the journals meant regular name recognition of the Press as a sponsor and distributor of scholarship and creative writing, and the increasing availability of journals online added further publicity value. Third, the journals became a platform for distinguished book series, such as the Rhetoric and Public Affairs Series, which began in 1994 and by 2005 comprised twenty-two titles. The successful journals program was paralleled by one initiated by then provost Lou Anna K. Simon where she provided multiyear support packages for faculty who could bring established, big-name refereed journals to campus and become their editors.

It took some time, but once the MSU Press had moved back to publishing an average of some thirty titles a year, the director and his associates could decide on a marketing strategy. Part of that has been already discussed: developing book series to parallel journals. Another part of the strategy was to build series on demonstrated faculty strengths and developing areas of expertise, as well as supporting a continuation of the Press's historical commitment to Michigan and the Midwest as well as the Great Lakes. The American Indian Studies Series and the Michigan Great Lakes Books are notable examples. Within each of these series are creative works of fiction and nonfiction. The Discovering the Peoples of Michigan Series (twenty books by 2005) covers the history, presence, locations, contributions, and cultures of ethnic, racial, and religious groups that constitute the peoples of the state. A Kellogg Foundation grant of $25,000 served as a startup for this popular monographic series.

What the Press has done notably well is to seize opportunities to publish books connected with university initiatives or long-standing commitments. Robert D. Vassen's edited *Letters from Robben Island: A Selection from Ahmed Kathrada's Prison Correspondence, 1964–1989* (with a foreword by Nelson Mandela) (1999) became a bestseller and was the focus of a national book tour. The university's connection with South Africa and its post-apartheid rebirth was located in collaborative programs involving MATRIX, the MSU Museum, and the commitments of individual faculty members such as Geneva Smitherman. MSU's long-standing commitment to the health of Michigan's people, animals, and resources can be seen in the publication of David Dempsey's *On the Brink: The Great Lakes in the 21st Century* (2004).

The university's connections to Africa and its collaborations there also set the groundwork for the MSU Press's role in the African Books Collective beginning in 2001, which has involved the Press distributing the books of 101 independent African publishers from over twenty African countries. Peter Limb, an adjunct associate professor of history and Africana bibliographer for the MSU Libraries, played the key role in this partnership of publishers with the salutary effect that the work of African scholars has received international distribution in North America and wider recognition.

The now sixty plus years of the MSU Press have been ones of determined directors, editors, and staff who have persevered in their mission to make the Press a valued asset to the university by producing high-quality books of scholarly and cultural significance. Its connections to faculty and academic programs have increased and been cemented by the journals program and the book series, and its reputation has been enhanced by publications that have found wide as well as specialized readership. The Press has responded to the fast-changing nature and challenges of the book market and shown how it can serve the scholarly and general public communities with equal facility. Its greatest contribution is that it serves ably as one of the many portals that disseminate and diffuse the knowledge, information, heritage, and artistic and creative expression that constitute the dynamic core of MSU's being and mission.

The MSU Museum

As the leading public natural and cultural history museum in Michigan and one of the foundational entities of Michigan State (established in 1857), the MSU Museum is a magnet destination on campus for school groups and visitors. Its accumulation of collections over the life span of the small college turned megaversity reflects the faith and trust donors have had and continue to have in its mission of stewardship and education. While its job is to preserve objects and artifacts, the Museum's main work occurs through its personnel, who research and interpret the collections and regularly exhibit them, thus providing for ongoing public education about the natural, material, and manmade world. That process involves ongoing research by a group of specialists who publish their own findings in their fields and who curate public exhibitions that seek a wide audience of viewers. Certain of those exhibitions attain a wide popularity, such as the "100 Seasons of Spartan Football" done by curator of history Val Roy Berryman and shown from September 1996 to early January 1997, or the "African American Quilting in Michigan" exhibit done by curator of folk arts Marsha MacDowell and shown from February through September 1991, then traveling to museums in Detroit, Flint, and Jackson during a two-year run.

The goal of the committed MSU curators has been to create excitement and curiosity about artifacts and objects, some of which visitors have never seen before and others that are familiar. Faraway places such as Tanzania have come to life through mammal fossils exhibited through the research of Professor Michael D. Gottfried, curator of vertebrate paleontology. He and Barbara Lundrigan, curator of mammalogy and ornithology, combined their talents to produce "Animal Weapons: Nature's Arms Race," exhibited from March through October 2000.

The MSU Museum has developed a national and international reputation for its particular strengths in folk arts, crafts, and traditions as well as material culture. The research and publications as well as exhibits of wife-and-husband team Marsha MacDowell and C. Kurt Dewhurst on Native American baskets and quilts and on religious folk art have been part of that reputation. Val Berryman, who curated annual exhibits of Christmas customs and objects that were installed at multiple sites in the greater Lansing area and at the MSU Museum, was also a noted collector and exhibited his holdings as part of the holiday shows.

By far the most important area in which the Museum has distinguished itself has been the collection, study, and exhibition of quilts. The 1991 exhibit on African American quilting in Michigan was followed in 1997 with an exhibition on Native American quilting, a collaboration between MSU and the National Museum of the American Indian with funding from the Smithsonian Institution, the National Endowment for the Arts, and the Lila Wallace–Reader's Digest Fund. The exhibit, titled "To Honor and Comfort: Native Quilting Traditions," opened in New York, came to the MSU Museum from April to October 1998, and then appeared at seven other locations across the nation from Massachusetts to Hawaii, with the last exhibit running from January to April 2001.

The MSU Museum staff also worked with the Smithsonian in 1987, the year of Michigan's sesquicentennial celebration of its statehood, to present cooks, storytellers, musicians, and craftspeople from the state as part of the Festival of Michigan Folklife on the National Mall in Washington, DC. That program then became part of the first Michigan Festival and then became the Festival of Michigan Folklife, which until 1998 brought a wide array of folk artists and performers to East Lansing to perform and demonstrate. From 1999 to 2002 the Museum and the City of East Lansing hosted the National Folk

Here MSU Museum director C. Kurt Dewhurst and curator Marsha MacDowell pose with the quilt exhibit. The Museum's quilt collection is one of its signature assets and is recognized nationally for its quality and importance to research and preservation. Image by Pearl Yee Wong, courtesy of MSU Museum.

Festival, and in 2002 the Great Lakes Folk Festival began its successful run as a Museum event, with each year having one or more themes, such as Maritime Traditions in 2005. This summer event has become part of the cultural fabric and tradition of summer life in East Lansing as well as providing experiences with living, ongoing folk art that people would not otherwise have had. It is a celebration of what people can do without technology or complex machines and plays a role in keeping folk arts, crafts, traditions, and performances alive and passing them on to a new generation.

The MSU Museum has also played a central role with its involvement with the Michigan Quilt Project established in 1984. Besides holding a collection of more than five hundred quilts, the MSU Museum staff is involved in doing tape-recorded interviews with quilters, taking photographs of them and their work, and gathering data and other information about the field. In 2005 an exhibit of the Museum's quilts was shown at department store locations in Tokyo, Osaka, Niigata, and Kyoto, Japan. Exhibits of the quilts have circulated throughout the state and nation, and in 1997 Marsha MacDowell edited *African American Quiltmaking in Michigan*, a volume in the Michigan State University Museum book series done with the MSU Press. African American and Native American quilts, and quilts with special ties to Michigan have provided the Museum with a great opportunity to educate the public in the material richness of this folk art and its connection to women and family as well as communities. The Quilt Index collection and documentation are available online with over 54,000 quilts displayed.

Another area where the Museum has been particularly strong is African studies. Some of the collections came by way of donations from faculty who participated in the Nigeria Project in the early 1960s. In 1989, MSU curator Raymond A. Silverman edited *Expressions from Africa: Selections from the Museum Collections of Michigan State University*, and Silverman also edited and contributed to two editions of his *Ethiopia: Traditions of Creativity* (in 1994 and 1999). The collaborative exhibit titled "Drinking the Word of God: Expressions of Faith and the Search for Well-Being in Two West African Communities" (March 2001 through January 2002) brought together the experiences and field research of Raymond A. Silverman and Robert S. Glew, who lived respectively in Bondouko, Côte d'Ivoire, and in Zinder, Niger, and studied Muslim identity and culture in those places. The Robert Glew Collection of Nigerian Culture at the MSU Museum includes seventy objects of ceremonial and religious significance related to Islamic religious identity and practices in South Central Niger. Other significant collections include the Cernyw and Morna Kline Collection of African Material Culture, the Simon Ottenberg Collection of African Art, and the Joseph Druse Collection of Nigerian Material Culture.

In 2001 the Museum gained Smithsonian Affiliation membership, furthering a relationship that prospered when the Smithsonian provided major funding for the "To Honor and Comfort: Native Quilting Traditions" national traveling exhibit of 1997–2001. The Museum was the first in Michigan to gain Affiliate designation.

Wiring the Campus and the Computer Culture

Between 1995 and 2003, Phases II through X of the Fiber Optics Project were carried out, with $26.5 million expended to complete the work of a high-speed system. MSU's ability to fund this critical program was made possible by one of the wisest targeted investments in higher education ever made by the State of Michigan. Starting in 1995 the state appropriation to MSU (and to the University of Michigan and to Wayne State University) included $10.4 million annually to be used for technology infrastructures, equipment, and programs. MSU was able to move from a $786,000 budget for Phase II of the Fiber Optics Project to a budget of $4 million for Phase III (Minutes, 19 April 1995 and 12 April 1996).

This focus on the needs of the state's three research-intensive universities and the commitment to an investment in technology had its origins in the High Technology Task Force, founded in 1981 by Governor William Milliken, on which President M. Cecil Mackey had served (Brace 56). That task force had identified and linked industry, business, finance, and the research universities as partners in fostering the healthy growth of the state's economy. Fast flow and transmission of large data volume were essential to linkages between the state research institutions, and necessary to advance projects like the Michigan Life Sciences Corridor, established by the state in 1999 to invest its tobacco lawsuit settlement of $1 billion in biotechnology research and business development. The Tobacco Master Settlement Agreement of November 1998 involved four companies that agreed to pay $206 billion with each state receiving a designated share. In the first round of funding from the Michigan Economic Development Corporation, MSU was awarded more than $40 million in grants, and in 2001 received more than $17 million to develop the Center for Structural Biology of Membrane Proteins to study the structure and function of proteins and their connections to diseases ("MSU Board Accepts"). Besides the three research universities, the Life Sciences Corridor also included the Van Andel Institute in Grand Rapids, a connection that later came into play in 2004 when MSU decided to establish a second College of Human Medicine in Grand Rapids.

On campus, the Fiber Optics Project provided a system that allowed for the establishment of a computer requirement for incoming freshman. The Board of Trustees mandated a requirement that would begin in the Fall semester 2001, with the result that 85 percent of freshman brought a computer and connected it to the campus network (Minutes, 21 September 2001). In June 2000 Bruce Magid was director of MSU's Global Initiatives. In Fall 2001 an online Master of Arts in Education program was launched. Instructors developed online resources and features for their courses (syllabuses, readings, homework, sample exams, visual materials, links to relevant websites, etc.). Blended or hybrid courses were developed involving online learning sessions and face-to-face class periods. Fully online courses would be developed, with offerings mainly available in the summer. That the digital world was becoming a reality is evident in WKAR-TV switching over to a digital format on the occasion of its fiftieth anniversary in January 2004, and the student-run radio station WDBM (known as IMPACT 89 FM) went digital in December 2004. The story of the incorporation, adaptation, and dispersion of new technologies at MSU and of their transformation of work and leisure is, of course, worthy of a complete study of its own. There is no doubt that the Fiber Optics Project and the system it established was the foundational act. When the network was almost complete in 2003, the university looked beyond it to the need for advanced connectivity between MSU and key Internet access points, and several strategic decisions were made that connected the MSU system to national nodes that increased its performance (Minutes, 11 April 2003).

Student Life and Activities

The lifestyle and activities of Michigan State students have had similar patterns regardless of the period of time in which they attended, from the 1960s to 2005. Almost all students began their life on campus by living in one of the residential halls and adjusting to roommates or floormates who might have widely different personalities, study and cleanliness habits, social and economic backgrounds, and so forth. Except for the students in the residential colleges, where there was more likelihood of commonalities, students had many social adjustments to make in their routine daily life in the dorms, particularly the reality of cafeteria food. One of the circulating myths was that of the

"Freshman 15," the number of pounds one would gain. The only day on which three meals were not served was Sunday, when the evening meal was up to the students' resources.

The challenge facing all students was that of navigating a large, spread-out campus, as well as management and allocation of time and effort. Up until the first issue of Mark Grebner's *Grading the Profs* in the early 1970s, news and information about professors and courses came by word of mouth and inquiry, not always reliable but nevertheless welcomed. Survival and study tips about passing so-called "weeder" courses (said to "weed" the weaker students out of certain majors) and information about professors' grading systems were also key parts of the regular ebb and flow of academic information. For some, the goal might be to avoid a course with "pop quizzes" or "killer" midterm and final exams, or requirements like daily homework or a research paper. Others sought out these same courses because of their rigor and academic challenge. For certain courses in the major there was little choice, since these were regularly taught by the same professors.

Michigan State students have always been known as highly social. For many years the university has carried the reputation of a "party school" and been ranked as such, to the dismay of the administration and parents. Social affiliations were sought through membership in fraternities, sororities, and other clubs and organizations. Some of the clubs in the 1950s and 1960s were extensions of majors, such as the Forestry Club or Dairy Club, while others were connected to special interests or activities, such as Block and Bridle (horseback riding), Orchesis (dance), Rifle Club (shooting), or Promenaders (square dancing). The club with the greatest number of members was the Ski Club. Activities in clubs allowed students to find others with like interests in a megaversity where chance or random social meetings were the normal experience. The value of attending a large university was the diversity and large number of interests, and the resources of the university, gathered through a student fee, to support such clubs, associations, and organizations with space and funding.

Intramural sports through the Men's IM and Women's IM programs provided a much-needed outlet for physical competition and exercise, as did club sports. The MSU IM program was one of the largest and best organized in the country. Touch football and softball games would be scheduled late into the night on lighted IM fields, allowing as many as possible to participate. Early in the development of intramural sports, women's activities tended to be indoors and featured volleyball, acrobatics, synchronized swimming, judo, and karate. Intramural sports provided friendships through teammates, "bragging rights" for dorm floors or groups when they proved to be the best in a league, and the opportunity to carry forward high-school sports interests but without all the glamour and adulation they had as high school athletes. Pickup basketball games at the IM were probably the most spirited and competitive because high school reputations carried over more strongly and the game (unlike touch football) was essentially the same. Teams had to win consecutive games in order to "hold" the court, and there were no referees to call fouls or keep the game under tight control. In the 1960s and 1970s handball was another popular and fiercely played game at the IM in singles or doubles. Reputations were made and talk widely circulated about players' styles, meanness, or toughness. Students could take on faculty members and faculty could challenge each other. Over time, as one would expect, individual preferences for exercise activities have changed or expanded, with running and physical conditioning or toning (including weight lifting, yoga, and aerobics) becoming prominent.

Another repeating pattern for MSU students was the move from the freshman year in the dormitories to off-campus apartments, duplexes, or houses in East Lansing neighborhoods. The selection of house or apartment mates became critical to the success of the arrangements, and new challenges and the potential for conflicts and misunderstandings increased regarding a range of domestic matters, including payment of the share of one's rent or the costs of a party. Often students would have three or four different addresses or types of residences from their sophomore year to graduation. Lessons were learned from these changing circumstances forged by the necessity of cooperative or group arrangements needed to live off campus. The more managed, organized, and routine dormitory life of the first year became something closer to actual life, where relationships and arrangements would have to be negotiated on a day to day basis with elements of unpredictability and change. The necessity for finding a job often accompanied the migration to off-campus living, and the

Social life and activities for students revolved around a regular succession of university-sponsored and student-run big events along with Greek Week. Because under the quarter system classes continued well into June, the IM Sports West Outdoor Pool, Lake Lansing's Dells Ballroom and amusement park and beach, and other spots were popular hangouts, as was the Coral Gables. Student club activities and intramural sports were also part of the rich mix. Courtesy of Michigan State University Archives and Historical Collections.

percentage of MSU students who work a substantial number of hours each week has increased every decade since the 1970s.

The differences in MSU student life and activities have been more notable at certain historical points than others, and these serve as kinds of dividing lines or points of departure. Before the mid-1960s there was a university- and organizations-sponsored social calendar year that involved the large majority of students. In the Fall quarter it included Homecoming and the Homecoming dance, Homecoming display competition between dorms, the Water Carnival with its parade of floats on the Red Cedar River, and the Union Activities Board Fashion Show. In the Winter quarter, the J-Hop and Vet's Winterland Whirl dances brought top-name national bands to campus for the premier formal social events of the year, each with a theme and an elaborate design and setting. The Winter Carnival featured ice-sculpture competition. In Spring quarter, Greek Week and Greek Fest—with competitions such as the Lamba Chi Alpha

The June 1958 Water Carnival was a major event on campus held at night under spotlights with crowds of spectators lining the banks of the Red Cedar River. The floats were as elaborate as those in the homecoming parades and were constructed by on-campus living unit residents. Courtesy of Michigan State University Archives and Historical Collections.

Junior 500 pushcart race and the Sorority Trike Race, and top notch entertainment as well as featuring of local music groups—took center stage. Pop Entertainment (part of ASMSU) brought in popular music groups, one each quarter. Because the Spring quarter ran until the second week in June with the arrival of spring and warm weather, the IM Sports West Outdoor Pool, the areas outside dormitories, and Lake Lansing became a popular gathering place for sunbathing and listening to music. The Union was a popular place for dates and study breaks from the library; it was also a place to shoot pool or bowl. This regular cycle of major campus events provided ritual and tradition as well as anticipation and social planning, such as getting or accepting dates, what to wear, how to pay for it, or what other couples to go with to the event. Other places such as the downtown East Lansing movie theaters, the Coral Gables with its "Show Bar" and local rock bands like the Woolies, and other events sponsored and funded by

the Union Activities Board or ASMSU or the many clubs or organizations meant a wide selection of places to go and things to do.

Over time, the hold of these big events and this regular pattern of a calendar of known activities lessened. The Water Carnival and the J-Hop disappeared in the early 1960s. Homecoming remained popular, especially with the success and nationally ranked prominence of the Spartan football teams in the 1965 and 1966 seasons, but even it lost some of its luster and appeal. Fewer students were attracted to formal dances and events, as big-name dance bands were no longer a major attraction. Student protests against the Vietnam War and the push for student and group rights came to the forefront. A more disconnected and discontinuous period emerged where the continuation of the past university social calendar and cycle seemed less important. The university's assumption of *in loco parentis* (acting in the place of the parents) was challenged all the way to the Supreme Court with the

The revival of the Water Carnival for 2005 Sesquicentennial Celebration represented a major effort to link with a past social event that began in 1920 as a Mardi Gras celebration. Courtesy of Michigan State University Photography Services.

The push cart races took place during Greek Week in the spring and pitted teams from the residence halls against fraternity teams in spirited competition. Courtesy of Michigan State University Archives and Historical Collections.

Dixon v. Alabama State Board of Education decision in 1961, spelling the beginning of the end for a doctrine that restricted students' activities and gave the university the absolute power to expel students. By 1967 the *Academic Freedom for Students at Michigan State University* report at MSU was issued, providing for due process and establishing students' rights and responsibilities in the pursuit of knowledge. It remains one of the most eloquent (and unfortunately one of the most unread) foundational documents in MSU's history.

As the student population became more diverse and activist, and as issues and concerns multiplied, it became harder to fashion a schedule of official university-sponsored events that captured the attention and participation of the large majority of students. Up through the mid-1960s students looked forward to a kind of secular liturgical year to direct their social life on campus, a life that was (until more students drove and owned cars) lived mainly on campus with infrequent trips home or elsewhere. If television was watched, students viewed it together in the dormitories, until the advent of portable televisions and later cable into the dorm rooms. The privatization and individualization of entertainment on campus was essentially not much different than what was happening in American society. Other patterns of communication, social connections, and leisure meant that life on and off campus mirrored larger cultural and commercial developments. Some of the special and individual qualities of life on campus for students changed or even disappeared, and now the university found itself serving and appealing to students with different social interests, needs, learning abilities, and activity patterns.

Student Activism and Concerns

It is virtually impossible for a history like this to capture and document student life in all its various expressions and venues. Certain things can be observed in terms of first-year students as they acclimated to a collective life in the dormitories and adjusted to a university that was becoming more racially and ethnically diverse. In Fall 1999, ethnic minority students constituted 19.2 percent of the freshman class (20 percent in 2001), or 16 percent of the total campus population (Minutes, 20 March 2001). In 2002, 15.5 percent of the tenure-system positions were held by minority faculty (Minutes, 12 April 2002). Moving the university positively in the direction of a multicultural, diverse society depended upon students understanding and embracing this institutional goal and valuing it as an asset. It depended upon Residence Life programs, initiatives, and positive experiences that fostered goodwill, flexibility, and openness on the part of students. It required well-trained student resident assistants (RAs) and dormitory personnel who could help students past the rough spots of ugly racial incidents, culturally insensitive acts, and thoughtlessness.

A significant development took place in Fall 2000 when the Department of Residence Life and University Housing moved to put the student staff into a mentor role rather than a disciplinary role. Rather than enforcing rules and regulations and assessing penalties for infractions, the student staff members took on the role of facilitator, assisting students in making choices and taking actions that benefited themselves and others. A new Community Standards initiative was

ACADEMIC FREEDOM FOR STUDENTS AT MICHIGAN STATE UNIVERSITY

Approved by Board of Trustees, March 16, 1967

Foreword

The foreword is not part of the document that follows. It supplies, however, a necessary perspective for interpreting the document.

Student rights and responsibilities at Michigan State University must be understood against the social and historical background of the University itself.

When, more than 150 years ago, the people of Michigan established this institution on the land-grant principle, they framed a new conception of the role of the university in American life. A land-grant university is a trusteeship of intellect in the service of society. It gathers society's creative and critical powers and uses them to advance the common good and to solve fundamental problems.

That is the special character that has caused the land-grant university to become one of the great transforming agencies of the American scene. When it honors its commission, it acts not for the sake of the academic community, but for the sake of society beyond the academy. All members of the academic community—trustees, administrators, faculty, staff and students—enact a trust of which society beyond the University is the proper beneficiary.

The real significance of this document, as we believe, is not that students have acquired rights, but that they have explicitly been made party to our social trust. The responsibility which lies upon the trustees, the administration, and the faculty continues. They remain guardians of the University, charged with preserving in it the genius of scholarship and the conditions of inquiry which society has entrusted to their care.

Article 1: Student Rights and Responsibilities

Michigan State University is a community of scholars whose members include its faculty, staff, students, and administrators. The basic purposes of the University are the advancement, dissemination, and application of knowledge. The most basic condition for the achievement of these purposes is freedom of expression and communication. Without this freedom, effective sifting and testing of ideas cease, and research, teaching, and learning are stifled. Knowledge is as broad and diverse as life itself, and the need for freedom is equally broad. Yet

introduced that had the residents of each floor establish their own standards for behavior promoting mutual respect and management of conflict, and for conditions promoting general well-being. Beyond everyday matters such as noise management and sanitation, students were encouraged to discuss community citizenship and cultural values. Ann Bolger, director of Residence Life; Angela Brown, director of University Housing; and Provost Lou Anna K. Simon took the lead in this initiative and worked with residence hall directors and staff to launch this program aimed at the development of leadership among students (Minutes, 22 September 2000).

Another residential hall–related program developed earlier in absolute freedom in all aspects of life means anarchy, just as absolute order means tyranny. Both anarchy and tyranny are antithetical to the purposes and character of the University. Therefore, the University always must strive to strike that balance between maximum freedom and necessary order which best promotes its basic purposes by providing the environment most conducive to the many faceted activities of instruction, research, and service.

Each right of an individual places a reciprocal duty upon others: the duty to permit the individual to exercise the right. The student, as a member of the academic community, has both rights and duties. Within that community, the student's most essential right is the right to learn. The University has a duty to provide for the student those privileges, opportunities, and protections which best promote the learning process in all its aspects. The student also has duties to other members of the academic community, the most important of which is to refrain from interference with those rights of others which are equally essential to the purposes and processes of the University.

The University cherishes many values, modes of thought, and standards of behavior that are better taught by example and rewards than by the threat of penalties. Regulations governing the activities and conduct of student groups and individual students should not be comprehensive codes of desirable conduct; rather, they should be limited to the prescription of procedures for meeting the practical, routine necessities of a complex community and to the prohibition or limitation of acts which cannot be tolerated because they seriously interfere with the basic purposes, necessities, and processes of the academic community, or with rights essential to other members of the community.

The student is not only a member of the academic community, but a citizen of the larger society, who retains those rights, protections, and guarantees of fair treatment held by all citizens, and which the University may not deny. The enforcement of the student's duties to the larger society is, however, the responsibility of the legal and judicial authorities duly established for that purpose.

April 1995 with the Multi-Racial Unity Living Experience (MRULE) program, founded by Jeanne Gazel (Student Affairs) and Professor Richard Thomas (History). MRULE meets weekly for roundtable discussions of social issues, participate in community service projects, and make trips away from campus to build group unity. From the outset the goal was to promote equity and social justice and to build genuine and solid interpersonal group relationships across all socially conditioned boundaries (Multi-Racial Unity Living Experience and Intercultural Aide Program). The group has engaged with such issues as HIV/AIDs, race relations, affirmative action, and orphaned and endangered children. By 2005 there have been at least three

Ann Bolger (*top*), director of Residence Life, and Angela Brown (*bottom*), director of University Housing, worked with then provost Lou Anna K. Simon to introduce the Community Standards Program in Fall 2000, putting students in charge of the culture and rules of their own dorms and making the resident assistant a mentor rather than an enforcer. Courtesy of Michigan State University Archives and Historical Collections.

generations of students who have gone through the MRULE program and graduated, and alumni of the program are invited back to campus for the end-of-year Recognition Ceremony.

One of the salient features of student life has been increasing involvement in volunteer work and community action programs. The "Into the Streets" program of ASMSU and the alternative spring break initiative have already been noted. Tower Guard, established in 1933 by May Shaw, began as an all-female honor society for women dedicated to serving the needs of the visually impaired students, and in 1977 men became eligible for membership. This group serves during their sophomore year and provides essential services for all students with impaired reading ability. The Beta Beta chapter of Alpha Phi Omega, an international coed service fraternity, was established in 1937, and has continued to provide volunteer services and carry out community projects for over seventy years. One of their projects, begun in 1993, was STATEWALK, which provided escorts for students with late classes. The Student Food Bank, sponsored by ASMSU and the Council of Graduate Students (COGS), opened in September 1992 as the only such fully student-run operation in the country. The Young Spartan Program began in 1993–94 as a three-year project involving MSU student volunteers in four Lansing schools, and due to its success the program continued until June 2005 and involved nine schools. The partnership ended due to school closings and changes in the Lansing School District's priorities (Casey). Students were also active in the MSU Recycling Coalition, the Green Lights Program (for energy-saving light bulbs), the Student Environmental Action Coalition, and Habitat for Humanity, which built its first local house in November 1993. The MSU Student Literacy Volunteer Corps, founded in 1985 by Professor Lois A. Bader (Education), works one-on-one with recent immigrants and others in need of English reading, writing, and comprehension skills.

Student volunteerism and community service were not something that sprang onto the scene due to a large-scale national movement, and of course they had strong roots at Michigan State with early organizations like Tower Guard and Alpha Chi Omega as well as the Center for Service-Learning and Civic Engagement (established in 1968), the oldest continuously operating service-learning center in the country. What students learned from service activities was that their world extended beyond their studies and concentration on degrees, and that these commitments provided opportunities for leadership and constructive social contribution. These experiences could complement and inform their formal studies and enhance their sense of citizenship.

Student activism also focused on issues of concern related to affirmative action, racism, student retention, and the needs of ethnic groups. In 1993 the North American Indian Student Organization (NAISO) expressed their concerns about the university's possible participation in the Mount Graham Observatory Project in Arizona on ecological grounds as well as the fact that Mt. Graham was considered a holy mountain by the Western Apaches as a "place of emergence" of the tribe (Minutes, 8 October 1993). This same concern was voiced at the 14 July 1995 Board of Trustees meeting. In 1997 MSU partnered with the University of North Carolina Chapel Hill, the National Optical Astronomy Observatory, and the country of Brazil to build and operate the SOAR (Southern Astrophysical Research) telescope located on a mountain top in Cerro Pachon, Chile, a facility fully operational in early 2005.

In December 1997 the Chicano/Latino Association issued a "Report Card" for the university and presented it to the Board of Trustees. The areas graded included recruitment and retention of Chicano/Latino faculty, staff, and students; academic support programs; the need for Chicano/Latino studies; and the university's support of positions taken by the United Farm Workers. Trustee Dorothy Gonzales responded to the ChiLA "report card," acknowledging the group's useful role as a "watch-dog" and its encouragement of the university to fulfill its commitment to access and inclusiveness. She acknowledged that MSU should support K–12 programs that positively benefit Chicano/Latino students, but at the same time pointed out progress that the "report card" had not cited (Minutes, 5 December 1997). The group's main concern, as was true with many minority groups, was that the university had acknowledged their concerns and reports but had failed to respond in terms of specific actions. A Chicano/Latino Studies program was instituted, with a program director, a PhD program, and an undergraduate specialization with a mentorship and volunteer program accompanying it. The Cesar Chavez Collection of the MSU Libraries was set up in February 1995 to provide a browsing collection of books and other materials and artifacts related to migrant farmworkers and their union as well as their collective actions. The College Assistance Migrant Program (CAMP) was initiated in 2000 and set up to assist entering students with migrant or seasonal farm-work backgrounds.

A Board of Trustees meeting on 11 April 2003 saw eleven groups speak to the board on affirmative action issues. Underneath the brief statements by individuals, who were limited to one and a half minutes each because of the large number assembled, there were strong undercurrents of student discontent, anger, and frustration. One focus was the retention rate for African American students, which at 43 percent was considered too low. Other issues included the need to strengthen academic support programs, more events for minority students, more faculty of color, more safety for women on campus, and a range of other concerns. One speaker asked "why there is a freestanding student athlete support building and there is not a freestanding multicultural center." A Multicultural Center in the lower level of the Union Building had been dedicated on 23 October 1998, and student groups had regularly complained about its limited and crowded space as well as its lack of visible presence on campus.

Before this confrontation of students and the Board of Trustees, another controversial issue developed—that of the Department of Police and Public Safety's use of undercover police to infiltrate student organizations. The organization involved was the Students for Economic Justice, which was urging the university to sign on with the Workers Rights Consortium rather than the Fair Labor Association. At issue were working conditions, unfair labor practices, and wages for workers in countries producing athletic apparel sold with the MSU logo. Rumors somehow started and circulated that the Students for Economic Justice group might have been involved in the arson at Agriculture Hall (Minutes, 20 April 2001). This may have prompted the campus police to have an officer infiltrate the group posing as a student, or it is possible that the police believed this group was too radical. At its 21 September 2001 meeting, the Board of Trustees approved the following resolution:

> Be it resolved that undercover surveillance of student organizations should occur only in extraordinary circumstances and should

> not be a part of normal police operations. No such undercover surveillance can be undertaken without the approval of the President. Implementation of this Resolution is the responsibility of the President and his/her designees.

What was established here was that even if the campus police believed that "extraordinary circumstances" existed warranting undercover surveillance of a student organization, they would first have to obtain the approval of the president. Since this policy made the president a party to undercover surveillance if it was approved due to "extraordinary circumstances," it also involved two sets of judgments and the president's power to disapprove of a request.

Student activism in the period of 1980–2005 focused on a wide range of issues and became more vocal and public. Concerns were presented directly to the Board of Trustees and to the president as well as to the media. Many of the issues focused on the status of minority groups and programs, and student groups held the university accountable for its position on diversity, access, and commitment to minority student success. For the administration there was always the question of the costs of new programs, their academic quality and sustainability, personnel to direct and staff them, and a concern that first steps not be rushed but rather be measured. The university could not move as quickly and decisively as student groups could, and what the administration saw as progress on a particular front could be viewed by students as inadequate. A more diverse student population meant more varied interests and concerns. MSU's success in attracting more minority students brought with it challenges as well as opportunities to advance its mission.

Black faculty scholarship and leadership developed in a remarkably productive way beginning in the early 1980s. Joe T. Darden, whose field was urban social geography with a focus on residential segregation, joined the Urban Affairs Programs and in 1984 became dean of that program, serving until 1997. Richard W. Thomas had been a part of UAP starting as an instructor, and by 1980 was a tenured associate professor. Dorothy Harper-Jones joined the School of Social Work as an instructor in 1981, and in 1990 after completing her PhD, which was a cross-cultural study of infants and mothers in Africa and the United States, she became part of the tenured faculty.

Professor Harper-Jones's contributions to MSU's diversity programs were essential to their success. She served as assistant dean for diversity in the College of Social Science, was named consultant to the provost on racial, ethnic, multicultural, and diversity issues, was cochair of the Martin Luther King Jr. All Celebration Committee, and was central to the establishment of the African American and African Studies (AAAS) Program. In 1997–98 she dedicated her consultant year to focusing on the issue of the loss of black programs and courses at MSU, and to curricular options for black students. She organized a meeting with Provost Lou Anna K. Simon and included Professors Geneva Smitherman and Gloria Randle from the Department of English, and Denise Troutman, who held appointments both in Linguistics and Languages and in American Thought and Language, to join the discussion of the issues. As a social activist, Professor Harper-Jones and the other three faculty members believed black students needed to know more about national conditions for black Americans, and internationally for all black people; that training researchers who would exert social responsibility was essential; and that black communities and families needed attention in terms of their changing needs.

In 1987 and 1989 two black women joined the faculty in the College of Arts and Letters. Darlene Clark Hine, a historian, came to MSU as a John A. Hannah Distinguished Professor and held that appointment for seventeen years until 2004, when she left East Lansing to become Board of Trustees Professor of African American Studies and professor of history at Northwestern University. Geneva Smitherman came to MSU in 1989 after several years of activism in Detroit dedicated to the betterment of education for black students and to the recognition of black children's language as "their own." She had taught at Harvard University and at Wayne State University, directing the Center for Black Studies in Detroit. Their incredible scholarly productivity was a continuation of the professional pattern already set, but its volume and impact while they were at MSU was nothing short of phenomenal.

Between 1987 and 2004, Professor Hine published twenty books, including comprehensive multivolume histories first of African Americans and then black women, two major studies of the Black Diaspora, a study of black women in nursing, and specialized studies

In 1987 Darlene Clark Hine came to MSU as the John A. Hannah Distinguished Professor of History and remained until 2004. During her seventeen years here, she published a succession of notable books on African American history, with a particular focus on black women and their roles and contributions. She moved to a new endowed position at Northwestern University in 2004, and in 2006 became a fellow in the American Academy of Arts and Sciences. At MSU, she was the director of the Comparative Black History PhD program. Professor Hine is shown with President Lou Anna K. Simon on the occasion of Simon's MSU inaugural. Courtesy of Michigan State University Photography Services.

of the Black Chicago Renaissance, the black professional class, and women and slavery in the Americas. She accomplished and exceeded what was hoped for from a Hannah Professor: to become a major scholar who changes a field and achieves distinction as a researcher. Hine has provided richly detailed narratives that set the black experience in the context of American history, but most importantly the history that black people and groups have created, shaped, and directed out of their own lives, cultures, and social institutions. As she shows, it is a record of remarkable achievement and progress against and in spite of all that acted to suppress it or deny its actuality.

Geneva Smitherman's work has focused on the rich and complex language patterns and expression of black Americans within the contexts of their communities, whether it is the streets, home, church, schools, or other institutions. Three books launched her as a scholar who would change thinking and understanding of black speech: *Talkin and Testifyin: The Language of Black America* (1980), *Black Talk: Words and Phrases from the Home to Amen Corner* (1994), and *Talkin That Talk: Language, Culture and Education in African America* (2000). In addition she has published over one hundred articles and essays in a wide variety of publications in order for her scholarship to

Geneva Smitherman's research and books on black people's language and culture have established her as a foremost authority in this field. Her prolific work on the speech and expression patterns of African Americans and her passionate advocacy of African American English have made her a scholar activist who seeks to transform a field that is also a culture. Since 1995 she has worked with scholars and activists in South Africa on language policy and education, and she has conducted workshops nationally and internationally. Courtesy of Michigan State University Photography Services.

reach the widest possible audience. She is a passionate and eloquent advocate for students' rights to their own language, whatever its variety or dialect, and believes that African American English is a cultural resource of identity and power as well as heritage. Her research and publications have always been activist, aiming at dislodging and overturning assumptions and practices that limit expression. In 1990 she established My Brother's Keeper, a program in which MSU students serve as mentors to Detroit males from the sixth to eighth grades, with the mentees coming to campus on the weekends and for overnight stays during the summers. She is regularly interviewed by local and national media, and she has worked in programs in South Africa that are part of that country's recognition of eleven official languages. Her work as a scholar and activist has been recognized by the National Council of the Teachers of English as "transforming," and as a "lasting intellectual contribution."

Carl S. Taylor rejoined the Department of Family and Child Ecology at MSU in 1994 after initially being appointed to the School of Criminal Justice in 1984, serving until 1990, and then working elsewhere for four years. He has worked extensively in the field with community and government agencies to reduce violence involving urban youths. Michigan State University Press published Taylor's *Dangerous Society* in 1990 and *Girls, Gangs, Women and Drugs* in 1993. He has studied the dynamics of gang membership and the alternatives needed by urban young people to direct their lives in positive and constructive directions. His work has been located in the Institute for Children, Youth and Families, and in 2004 he moved to the Department of Sociology at MSU and has been the editor of the online *Journal of Urban Youth Culture* since 2003. Former MSU president Clifton Wharton Jr. provided the guest editorial to the first issue of the journal.

Curtis Stokes was the founding director of the graduate program in African American and African Studies, which began in 2002. He teamed with Joe T. Darden and Richard W. Thomas to edit and contribute to *The State of Black Michigan, 1967–2007* (MSU Press), which was an update and continuation of a volume of the same title issued in 1984 by the Center for Urban Affairs. Stokes's work has focused on black politics in Michigan and the nation, and in 2003 the MSU Press published his *Racial Liberalism and the Politics of Urban America*.

Significantly, these black faculty were, of course, affiliated with the African American and African Studies Program, and directed graduate student research and dissertations after 2002 as well as participated in symposiums and national conferences on campus sponsored by AAAS, such as the "Black Religion and Spirituality" Conference held annually starting in 1996, and the "Race in 21st Century America" Conference that began in 2006. What gradually developed over the period from the early 1970s was a solid and expanding core of black scholars, teachers, and activists who gained national visibility and recognition in their fields and who provided a wider base of disciplines. Much of the direct involvement and research focused on Detroit and other Michigan cities, and thus the university was at last substantially and continuously doing what President Walter Adams had urged in his December 1969 commencement address when he stated that the university must change to meet "the crisis in the long neglected urban centers of our society" (Adams 278). The Urban Affairs Programs had kept that mission alive and circulating, even after the College of Urban Development had been eliminated.

The single most dramatic event that impacted the campus was undoubtedly the terrorist airplane hijackings and attacks on 11 September 2001. This collective experience linked students, faculty, and staff to the generation who were on campus during the Japanese attack on Pearl Harbor in December 1941. Both attacks were shocking and unexpected, shattering a sense of national security and personal safety. As events developed on September 11th, there was a sense of things spinning out of control, and then horror with the collapse of the World Trade Center towers, the plane slamming into the side of the Pentagon, and a hijacked plane crashing in a Pennsylvania field. For a few uneasy hours there was a sense of helplessness, as well as an undeniable awareness that catastrophic events had taken place with the terrible finality of a great human toll. It was hard to process what had happened, let alone consider why it happened or who was responsible. ASMSU organized a candlelight vigil at The Rock with about one thousand students participating, and on 14 September, on the designated National Day of Prayer and Remembrance, a campus-wide service was attended by about four thousand people. Associate General Counsel Sally Harwood gave a carillon concert at Beaumont

The candlelight vigil organized by Associated Students of Michigan State University and held at The Rock on the evening of 11 September 2001 was a somber but calming memorial for those who had been killed at three different sites by terrorists that morning. The day's events had been staggering and shocking as well as surreal, but The Rock provided a place where thoughts and prayers could steady sorrow and bewilderment. Courtesy of Michigan State University Photography Services.

Tower in memory of the victims (Minutes, 21 September 2011). At its meeting on September 21, the Board of Trustees established eleven full four-year scholarships for tuition and fees for "children whose parents lost their lives as the result of terrorist acts and rescue efforts in New York, Washington, D.C., and Pennsylvania." President McPherson reached out to the Muslim community and assured them of the university's commitment to them as part of the community, and the Muslim Student Association put on a program that was attended by almost one thousand people. Professors helped students sort through their emotions of confusion and anger, and collectively the university community realized that a different time had dawned, and that being part of a global political and ideological world would not be an easy course or certain future. From this departure point, the academic year of 2001–02 continued.

Intercollegiate Athletics

The period from 1995 to 2005 involved a number of transitions and changes in MSU athletics. George Melvin "Jud" Heathcote coached his final season in 1994–95, with the Spartans tied for second in the Big Ten Conference at 14-4 and finishing at 22-6 for the season after a first-round loss in the NCAA tournament. After serving five years as an associate head coach under Heathcote, Tom Izzo became head coach on 30 June 1995, and after knocking on the door in the 1998 and 1999 NCAA tournaments, the Spartans claimed the national championship in 2000 in Izzo's fifth season as coach. Heathcote had his national championship in his third season at MSU. But Izzo was performing his specialty, which was winning Big Ten championships and going to the Final Four. From 1997–98 to 2000–01 the Spartans won four consecutive conference championships (one outright in 1998–99). They went to three consecutive Final Fours and to another one in 2005.

Women's basketball coach Karen Langeland finished the last of her twenty-four seasons in 1999–2000. Three of her teams in the 1990s went to the NCAA tournament, and the 1996–97 Spartans recorded a 22-8 season record while claiming a share of the Big Ten title at 12-4. Succeeding Langeland was Joanne P. McCallie, who at the University of Maine had established a reputation for winning regular season titles (five in eight years as head coach) and for taking her team to NCAA tournaments (six straight in eight years). "Coach P," as she was known, brought intensity and a winning system to a program that had shown definite promise in the 1990s for moving up into top-level national competition. In McCallie's third year at MSU, the Spartans made the NCAA tournament and lost in the first round, and in 2004 again made the "Big Dance" and won their first-round game but lost in the second round. In 2004–05 the women's program made a big jump forward, winning the Big Ten championship and receiving the no. 1 seed in the Kansas City Regional. The Spartans beat the no. 2 seed Stanford 76-69 to claim a regional title, beat the no. 1 Philadelphia Regional Seed and champion Tennessee (a team in its sixteenth Final Four) in the national semifinals, but lost to Baylor 84-62 in the national championship game in Indianapolis, where Izzo's team had claimed its national championship in 2000. It was a

Tom Izzo became MSU head basketball coach starting with the 1995–96 season and established the Spartans as a national powerhouse, winning four consecutive Big Ten championships and going regularly to the NCAA Final Four, claiming the national championship in 2000. The Izzone student cheering section became an important part of the successful program. Courtesy of Michigan State University Photography Services.

stunning and exciting rise to the top, built on the platform of a shared Big Ten regular season title and a first-ever conference tournament title and a record of 28-3 going into the NCAA competition. The look and style of a nationally competitive program had arrived in East Lansing at the Breslin Center.

Another transition took place when Ron Mason concluded his twenty-three seasons as MSU's hockey coach in 2002 and his thirty-fourth as a head coach. He amassed 924 career wins, and in December

From 2000 to 2007, Joanne P. McCallie brought the women's basketball program to a new level of performance and consistent winning, taking her teams to five straight NCAA appearances and to a 33-4 season record in 2004–05 and a runner-up role to the national champion. She was well known and appreciated for her community service on behalf of homeless people, young people with cancer, and adults with Alzheimer's. Courtesy of Michigan State University Photography Services.

1997 (five years before his retirement) he notched his 500th career victory as a Spartan. He would become athletic director in 2002, and with the steadiness and consistency he had as a coach would guide intercollegiate athletics through some challenging times until his retirement in 2008. In April 2002 Rick Comley succeeded Mason as hockey's head coach.

Before Mason's five years as athletic director, this position experienced an unsettled period as well as posed a challenging job for two individuals. In 1992 Merrily Dean Baker was hired as athletic director, coming directly from four years of working in the NCAA main office, and before that six years at the University of Minnesota as athletic director of women's intercollegiate athletics. She was the first woman athletic director in the Big Ten Conference and the second woman athletic director at a Division 1 football-playing school (Ruiz). Baker's three years as athletic director were complicated by the fact that President DiBiaggio, who had accepted Provost David K. Scott's recommendation that she be hired, left MSU immediately after she began in the position. Scott left his position as provost and by 1993 had moved to the University of Massachusetts Amherst, and a contentious presidential search was underway while Gordon E. Guyer served as president. George J. Perles was continuing as head football coach after a short period of time also serving as athletic director. It was a "perfect storm" of instability and change, one that would test the mettle of any new administrator. As Baker remembered it, "These were people fighting for personal egos and self-serving agendas, not simple turf. I did not come in here naive to the realities; I knew of the chaos. What I did not know was the president who hired me was going to leave the first day I was here. No question, I wouldn't have come if I had known that, even if I learned it as little as a week before" (qtd. in Perles 184). Almost everything Baker did was subject to scrutiny and criticism, including the color of her outfits for certain occasions where she was representing MSU. She resigned in 1995, and Merritt J. Norvell Jr. took her place.

Norvell had played football at the University of Wisconsin and was a member of the Badgers squad that won the 1962 Big Ten championship and played University of Southern California the Rose Bowl (and ended up ranked no. 2 nationally to no. 1 USC in the final poll). Prior to becoming MSU's athletic director, Norvell had worked for the IBM Corporation and been involved with IBM's Academic Information Systems, where he had business and sales contacts with universities. He earned three degrees, including the doctorate, from Wisconsin and served as an assistant dean of the Graduate School Administration. He was successful in executive leadership positions at IBM for eighteen years, but his role as athletic director (one of only four African American athletic directors in the United States at major schools) would last three years and nine months. He resigned on 15 April 1999 and joined one of the top U.S. executive search firms and remained with his family in the Lansing area. Norvell headed intercollegiate athletics when its budget was expanding as costs increased. A budget that was $20.9 million in 1997–98 had grown to $24 million in 1998–99. Norvell encountered the same problems and challenges that Baker had, many of which had to do with administrative style and interpersonal communication. Both Baker and Norvell preferred some distance and separation as administrators, which opened them up to charges of being aloof. Both were aware of the complexities of institutional politics and were careful about seeking advice or giving personal counsel. They did not seek to line up or gather loyal supporters who could advocate for or protect them if needed. But at bottom, their biggest limitation was that they were not originally "Spartans," not products of a culture that expected fervent loyalty, deep roots, and unabashed pride in being "green and white." Douglas "Doug" Weaver, who had proceeded them as athletic director from 1979 to 89, was such a Spartan.

In September 1996 the NCAA Committee on Infractions issued a 21-page report with findings against MSU that resulted in a four-year probation and the loss of two athletic scholarships in 1996 and seven in 1997. Because of a thorough internal investigation ordered by President Peter McPherson, which cost an estimated $1 million and involved about two hundred interviews, the NCAA allowed MSU to play in bowl games and be on television. The infractions involved illegal cash payments to recruits by boosters, and academic cheating directed by a student advisor in the athletic department in order to keep athletes eligible. In response to the report, President McPherson accepted the sanctions, indicated there would be no appeal, and offered to forfeit the five football games won in 1994, four of which had been Big Ten victories (Bagnato). The NCAA accepted the offer, making the Spartans' record 0-11 in Coach Perles's final season. On 8 November 1994, after a Spartan win at Northwestern, McPherson called Perles to tell him he was fired. In his 1995 autobiography, Perles admitted a certain relief that the matter was decided, because he had been experiencing unhealthy anxiety (Perles 200).

Following Perles was Nicholas "Nick" Lou Saban Jr., who coached the Spartans for five seasons and did not have a losing season, although his teams were 6-6 in both 1996 and 1998. His teams went to bowl games four of the five seasons, although he did not coach in the 1 January 2000 Citrus Bowl because he had taken the head coaching job at Louisiana State University. Saban was totally focused on football and stayed out of the politics swirling around. He also knew that with the loss of nine scholarships he had been handed a difficult task of restoring a winning tradition. The coaching he and his staff did in the 1999 season may just be some of the finest ever. The Spartans beat three teams they had lost to in 1998 (University of Oregon, University of Michigan, and Penn State) and again beat University of Notre Dame and Ohio State University as they had in 1998. The only losses in a 9-2 regular season came at Purdue, which led the Big Ten in passing offense for the season, and at Wisconsin, which won the

Nicholas "Nick" Lou Saban Jr. had served as a defensive coordinator at MSU under George Perles from 1983 to 1987 and had four years of professional coaching experience in the NFL before becoming head coach of the Spartans in 1995. He turned a program with a record of losing seasons and under the cloud of NCAA sanctions into a winning program with four bowl appearances in Saban's five seasons. The 10-2 record for the MSU team in 1999 was the best since 1965. He went on to LSU, where he won a national championship in his fourth season there. Courtesy of Michigan State University Archives and Historical Collections (*Red Cedar Log* 2000).

conference and finished fourth in the final national polls. The 1999 season was capped off with a Citrus Bowl win, 37-34 against Florida, and a seventh place final national ranking.

Bobby Williams coached the Spartans in the bowl win and became head coach after Saban's departure. He was a popular choice of the players, who showed up at Cowles House in support of him, and McPherson said that he had selected Williams to maintain consistency and continuity in the program (Minutes, 10 December 1999). Saban had not been able to convince any of the assistant coaches to join him in Baton Rouge, and the assistants were unified behind Williams. The football program had succeeded in overcoming the limitations imposed by the 1996 NCAA sanctions, and the 10-2 season of 1999 signaled a return to national recognition. What followed were a 5-6 season in 2000, a 7-5 season in 2001 with a bowl win over Fresno State, and then a 4-6 season in 2002 with Williams being fired after a 49-3 loss at Michigan in the ninth season game. The critical factor in Williams's firing was the poor Big Ten record, which up to the 2002 game with Michigan was 6-15, and the public's perception that somehow Williams did not fit the demanding role of head coach and could not make the transition from a positions coach to the main man. Others believed that Williams was not given the time or support he needed to win.

Into the picture came John L. Smith in 2003, coming from the University of Louisville, where his teams compiled a 41-21 record in five seasons, went to five bowl games, and won two Conference USA championships. He came to MSU with fourteen seasons of head coaching experience and a reputation as an adventurer and rugged Westerner. In his first season at MSU the team compiled an 8-4 record, went 5-3 in the Big Ten, and went to the Alamo Bowl. His team outscored their opponents in cumulative season points 360-276, and he was named Big Ten Coach of the Year. What followed the next three seasons were records of 5-7, 5-6, and 4-8. In 2005 the Spartans started 4-0 but then only won one more game out of seven, and in 2006 after winning the first three games won only one of the nine remaining games, winning only one Big Ten game. In five games decided by four or less points the Spartans were 1-4. The only Big Ten win was an NCAA comeback record victory over Northwestern when

Bobby Williams became MSU's head football coach in December 1999 when Nick Saban left for Louisiana State University. Williams had been the running backs' coach at MSU since 1990 and was a popular choice. In his almost three seasons, his record was 16-17, with seven conference wins and with two bowl victories. He has worked subsequently as an assistant under Saban at LSU, for the NFL Miami Dolphins, and at Alabama. Courtesy of Michigan State University Archives and Historical Collections (*Red Cedar Log* 2003).

MSU came back from a 38-3 deficit in the third quarter to win 41-38. It was the last win for the season, which ended with Smith being fired with two years left on his six-year contract. In the seven seasons from 2000 to 2006 MSU was 38-45 overall and 19-37 in the Big Ten. An expanding sports program with a need for revenues could not afford what had unfortunately become below-mediocre football teams.

Another major story in intercollegiate athletics had nothing to do with teams or coaches but involved facilities. In February 1994 the Board of Trustees approved Phase I of the Spartan Stadium Renovation Project, and by 2002, when the project was completed, the total cost was $15 million. Like many other aging college football stadiums, Spartan Stadium needed renovation (Sheehan 134). The support columns were showing signs of deterioration and crumbling. In September 2003 the Spartan Stadium Expansion project was approved at an estimated cost of $50 million. The project was seen as a revenue-enhancing one, with club seats in the indoor-outdoor club, box suites, and a large event area for rent year round. A portion of the facility would house University Development, the MSU Alumni Association, and the MSU Foundation. It was a bold step forward at a time when extreme caution seemed called for, but the plan, as presented by athletic director Ron Mason, showed how collaboration and coordinated planning across units could win the day. Athletic director Mason, Provost Simon, Charles "Chuck" H. Webb of University Development, Keith Williams of the MSU Alumni Association, and Vice President Fred L. Poston combined efforts to produce a new-look Spartan Stadium with first-rate facilities capable of generating a steady flow of additional revenues.

Other revenue-generating moves included a reseating plan for Breslin starting in 2000–2001 and the Spartan Stadium Scholarship Plan in May 2003. New rules guided the availability and selection of choice seats, and the fans' willingness to pay a premium in addition to ticket cost was the guiding factor. A system of accumulated points or credits determined eligibility for various levels of seats. Fan loyalty over a long period of time and the purchase of the same seats year after year were no longer the determining factors. In 1995–96 the average profits at Division 1A football schools were slightly in excess of $3 million annually, with average profit increases of 7.6 percent per year (Sheehan 138). By 2011–12, MSU revenues from football were

The Spartan Stadium Renovation Project (1994–2002) and the Spartan Stadium Expansion Project (beginning in 2003) gave the university a first-class sports facility and coincided with the substantial increase in revenues from athletics. In all, expenditures for renovating, upgrading, and building sports facilities from 1994 to 2005 totaled about $94 million. Courtesy of Michigan State University Photography Services.

just over $45 million, and basketball generated $17 million (Equity in Athletics Data). The decisions made to renovate and expand Spartan Stadium before the start of the 2005 season brought its capacity to 75,005, recovering some 3,000 seats that had been lost in the 1990s (MacCambridge 79).

Other new facilities included the $6.5 million Student Athletic Academic Center, named the Clara Bell Smith Center after Spartan basketball player Steve Smith's mother. Smith donated $2.5 million for the facility. The expanded Jack Breslin Student Events Center featured two gymnasiums, offices, and conference facilities and became known as the Alfred Berkowitz Basketball Complex. Berkowitz had contributed $2 million of the $7.5 million cost. The two practice gymnasiums were named after Forest Akers and Jud Heathcote, with the Forest Akers Trust donating $1 million and Heathcote's friends donating $1 million (Minutes, 7 December 2001). In December 2001 a new running track and artificial turf were approved at a cost of

$3.3 million for Ralph Young Field. The women's field hockey teams now had a new, well-scaled facility and escaped playing in cavernous Spartan Stadium. Off campus on the Grand River, a new boathouse facility was built at a cost of $600,000 for MSU's varsity crew. Expenditures on new sports facilities, renovations, upgrades, and additions from 1994 to 2005 totaled in the area of $94 million, invigorating the athletic program across many sports and extending the modernization that began with the Jack Breslin Student Events Center.

Sports other than football and basketball had a resurgence and experienced success. Leading the way was Coach Michele Madison's field hockey team, which won the Big Ten championship in 2001 and reached the NCAA Elite Eight, and then in 2002 reached the national semifinals after winning the conference tournament title. In 2003 the team shared a Big Ten championship and won the tournament and another NCAA quarterfinals appearance, and 2004 brought another share of the Big Ten championship and a second appearance in the NCAA semifinals. It was a remarkable run from 2001 to 2004 in which Madison's team compiled a 74-18 record. The women's golf team won a Big Ten championship in 2001, and in 1995 Coach Chuck Erbe's women's volleyball team made it to the NCAA semifinals. Erbe took his teams to the NCAA tournaments ten of twelve years from 1993 to 2004. Teams in cross-country, women's rowing, softball, and men's golf claimed tournament championships. In a club sport, the men's water polo team won a national championship.

The university continued to work on a gender-equity plan in order to comply with Title IX as well as the NCAA and Big Ten Conference, with the goal of balancing out the number of men's and women's sports and the numbers of athletes. This goal had to be reached within the scope of revenues and expenses produced by all sports. The last men's varsity sport to be dropped was lacrosse.

Two events highlight MSU sports in this period as well as any, one that was highly visible and the other not as visible. In October 2001, MSU played University of Michigan to a 3-3 tie on an ice rink installed on the field of Spartan Stadium. A then world-record crowd of 74,544 for an outdoor hockey game turned out for the "Cold War" event, which was the brainchild of assistant athletic director Mark Hollis, and the game received national and international television coverage. The other event took place on campus the weekend of 9–10

February 2002. Women athletes who had played sports but never received varsity letters were invited to campus to be recognized and honored; under the rules of the Association for Intercollegiate Athletics for Women (AIAW), which governed women's sports from 1971–83, female athletes were not allowed to earn varsity letters. At the women's basketball game, the returning athletes were introduced, and on Sunday at the Kellogg Center they were introduced one by one and came across the stage to receive a plaque with the varsity "S" letter attached (Underwood 323–24). About two hundred women athletes attended and, although belatedly, were recognized as Spartan athletes. The committee that recommended to Clarence Underwood the award of the varsity letters included Shelley Appelbaum, Karen Langeland, Sally Belloli, and Lori Schultz (Underwood 323). It was one of those moments where the university's history was adjusted and corrected to the betterment of all.

The Campus of the Future

What began as a south campus beautification project with a tree-planting initiative turned into perhaps the most important and long-lasting plan in the university's history. After the MSU Department of Horticulture moved into the new Plant and Soil Sciences Building in 1986, the Horticulture Demonstration Gardens moved to a space behind the new building. An area of plant diversity and beauty that had formerly been located on the northern edge of campus now anchored one of the main southern boundaries. The Plant and Soil Sciences Building was beautifully landscaped and the path from Eustace Hall to the Old Horticulture Building to south campus was complete. Attention turned to the planting of trees, and Peter and Joanne McPherson as well as trustee Robert E. Weiss and his wife Vickie responded generously to the call for donations from University Development.

What followed in December 1999 was a Board of Trustees resolution to establish a Public Art on Campus Committee that would initiate the process to commission or acquire "enduring works of public art" as a meaningful way to commemorate MSU's Sesquicentennial (2005–06). This resolution followed the 9 September 1999 submission of the Ad Hoc Artwork on Campus Committee Report. The resolution provided funding by stipulating that 0.5 percent of the cost of major renovations or new buildings be dedicated to public art "up to a maximum of $250,000." Funds not spent on specific artwork would go into a common fund for acquiring more costly or additional works (Minutes, 10 December 1999). The first Public Art on Campus Committee was chaired by Jeffrey R. "Jeff" Kacos, the director of Campus Parks, and Susan J. Bandes, director of the Kresge Art Museum. A statue of John A. Hannah, proposed by trustee Bob Traxler, would be the first in a series of Sesquicentennial art projects (Minutes, 28 April 2000). The resolution passed on 10 December 1999 began, "WHEREAS the creative work of sculptors, painters, and graphic artists enriches a learning environment, stimulates lively discussion and evokes aesthetic appreciation . . ." Public art was also declared to be "integral to a well-constructed campus plan."

By 7 December 2001, the "2020 Vision: A Community Concept for the MSU Campus" was ready for presentation to the Board of Trustees. That plan was aimed at (1) preserving the campus environment and its natural beauty as well as increasing it; (2) balancing vehicle traffic with pedestrian use of space; (3) allowing for growth while maintaining the open space quality of the north campus; (4) conserving finite land resources with environmental sensitivity; (5) maintaining and continuing a campus that reflects a community's aspirations and aesthetic sense. New zoning ordinances were passed to guide and regulate the plan. Updates in the Campus Master Plan would be made every five years to keep the vision and goals visible to the campus and East Lansing community. Those most directly involved were William J. "Bill" Latta, then assistant director of the Office of Planning and Budgets, who chaired the 2020 Vision Committee; Ronald T. "Ron" Flinn (Physical Plant); Chuck Gagliano (Housing and Food Services); Charles J. "Chuck" Reid (Land Management); Jeffrey R. "Jeff" Kacos (Campus Parks and Planning); and Kathryn E. "Kathy" Lindahl (Finance and Operations). Vice President Fred L. Poston, Provost Lou Anna K. Simon, and the hired outside consultants from Sasaki Associates, Inc. were also key players. The plan had been presented and discussed across campus, and the committee had received substantial response and input. It was the first time the entire sprawling campus with its distinctive areas and their growth histories was considered comprehensively for what it had become and what it could be in terms of aesthetic, social, and ecological values. As President M. Peter McPherson put it,

> It [the campus] has the potential to define a collective experience of place and community, which is an essential part of the teaching and learning experience for students, faculty, and staff. At its best, the campus can be a rich expression of tradition and history, a fundamental resource to the current educational enterprise, and an invaluable reference point in helping to define the future. Perhaps more than any other single aspect of the University, the physical environment has the power to embody and express the purpose and mission of Michigan State University. (Campus Master Plan)

In its earliest days, the land south of the Red Cedar River had been the farmlands where students did their agricultural practice, the work in the fields to which many would return. Now, in the twenty-first century, much of that land had been transformed into the extension of a modern university replete with research facilities, laboratories, classroom buildings, and a clinical center. What had once fit into five brick buildings on a circular drive had become over twenty buildings stretching across the campus west to east. The Campus Master Plan sought to extend the "park-like quality of the campus landscape" from north to south, from west to east, so that its original beauty and heritage could be felt and experienced by successive generations. Again, the potential of the entire campus for thoughtful and purposeful planning was demonstrated.

The McPherson Presidency—An Overview

Except for the five plus months between May and the end of the first week in October 2003 that he spent in Baghdad as director of economic policy for the Office of Reconstruction and Humanitarian Assistance in Iraq, M. Peter McPherson was a full-time on-campus president. He did not log the extensive and far-flung international travels of DiBiaggio, but when the call came to use his knowledge of currency systems and banking, he went to work on assignment in the "Green Zone" of Baghdad, the Iraqi capital that had only been taken by American military forces in April 2003. The job he and his staff had was to establish the printing of currency for the postwar recovery, to restore banking and financial institutions and make them operational, and to bring some measure of public confidence or trust in a functional economy to the degree possible under the circumstances. The university's struggles with its budget reductions in early 2003 certainly paled by comparison with the monumental task McPherson and every other American, civilian or military, faced in Iraq. In April 1998 he had been nominated to the Dow Jones and Company Board of Directors, and in December 2000 he spoke at the Detroit Economic Club and at the national Republican Governors Association conference (Minutes, 10 April 1998 and 8 December 2000). His reputation or usefulness had not been forgotten, and the world in which he spent twenty-five years before coming to East Lansing would eventually pull him back into its orbit. This process started with his work in Iraq.

One of the most significant developments during McPherson's presidency was the arrival of the law school. Earlier, John A. DiBiaggio had tried to make Thomas M. Cooley Law School in Lansing a part of MSU. He envisioned MSU downsizing the school and being more selective in admission, but keeping the school in downtown Lansing. However, Thomas E. Brennan, who founded Cooley Law School in 1972 and became its first full-time dean in 1974, would not enter into an agreement. Brennan had a different vision and mission for the school, which he pursued after becoming its president in 1979 and serving until 2002. Brennan wanted to remain in charge and retain his own board. After that nonstarter, MSU began conversations with the Detroit College of Law (DCL), but with a large number of pressing needs demanding attention, DiBiaggio decided to concentrate on them (SOHP interview, 12 July 2000).

At the 11 June 1993 Board of Trustees meeting, trustee Robert E. Weiss moved that the "administration . . . create an appropriately constituted select committee to analyze options for the involvement of Michigan State University in legal education and requests that the Board receive through its Policy Committee periodic reports on the progress of the deliberations with the expectation that the select committee will conclude its work as quickly as possible after the

The movement of the Detroit College of Law to its campus location and its incorporation into the university as the MSU College of Law is one of the most notable success stories of the contemporary period. President McPherson called upon former MSU president M. Cecil Mackey to facilitate the transfer, which he skillfully accomplished, and Provost Lou Anna K. Simon saw to its organizational movement into academic governance. Courtesy of Michigan State University Photography Services.

beginning of Fall semester." At its 27 February 1995 meeting, the Board of Trustees was ready to act on a recommendation that a law affiliation between MSU and the Detroit College of Law be established and that a formal agreement be prepared. Professor and former MSU president M. Cecil Mackey would be the facilitator for law affiliation. The Board of Trustees approved the specific guidelines that had been set forth in the task force report, and a formal status report was requested in twelve months (Minutes, 27 February 1995). In its initial appearance on campus, the Detroit College of Law (DCL) would retain its identity and name and would provide all operational and building funds. The motion and plan were unanimously approved.

In April 1995 MSU's Architectural and Engineering Services were contracted for the building to house DCL. By February 1996 the cost of a building for the law school and its library was set at $28.4 million. By July 1999 the law school became Michigan State

University-Detroit College of Law, and by April 2004 the name had become MSU College of Law and Provost Simon could announce the full integration of the faculty into regular academic governance. From the Board of Trustees' approval of a select committee to "analyze options for the involvement of [MSU] in legal education" on 11 June 1993 to the April 2004 full incorporation, twelve years had passed smoothly and progressively due to intelligent and purposeful planning, the trust and goodwill of those involved, the fact that DCL's relocation and operation did not impose any financial demands on MSU, and the fact that a good law school survived and thrived in a new setting and found its place on a university campus that wanted and welcomed it. The work of Cecil Mackey, done with his characteristic thoroughness and persuasive clarity of presentation, was critical to the project's success.

Another major success during McPherson's presidency was the Campaign for MSU, with a goal of $1.2 billion to be raised by 30 June 2007. The three year "silent phase" of the capital campaign raised $600 million, and by the end, $1.439 billion was raised, with over two hundred gifts of $1 million or more that totaled almost $700 million ("1.4 Billion Exceeds"). The campaign focused on raising the university's net endowment portfolio as well as strengthening instruction and research. The constant flow of positive news about MSU was critical to the capital campaign's resounding success.

Like John A. Hannah, McPherson strongly believed that students needed to be interested in politics and economics, to be aware of issues like world hunger and the needs of developing countries, and to move beyond their culturally determined viewpoints. He invited political commentator Chris Matthews to bring MSNBC's *Hardball* program to campus, and it was televised from the MSU Auditorium. He invited Vice President Richard "Dick" Cheney to deliver the commencement address, which he did in May 2002. Working with student housing, McPherson endorsed a newspaper readership program that provided the *New York Times*, the *Wall Street Journal*, and a Detroit paper free for students daily. The *New York Times* became part of the reading curriculum in many courses, from first-year American Thought and Language writing to higher-level courses. Music Television (MTV) brought its "MTV Rock the Vote, Choose or Lose" bus campaign to the MSU campus in September 1996 as part of an effort to boost student voter registration for the presidential election.

President McPherson also involved students in addressing and proposing solutions to campus problems like policies on alcohol consumption or riotous behavior and destruction. Two student liaisons sat with the Board of Trustees, as did faculty liaisons, and provided connections back to student organizations. Their individual contributions and perspectives were acknowledged and valued. In his first meeting with the Board of Trustees as president, McPherson had indicated that he would like to make board meetings more open and accessible to public participation, recommending that direct responses to individuals or groups during the meeting from Board of Trustees members or administrators be possible, and that participants be able to sign up to address the board the morning of the meeting (Minutes, 8 October 1993). Without a doubt, more individuals and groups brought issues and concerns before the Board of Trustees, and meetings could and did at times take on a contentious and confrontational tone as groups pressed their cases. Overall, however, this opening up of the meetings made them more of a public forum rather than a carefully managed formality.

The last major issue that McPherson dealt with was the proposed expansion of the College of Human Medicine (CHM) to Grand Rapids. This proposal galvanized vocal opposition, with concerns being expressed that this was a decision made by central administration, which failed to seek faculty input. Concerns were voiced about accreditation, a possible decrease in health care locally, the impact on research and multidisciplinary teams on campus that could be disrupted by shifting personnel, the need for an oversight committee to guide the process and ensure balanced interests, and a fear that CHM might be privatized (Minutes, 16 April 2004 and 7 May 2004). McPherson took the position that this was "a true expansion to Grand Rapids, rather than a transfer of a vast number of people," and that oversight by CHM faculty would regulate the process (Minutes, 7 May 2004). Fundamentally there were two questions: (1) Would expansion to Grand Rapids weaken or impair biomedical research on the East Lansing campus or decrease the quality of health care? (2) Were the financial projections sound, and if they were not, could the East Lansing CHM be endangered? Of course, no immediate answers could be had; only reassurances could be offered, as well as a belief that the preparatory work for the project was sound and reliable. Here was a case where multiple interests intersected and were focused, and where the larger community was involved and had a stake. The Board of Trustees voted to adopt a resolution for the expansion of the College of Human Medicine in Grand Rapids, and set the conditions and requirements for the implementation of the plans with their authorization in a separate action by the Board of Trustees at a later meeting (Minutes, 7 May 2004). As the board was aware that President McPherson was nearing the end of his presidency and would not see this expansion completed, it moved quickly and decisively to make Lou Anna K. Simon "president designate" as part of a transition in the last three months of McPherson's eleven years of service to MSU. Simon had worked with the Board of Trustees to do the difficult work of program and budget cutting, and in the process gained the trustees' respect and confidence in her abilities. In her work as provost, the trustees already knew her comprehensive and thorough knowledge of curriculum.

McPherson's final meeting with the Board of Trustees came on 10 December 2004, and he expressed pride in his service. His wife, Joanne, was an important part of his success, and she had made her own contributions with her key role in the establishment of the MSU Safe Place in 1997 for women and children needing safety from domestic abuse, and with her involvement in alcohol and drug abuse education on campus. McPherson left campus to join Dow Jones and Company, where he had been serving as an independent director since 1998, and to become the chairman-in-waiting for the company. McPherson had provided the university with eleven years of consistent and committed leadership at a time when college presidents were coming and going every five to seven years. That stability had benefited MSU greatly and taken it through another period of trial and testing.

CONCLUSION

Looking Back through the Lens of the Sesquicentennial and Looking Ahead

On 17 September 2004, three months before his final meeting with the Board of Trustees, President M. Peter McPherson presided at the unveiling and dedication of the sculpture honoring President John A. Hannah. The 7-foot bronze statue weighing in excess of 700 pounds and standing on a granite base was the first project of the Public Art on Campus Committee and heralded the beginning of events that would commemorate the university's Sesquicentennial. The Hannah Administration Plaza had been renovated for the occasion, and Hannah's son, Thomas, was present. In his remarks, McPherson focused on how Hannah built a university by building on land-grant values that anchored and guided all developments.

> John Hannah built on land-grant values when he proclaimed that greatness in basic science must be united with the land-grant ideal of applied science. His commitment lives on in the cyclotron to plant research Labs to our quest for a Rare Isotope Accelerator. Hannah built on land-grant values when he called upon MSU to be global in thought and action. He made the world our campus, and named the nation's first dean of international programs. ("John Hannah and Land-Grant Values")

It was certainly appropriate and fitting that President McPherson should preside over this dedication. They had both served as presidentially appointed administrators of the Agency for International Development (USAID) and as president of the Association of Public and Land-Grant Universities (APLU). Those viewing the sculpture created by California artist Bruce Wolfe agreed that it dynamically captured the forward-moving spirit of Hannah, his daily sense of

The John A. Hannah sculpture in the Hannah Plaza in front of the Hannah Administration Building was dedicated on Friday, 17 September 2004 as the first official event of the Sesquicentennial celebration. The $300,000 statue was privately funded and the first project of the Public Art on Campus Initiative. President M. Peter McPherson, who had announced on 17 June 2004 that he would step down, presided at the ceremony, while incoming president Lou Anna K. Simon would preside over the Sesquicentennial. Courtesy of Michigan State University Photography Services.

purpose, and his dignified bearing. It was also appropriate that at 7 feet high and more than 700 pounds, it was larger than life and was elevated on a base. People saw Hannah as larger than life and looked up to him as if he was on a pedestal. The only criticism heard was that the statue had Hannah going in the wrong direction, and that he should have been headed in the direction of the old Administration Building (Linton Hall), where he had his office on the second floor and where the Board of Trustees met with him in the conference room. Hannah's *A Memoir* (1980) concludes: "There are few people who have had an opportunity to live a more interesting life than I. It was all made possible as a result of my role at Michigan State University. For that I am grateful to the university and the people there who helped make it possible" (143).With the dedication of this impressive statue, MSU's 150th celebration got off to a good start.

Hannah's statue was not the first free-standing large bronze

On Saturday, 1 November 2003, Earvin "Magic" Johnson unveiled the 12-foot bronze statue of himself in front of the Jack Breslin Student Events Center, which honored the dynamic playmaker who helped Jud Heathcote's Spartans claim an NCAA championship in 1979. Titled *Always a Champion*, the statue recognized a man who developed and maintained the class and dignified presence of a champion as he added NBA championships and personal success to his achievements at MSU. Courtesy of Michigan State University Photography Services.

sculpture of a prominent Spartan to grace the campus. On 1 November 2003, a 12-foot statue of Earvin "Magic" Johnson was unveiled outside the Jack Breslin Student Events Center. Johnson and his coach and teammates on the National Championship team (which also had two Big Ten championships) were present to begin a season-long celebration of the 25th anniversary of the 1979 championship. The statue shows "Magic" in motion, dribbling and directing the offensive set with his incredible court vision and superb playmaking. The $250,000 work was funded by private donations, and the statue's designer, Omri Amrany, had earlier created the 16-foot sculpture of NBA superstar Michael Jordan for installment outside the United Center, home of the Chicago Bulls. After he received a standing ovation, Johnson said, "I did not achieve this alone. It's about all these guys, it's not about me. It was always about being a Spartan" ("Michigan State Dedicates"). Magic Johnson has gone on to become one of the great representatives of MSU and a public ambassador for the university because he sees himself as a Spartan, just as he saw himself as a member of a remarkable Spartan basketball team for two seasons.

The celebration of the 25th anniversary of MSU's first national championship in basketball was, in fact, one of many anniversaries taking place between 1998 and 2004. A sampling of some of these include:

- 1998: 50th anniversary of admission into the Big Ten
- 1999: 40th anniversary of Kresge Art Museum
- 2000: 75th anniversary of MSU Union Building
- 2002: 50th anniversary of first national championship in football
- 2002: 50th anniversary of School of Packaging
- 2002: 50th anniversary of Alumni Memorial Chapel
- 2003: 75th anniversary of Beaumont Tower
- 2003: 40th anniversary of Abrams Planetarium
- 2003: 50th anniversary of first Big Ten football title
- 2004: 50th anniversary of WKAR-TV
- 2004: 40th anniversary of MSU becoming an AAU institution

Other significant heritage developments preceded the Sesquicentennial celebration. In June 1994 the proposed renovation cost for Beaumont Tower and restoration of its carillon was $513,000, and the Board of Trustees approved the project in July 1995. The rededication took place on 3 May 1996 in the afternoon between the undergraduate and graduate commencements, with Margo Halsted presenting a seven-selection concert that began with the "MSU Fight Song" and concluded with "MSU Shadows." The clock was renovated along with the Westminster chimes that mark the quarter hours ("Restored Beaumont Bells"). For almost ten years since 1987, Beaumont Tower had stood silent, marking only a place and not marking the passage of time for the campus and East Lansing neighborhoods. The carillon that Wendell J. Westcott made famous through his 45-minute Sunday concerts simulcast on WKAR Radio was now restored and improved (Galik). The rededication concert that university carillonneur Margo Halsted played on 3 May 1996 was shared with a worldwide audience over the Internet ("Restored Beaumont Bells"). The heart of the campus began to beat again, and the marking of time by the most

Wendell J. Westcott was the university carillonneur from 1941 to 1987 and remained active through playing popular Sunday afternoon recitals at Beaumont Tower until age 96. He was a gifted professor of piano, and he directed the Spartan Bell Ringers and popularized hand-bell ringing as a performance art. His 1970 book titled *Bells and Their Music* is still considered the authoritative work on its subject. Courtesy of Michigan State University Archives and Historical Collections.

awe-inspiring and inspirational building on campus was restored. Milton E. Muelder, who served as dean of the College of Science and Arts, vice president for research development, and dean of the Graduate School, along with Kathleen D. Muelder established the Muelder International Summer Carillon Recital Series endowment in 1996, bringing artists from all over the world and the United States to present a rich program. Wendell Westcott continued to play the Beaumont carillon until the age of 96, when finally his health would not permit him to climb the four flights of narrow stairs (Obituary). He was a virtuoso performer and artist, with dedicated and adoring fans and devoted music students who learned piano, carillon, or bell-ringing from him. His free concerts became a summer tradition of music enthusiasts meeting and spreading out blankets on the lawns and enjoying food and refreshments as the bells rang in musical compositions.

Two historic buildings, Eustace Hall and Marshall Hall, underwent extensive renovation and restoration due to the contributions of generous alumni. Jeffrey N. Cole (1970 Honors College BA) and his wife Kathryn C. Cole (MBA 1990) donated $3 million to the Honors College in September 1998 with the goal of preserving Eustace Hall's historical integrity while adding a technology room and handicapper accessibility. The new Eustace-Cole Hall became a place of pride and continuing intellectual excitement and exploration for the three

Randall L. Pittman received a BA degree in political science and pre-law from MSU in 1976, and an MBA in finance from the Eli Broad College of Business. He founded a successful health services company in 1992, and in February 2002 joined the Board of Trustees, appointed to replace Robert E. Weiss. He and his wife, Mary E. Pittman, gave $6 million in 2002 for the restoration of Marshall Hall and requested the building be renamed Marshall-Adams Hall to honor Walter Adams for his service as professor and president. Trustee Pittman had worked for Adams as a graduate assistant. Courtesy of Michigan State University Photography Services.

thousand MSU students involved in the Honors College. Just over half of the Coles's bequest was directed to endowed scholarships.

Marshall Hall was renamed Marshall-Adams Hall when the restoration and renovation of the 1902 building was complete. MSU trustee Randall L. Pittman and his wife Mary donated $6 million for the work, which was completed for $5.2 million in 2005 with the dedication occurring on 1 October 2005 as part of the Sesquicentennial celebration. Pittman requested the building's renaming for Professor and President Walter Adams, and Pittman stated that he and his wife were making this gift to his former economics professor "on behalf of all the students who had the privilege of spending time with Dr. Adams in the classroom" (Minutes, 20 September 2002). Pittman recalled Professor Adams's annual final lecture when he would say: "I'm tired. I'm passing on the torch. Which of you will pick it up and carry it on?" Jeffrey N. Cole, when speaking to the Board of Trustees, recalled the speech that President Frank S. Kedzie made at the dedication of the new Olds Hall, rebuilt from the foundation up after the devastating fire in 1916 with the $100,000 donation of Ransom E. Olds. In that speech, President Kedzie talked about the future value of the "private bequest" to building and strengthening the college. Cole told the trustees: "My commitment to the university is really a revival of Dr. Kedzie's prophecy. MSU might not merely serve as a place where lifelong learning might be obtained, but as a place where lifelong service might be done. People like myself are merely the newest of those standing in a long green line of support" (Bao).

These two stories of major gifts illustrate how donors make personal connections to their experiences at MSU and what they learned of significance that registered in the future after they became successful. These same stories were repeated in various ways with everybody who contributed to the Capital Campaign that raised $1.4 billion. Alumni, friends, corporations and businesses, administrators, faculty and staff understood the value of MSU as a public good and as a socially transforming agent through education, research, outreach, professional and public service, and creative and performing arts. When the university was in danger of losing ground due to drastic budget cuts and reduction in state appropriations, the people shaped and influenced by Michigan State stepped forward so the legacy they received could be passed forward to future generations. By no means

MSU's first Magnetic Resonance Imaging (MRI) scanner was installed in 1977 soon after E. James Potchen became chair of the new Department of Radiology and W. Donald Weston, MD became dean of the College of Human Medicine. The MSU Clinical Center became a central locus of medical services and clinical treatment aided by the best equipment available. Courtesy of Michigan State University Archives and Historical Collections.

did the $1.4 billion gathered solve the university's ongoing budget concerns, nor was it intended to do so. What it did was to provide a collective statement of faith in the future of MSU, and public testimony to its positive past influence and ongoing connection.

The Sesquicentennial provided the 150-year marker to pause and take stock of the past—to take a fresh look at the whole history as well as at the fifty-year period since the Centennial. This volume's historical narrative has attempted to show that MSU's history featured a variety of developments that have shaped the institution and its people. No argument for uniqueness or specialness has been made. What happened at MSU occurred at other large and growing institutions of higher education with aspirations to distinguish themselves and garner recognition for excellence. The same problems of bigness or rapid development affected all universities that became

The Sesquicentennial "A Parade of Memories" took place on Saturday, 8 October 2005, starting at the Frandor Shopping Center, and coming up Michigan Avenue and Grand River to campus. The previous evening featured the Water Carnival on the Red Cedar River and fireworks. Prominent members of MSU sports teams past and present were on hand, and top-flight entertainers such as jazz artist Dave Brubeck and comedian Jay Leno were featured in the evenings. Courtesy of Michigan State University Photography Services.

"megaversities." The challenge of maintaining and expanding a revenue stream in order to maintain quality, to innovate, to change in a technological and digital world has been and is faced by almost every public institution of higher education, and by many private ones. But what does make the story unique or different is its particular and individual qualities. With that telling it becomes our story, set within the place that Spartans know.

One of the recurring patterns in MSU's history has been groups of individuals coming together as committees and being charged to act on behalf of the university for its common good and its future. It happened on 3 March 1959, when President Hannah announced the appointment of the sixteen individuals who constituted the Committee on the Future of the University. That committee issued its report on 28 July 1959, which was the basis for MSU's transformation, already underway by then, into a research-intensive and graduate studies institution, and its continuation of national leadership in land-grant philosophy and application. The Committee on Undergraduate Education was appointed by Hannah on 8 February 1967, and its report titled *Improving Undergraduate Education* was issued later that year. The Council to Review Undergraduate Education, involving forty-one people, issued its report titled *Opportunities for Renewal* in 1988. It is inaccurate to state that no politics, agendas, or heated debates or conflicts were involved in the writing of these documents, or that they produced a consensus behind which almost everybody rallied. What these reports (and others) did do was to bring issues, avenues of choices or directions, and critical self-examination into the open arena of debate and discussion. The 2020 Vision Committee developed a Campus Master Plan that would unify and harmonize north and south campus and provide a comprehensive vision focused on aesthetic, social, and ecological values. As revised and updated, the 2020 plan has already produced discernible results in terms of tree plantings, landscaping, and returning to green spaces what had been car parking areas. What is significant to note here is that committee reports were made after intensive periods of discussion and consultation and were usually issued within the same year of the committee's formation. As a result, reports were circulated when the matters under review or investigation were still fresh and under discussion by the campus community. Thus, protracted wrangling was avoided, as was the forming of entrenched factions that might make any forward movement difficult. As President Hannah had often put it, the goal was to move forward in an "informed and well reasoned way" on the basis of a report, but to move ahead when purposeful movement was necessary or desirable ("To the University Faculty").

Another key development in the period from the late 1960s to 2005 was the solid commitment to developing a diverse and multicultural university. This began with the selection of Clifton R. Wharton Jr. as president in 1970, and President M. Cecil Mackey brought Moses Turner and Connie W. Stewart into his administration as vice presidents in key roles. In DiBiaggio's presidency, the MSU IDEA I and II in 1988 and 1992 made that commitment in a way that only pointed forward: "Diversity and pluralism are essential for MSU's continuing world-class distinction as a progressive land-grant/AAU institution committed to excellence and equity" (MSU IDEA I). The

Paulette Granberry Russell graduated from MSU and earned a JD degree from the Thomas M. Cooley Law School. Since 1998 she has served as senior advisor to the president for diversity, and as director of the Office for Inclusion and Intercultural Activities. She is the university point person and leader for the institution's commitment to advancing diversity and inclusion, and has given presentations in South Africa and Brazil on affirmative action and programming for equity and inclusion. Courtesy of Michigan State University Photography Services.

increase in minority enrollments and in international student enrollment, which was 7.4 percent in 2004, brought with it the challenges of providing support services as well as the fostering of a culture and day-to-day working environment, making it clear that "Racism, sexism, denigration of the worth or abilities of handicappers or other painful manifestations of inequity cannot be tolerated at Michigan State University" (MSU IDEA I). This commitment was kept in focus by regular reports to the Board of Trustees by Ralph W. Bonner and later by Paulette Granberry Russell and by those in the area of Academic Student Services and Multicultural Issues under the leadership of Associate Provost Lee June. Members of the Board of Trustees who are minorities also contributed significantly to keeping this goal in focus. The commitment to pluralism and diversity also included issues of sexual preference or orientation. On 9 November 1995, the Board of Trustees discussed same-sex domestic partner benefits and voted 8-0 to postpone any consideration of benefits for a period of not more than 24 months. On 12 September 1997 the policy establishing this full range of benefits for same-sex domestic partners was passed by the Board of Trustees on a 5-3 vote.

Over the past three decades, affirmative action and the civil and personal rights of the gay population have witnessed progress, as well as retrograde movement and various forms of legislation or policies reflecting shifting positions. The Michigan Civil Rights Initiative or Proposal 2 was passed by voters as a ballot initiative in November 2006 and became law the following December. While the language, scope, and application of the law has been and is still being debated (and the law's constitutionality has been questioned), the impact of the law was that all state universities or colleges, junior colleges, or school districts "shall not discriminate against, or grant preferential treatment to, any individual or group on the basis of race, sex, color, ethnicity, or national origin in the operation of public employment, public education or public contracting." Brought into question were financial aid, scholarships, and admissions policies or practices, as well as the issue of hiring or contracting by state educational institutions at all levels.

Another measure with an impact on MSU and other institutions of higher education was the Michigan voters' approval in 1992 of a constitutional amendment that limited the number of total terms that state officials can serve in office—with senators limited to two terms starting in 2002 (a total of eight years) and representatives to three terms starting in 1980 (a total of six years). This law has contributed to large turnover and has affected the stability and continuity of the appropriations committees with which university officials deal for budgets. State politics and constitutional initiatives originating from voters have had a significant impact on higher education and made it more challenging for MSU to maintain and pursue its institutional goals. Formerly, periodic state budget crises had great impact, and these, of course, did not go away. Increasingly, the university's facility for making the case for MSU as a social good and as a source of economic innovation and growth became critical. Its own perception and understanding of its goals, principles, and aspirations could and sometimes did differ from the political climate and realpolitik. That reality required diplomacy and public relations that recognized the power of legislators and the people, but that also did not compromise institutional gains and vision.

Another important institutional characteristic was the university's not being afraid to make new investments in the form of new departments, or to find new organizational combinations. In February 1997 the new Department of Epidemiology was established, with the Department of Radiology established four months later. In early 2000 the Department of Neurology and Ophthalmology was approved. These departments were developed to provide a greater medical-science research base, more community health services, and an even greater concentration of medical specialists who could compete for grants.

In November 2003 three departments in the College of Agriculture and Natural Resources were restructured and integrated into the Department of Community, Agriculture, Recreation and Resource Studies. In July 2004 four departments were combined into the School of Planning, Design and Construction. The Department of Material Science and Mechanics was folded into Chemical Engineering and Materials Science, and Biosystems and Agricultural Engineering came about with a merger. These changes were, in part, justified by budget savings and economics, but they also reflected the need for new combinations that could bring energy and a new mission to faculty in what had developed as related or intersecting fields. One thing

Lee June served as MSU's vice president for student affairs and services and as associate provost for academic student services and multicultural issues starting in 1994. Among minority student groups he was widely known for his advocacy for underrepresented students and his commitment to equity. He directed the MSU Counseling Center for nine years and is a professor in the College of Education as well as a faculty member in the African American and African Studies Program. His published scholarship focuses on African American churches and the importance of religion and leadership in black communities. Courtesy of Michigan State University Photography Services.

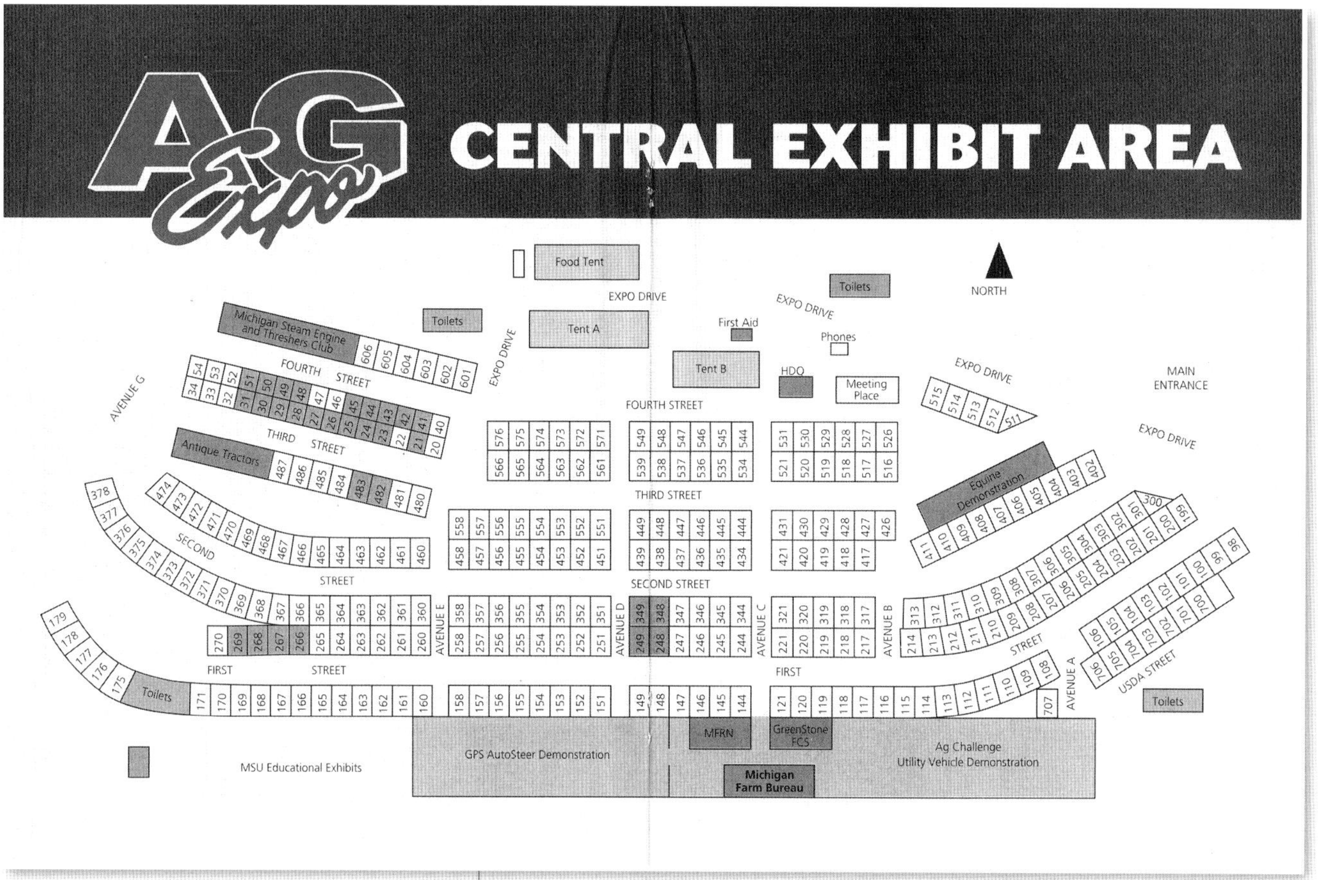

The Ag Expo began its run on MSU's campus in 1979 as Michigan's largest outdoor farm show, with exhibitions of products and services for the agricultural community, demonstrations, information sessions, and presentations by MSU Extension experts. New technologies and equipment were a major source of interest, and the Ag Expo was a major social gathering in the tradition of rural fairs. Courtesy of Michigan State University Archives and Historical Collections.

was certain in uncertain economic times and fast changing fields: departments could disappear or undergo mergers or absorption, and new departments could emerge in fields commanding attention.

In a way, what was happening in the corporate and business worlds was occurring in the university. Adaptation and change were now part of the structural and administrative world of the university. Faculty were encouraged and supported in developing spinoff companies and for-profit services based on their research. While many faculty bridled at what they saw as the imposition of a business or corporate model on the sacrosanct traditional university, there is no question that the university became more open to working with the outside economic world. The need to find new sources of revenue for basic operating expenses, research, and service is in part responsible, but there was also an increasing realization that students' educations needed to be grounded in real-life projects, short-term practicums in workaday environments, service-learning, and internships of all kinds and durations. Technology also has made it easier to bring the real-time world into the classroom, providing a dynamic immediacy. Much of this progress has already been made, but there are new combinations, circumstances, and models to explore for learning and personal-growth experiences.

Perhaps the most important ongoing development at MSU over the past forty years has been the periodic assessment of the institution's land-grant identity and the reach involved in that identity. As the numbers of farmers and family farms in Michigan fell due to land consolidation, crop and animal specialization, imported food, and corporate agriculture, the group utilizing the diverse services and information provided by MSU shrank significantly. The same agricultural problems and challenges continued: effective and productive land use, soil and water issues, use of chemical fertilizers, applications of available technologies and equipment, and so forth. Where livestock are involved, another set of issues exists. But the central fact remained evident. What had once been a broad base of support for the land-grant university was now narrower; what had once been a rather distinct and central mission in an agriculturally diverse state was in need of some redefinition.

Research and extension work in agriculture, of course, has remained an important part of MSU's land-grant heritage. MSU remains the place where the groups of young Future Farmers of America and 4-H'ers come as part of a long tradition of meeting on campus to share talents and interests. The Ag Expo held annually starting in 1979 was such an established event that the site is permanently marked on the campus map. The various farms and their specialized laboratories stretching southward from campus remain as important as they ever were. Specialized two-year certification programs remain part of the curriculum.

The basic concept many people have of a land-grant institution is that it was created from lands controlled by the federal government (the grants given to states that could be developed or sold to raise funds to endow colleges) and that the institution would serve the people on and off the land, that is, the agriculturalists and rural farm communities. The science and the engineering taught would largely serve the purposes of facilitating agriculture and food production by making it more efficient, productive, and stable to meet the needs of an expanding national population.

President Hannah expanded this concept for MSU when he connected the land-grant mission to President Harry S. Truman's Point Four Program of 1949. This technical assistance program would share American "know-how" with countries seeking economic development. Michigan State could help by making its technical knowledge available to governments and universities by putting agricultural experts into the fields and by assisting in the upgrading of curriculums and instruction that would produce native experts. If new institutions of higher education were needed, Michigan State could provide assistance in terms of expertise in curriculum and administration, as it did with the University of Ryukyus in Japan. Individuals and groups could be brought to East Lansing for graduate education, establishing a back-and-forth flow of knowledge and expertise as well as creating a new body of Michigan State alumni across the world. As the Vietnam Project had revealed, problems could result from such exchanges and contracts with governments and their leaders. Land-grant service was no longer confined to the counties of Michigan, but extended to countries struggling with hunger and starvation, and particular problems of land, food distribution, and limiting agricultural practices. Michigan State would learn to work with federal and international agencies and programs involved in the same work. The land-grant mission also included addressing other problems and issues requiring expertise not yet available in a country.

After Hannah, the university's commitment to, and embracing of, this wider land-grant mission was evident in the selection of Clifton R. Wharton Jr. as president in 1970, with his expertise in the economics of subsistence agriculture and his work in Latin America and Southeast Asia with the Rockefeller Foundation. Later M. Peter McPherson would become president after his seven years of heading USAID and his direction of programs to respond to famine in Africa. John A. DiBiaggio carried out an ambitious agenda of international trips to reconnect with all the countries and universities with which Michigan was working—contacts and relationships that Hannah had started. Cecil Mackey made a landmark trip to China, and in his one year Gordon E. Guyer made a visit to Central America. All of these presidents mentioned had networks of contacts in Washington, DC.

In 2005 Lou Anna K. Simon became MSU's 20th president thirty-one years after receiving her PhD in administration and higher education here, and after eleven years of serving as provost in the administration of President M. Peter McPherson. No president other than John A. Hannah began with the institutional knowledge and experience that she had acquired and mastered. Courtesy of Michigan State University Archives and Historical Collections (*Red Cedar Log* 2005).

The land-grant mission and heritage in many ways influenced the selection of the university's presidents and kept its part of the overall mission in the forefront, as well as shaping and directing new developments, such as the medical school's emphasis on family practice and attention to rural medical needs, or the goal of making affordable Study Abroad programs available to as many students as possible.

In 2005 President Lou Anna K. Simon announced the "Boldness by Design: Strategic Positioning of Michigan State University" plan that was to guide the institution in the first eight years of her presidency and take it to the sesquicentennial of the Morrill Act of 1862. MSU's goal was to become a "world-grant" institution, with the transformative process taking the university to a recognition worldwide "as the leading land-grant research university in the United States." One of the five identified areas for excellence and innovation was to "expand international reach." MSU was committing itself to renewing "public trust in the value of land-grant universities and the vital role they play in leading the nation—and the world—to a better tomorrow" ("Boldness by Design").

In his 12 March 1959 charge to the faculty on the Committee on the Future of the University, President Hannah had written: "The University is a social institution and its role cannot be assessed without reference to the society—state, national, and world in which it rests. This fact has meaning for its instruction, its research, its service. How to keep it respondent to those social needs is of vital importance" (*Report to the President* x). "Boldness by Design" also includes two other areas: "Enrich community, economic, and family life" and "Strengthen stewardship." The Sesquicentennial celebration and the beginning of the term of MSU's twentieth president provided the perfect opportunity for the next chapter in the institution's definition of its land-grant identity and its goal of worldwide recognition. That was indeed a bold goal and target, and it is important to note that the field of comparison is the other forty land-grant universities. The goal is actually not a top ranking or rating but rather a recognition as the "leading" one—that is, the land-grant research university that leads by example, that changes and adapts boldly, that is unafraid to venture into new territory and that values advancing, and that works within its resources and abilities while utilizing them most effectively to progress.

Here, then, is the story of Michigan State University from the mid-twentieth century into the first years of the current century. It is the story of growth and development into a major research university guided by and anchored in the land-grant identity that was central to its place in the state and to expectations of it. It is a story of the rapid growth into a "multiversity" or "megaversity" that could provide a college education for an increasing number of students. Its graduate programs developed, as did its research infrastructure and facilities. At certain junctures in this story, state budget crises reduced, froze, or severely limited appropriations and resulted in the elimination and reduction of programs. Such a history called for resilience, adaptation, steadiness of purpose, and vision, looking ahead past exigencies. Limited resources called for great resourcefulness. Individuals continued in or stepped into roles that prompted confidence in the future, not a diminished one but one of new or unimagined possibilities.

Out of that recurring set of circumstances came a solid and certain Michigan State identity and culture. The striving for excellence in science produced two world-class research facilities: the National Superconducting Cyclotron Laboratory and the MSU–Department of Energy Plant Research Laboratory. Along with these two facilities came some of the strongest graduate programs in the country, and iconic researchers and faculty such as Henry Blosser and Anton Lang.

The commitment to service coming out of the land-grant identity resulted in the College of Human Medicine and the College of Osteopathic Medicine, as well as a whole host of research and treatment centers for agriculture and animals. The overall health

The College of Human Medicine (CHM) graduation class of 1972, numbering twenty-one, could be seated on the floor of the Erickson Hall Kiva, but by 1976 this was no longer possible, as the number of new physicians grew to a class of almost seventy. Andrew D. Hunt was the founding dean of CHM and served from 1964 until 1977, and Dean Hunt developed a curriculum that focused on the patient and that emphasized personal psychology and behavior playing a key role in treating disease with the best of biomedical science. Courtesy of Michigan State University Archives and Historical Collections.

The College of Osteopathic Medicine (COM) class of 1974 is shown here at their hooding ceremony with their dean, Myron S. Magen (*third from left in front row*). As the COM founding dean, Magen led the relocation of the privately funded Michigan College of Osteopathic Medicine in Pontiac to a place at MSU, and for twenty-five years until 1991 Dean Magen provided vision, leadership, and energy that made COM the flagship college of the profession. He developed connections between MSU and osteopathic programs in over sixteen countries, more than half of these in Africa. Courtesy of Michigan State University Archives and Historical Collections.

and well-being of society remained a central core of the land-grant mission of contributing to the betterment of society. That effort was extended to parts of the world that needed assistance in elemental or fundamental processes in order to become stable or to establish favorable circumstances for economic development.

Another part of the MSU identity has been its commitment to affirmative action, diversity, and multiculturalism, and its efforts to make these realities. This has, of course, not been without challenges and difficulties, and such a commitment requires steadiness of purpose and a strong and immediate response to any incident or development that compromises the effort. This commitment has been furthered by strong leadership and activism of minority administrators, faculty, students and student groups, and community leaders.

The MSU outlook involves valuing the past and learning from it, but not being tradition-bound or inflexible when it comes to needed changes or adjustments. The same experiential outlook of those involved in running the university is encouraged and fostered in its students. In *Walden* (published in 1854, the year before MAC's founding), Henry David Thoreau wrote: "If you have built castles in the air, your work need not be lost; that is where they should be. Now put the foundations under them" (324). The story of Michigan State has been one of building foundations under the dreams that various individuals and the collective group have had for the small agricultural college that became a nationally and internationally recognized university. Those foundations have supported the aspirations of the past and present, and will do so until the university's bicentennial is celebrated.

The new bronze statue of Sparty was unveiled on 25 August 2005 in a new location at the northern edge of Demonstration Hall field and was formally dedicated on 8 October 2005 after the Sesquicentennial parade. Going to Sparty for graduation pictures and for other notable family events is a rich part of campus tradition.
Courtesy of Michigan State University Photography Services.

Bibliography

Chapter One. The Emergence of the Research University in the 1950s and 1960s

Chapin, Richard E., and Ralph E. McCoy. "The Emerging Institutions: Michigan State University and Southern Illinois University." *Library Trends* (October 1966): 266–85.

"Chemical Genealogy." http://www2.chemistry.msu.edu/Genealogy/chem_gene.shtml.

Geiger, Roger L. *Research and Relevant Knowledge: American Research Universities since World War II.* New York: Oxford University Press, 1993.

Hannah, John A. *A Memoir.* East Lansing: Michigan State University Press, 1980.

John Hannah Papers. Association Files. Association of American Universities, 1964–1965. MSU Archives and Historical Collections. UA 2.1.12, Box 74, Folder 25.

Lang, Anton. "The Beginnings (1965–1978)." MSU-DOE Plant Research Laboratory: History: The First Forty Years (1965–2005). http://www.prl.msu.edu/uploads/files/PRL_History_1995-2005.pdf.

Mallmann, W. L. *Recollections of Early Microbiology at Michigan State University.* East Lansing: Department of Microbiology and Public Health, 1974.

Michigan State College Faculty and Staff Directory, 1949–50.

Michigan State University Directory of Faculty and Staff, 1955–56.

Michigan State University Directory of Faculty and Staff, 1960–61.

Michigan State University Faculty and Staff Directory, September 1964.

Michigan State University Faculty and Staff Directory, September

1967.

Progress Report to the President from the Committee on the Future of the University. 7 November 1960. Committee on the Future of the University Records. MSU University Archives and Historical Collections. UA 2.1.12.3, Box 458, Folder 25.

A Report to the President of Michigan State University from the Committee on the Future of the University. East Lansing: Michigan State University, 1959.

Roose, Kenneth D., and Charles J. Anderson. *A Rating of Graduate Programs.* Washington, DC: American Council on Education, 1970.

Sesquicentennial Oral History Project (SOHP). MSU University Archives and Historical Collections. http://onthebanks.msu.edu/sohp/.

- Transcript of Interview with Henry Blosser on 9 August 2000.
- Transcript of Interview with Richard E. Chapin on 9 November 1999.
- Transcript of Interview with Barnett Rosenberg on 2 February 2001.
- Transcript of Interview with Larry Von Tersch on 2 May 2001.

Chapter Two. The University in the Vortex of History and Social Change

Adams, Walter. *The Test.* New York: Macmillan, 1971.

Chambers, M. M. *Appropriations of State Tax Funds for Operation Expenses of Higher Education, 1970–1971.* Washington, DC: Office of Institutional Research, National Association of State Universities and Land Grant Colleges, 1970.

Clegg, Helen. "Protestors Deaf to Wharton." *Lansing State Journal,* 11 May 1972.

Geiger, Roger L. *Research and Relevant Knowledge: American Research Universities since World War II.* New York: Oxford University Press, 1993.

George and Nancy Axinn International Scholarship Fund. http://www.studyandscholarships.com/2012/11/george-and-nancy-axinn-international-scholarship-fund.html.

Griffore, Robert J., and Lillian A. Phenice. "Human Ecology in American Higher Education." Fall 2005. http://tfpa.cafcs.org/documents/Griffore-Phenice-article-MSU-Col-of-HUMAN-ECOLOGY.pdf.

Heineman, Kenneth J. *Campus Wars: The Peace Movement at American State Universities in the Vietnam Era.* New York: New York University Press, 1993.

Minutes of the Michigan State University Board of Trustees, 1969 through 1978. MSU University Archives and Historical Collections. http://onthebanks.msu.edu/Browse/Contributor/Offices%20of%20Board%20of%20Trustees%20and%20President/Date/.

MSU Agricultural, Food, and Resource Economics. "AFRE Faculty Specializations." http://www.afre.msu.edu/projects/afre_faculty_specialization_areas.

"MSU Athletics Hall of Fame Class of 2010: Jim Bibbs." http://www.msuspartans.com/genrel/093010aau.html.

Office of the Registrar—Michigan State University. Archived Course Descriptions for 1974 and 1983. http://www.reg.msu.edu/UCC/DescYearIndex.asp.

Rogers, Ibram Henry. "The Black Campus Movement: An Afrocentric Narrative History of the Struggle to Diversify Higher Education, 1965–1972." PhD diss., Temple University, 2010.

Sesquicentennial Oral History Project (SOHP). MSU University Archives and Historical Collections. http://onthebanks.msu.edu/sohp/.

- Transcript of Interview with Gladys Beckwith on 9 October 2000.
- Transcript of Interview with John Cantlon on 27 March 2000.
- Transcript of Interview with Lois Lund on 14 March 2000.
- Transcript of Interview with Blanche Martin on 31 March 2000.
- Transcript of Interview with Don Stevens on 19 April 2001.
- Transcript of Interview with Richard Sullivan on 23 March 2000.

Sinclair, Norman. "Kids Hold Block Party: MSU Students Take Over Grand River." *Lansing State Journal,* 11 May 1972.

Smuckler, Ralph H. *A University Turns to the World: A Personal History of the Michigan State University International Story.* East

Lansing: Michigan State University Press, 2003.
U.S. Inflation Rate—1948 to 2010. http://www.miseryindex.us.
Waggoner, Mike. "Arrest Threat Clears Downtown East Lansing." *Lansing State Journal*, 11 May 1972.
Wilbur, Ellie, Professor Emeritus. E-mail communication on 2 September 2011.

Chapter Three. Financial Crisis and Its Impact

Anderson, David D. Personal interview, July 2011.
Brace, Paul. *State Government and Economic Performance*. Baltimore: Johns Hopkins University Press, 1993.
Crawley, Nancy. "M. Cecil Mackey: Controversy and Conflict for Michigan State's New President." *Change* (November/December 1980): 39–47, 56.
Geiger, Roger L. *Research and Relevant Knowledge: American Research Universities since World War II*. New York: Oxford University Press, 1993.
McCormick, Justin. E-mail communication on 21 October 2011.
Minutes of the Michigan State University Board of Trustees, 1974 through 1984. MSU University Archives and Historical Collections. http://onthebanks.msu.edu/Browse/Contributor/Offices%20of%20Board%20of%20Trustees%20and%20President/Date/.
"MSU Loses Pioneer in Athletics, Academics, A 'University Jewel.'" 15 June 2004. http://msutoday.msu.edu/news/2004/msu-loses-pioneer-in-athletics-academics-a-/.
Nosow, Sigmund. *Professional Self-Images and Organizational Orientations of a General Education Faculty: A Case Study of the University College of Michigan State University*. East Lansing, MI: University College, 1969.
A Report to the President of Michigan State University from the Committee on the Future of the University. East Lansing: Michigan State University, 1959.
Sesquicentennial Oral History Project (SOHP). MSU University Archives and Historical Collections. http://onthebanks.msu.edu/sohp/.

- Transcript of Interview with Blanche Martin on 31 March 2000.
- Transcript of Interview with Lawrence Sommers on 24 July 2000.
- Transcript of Interview with Richard Sullivan on 23 March 2000.
- Transcript of Interview with Clarence Winder on 20 September 2000.

Smuckler, Ralph H. *A University Turns to the World: A Personal History of the Michigan State University International Story.* East Lansing: Michigan State University Press, 2003.

Underwood, Clarence, with Larry Paladino. *Greener Pastures: A Pioneer Athletics Administrator Climbs from Spartan Beginnings to the Top at Michigan State.* No publisher cited, 2005.

Chapter Four. A Steady State Period and Its Salutary Effects

Bresnahan, Roger. E-mail communication on 3, 6 February 2012.

Campbell-Kelly, Martin, and William Aspray. *Computer: A History of the Information Machine.* New York: Basic Books, 1996.

Graham, Hugh Davis, and Nancy Diamond. *The Rise of American Research Universities: Elites and Challengers in the Postwar Era.* Baltimore: Johns Hopkins University Press, 1977.

"Historical Timeline." Department of Forestry. http://www.for.msu.edu/about/historical_timeline.

Hospitality Business Leader (Fall 2005/Winter 2006): 1, 3.

Jones, Lyle V., Gardner Lindzey, and Porter G. Coggeshall, eds. *An Assessment of the Research-Doctorate Programs in the United States: Humanities.* Washington, DC: National Academy Press, 1982.

McLaughlin, Judith Block, and David Riesman. "The President: A Precarious Perch." In *Higher Learning in America: 1980–2000,* ed. Arthur Levine. Baltimore: Johns Hopkins University Press, 1993.

McVey, Susan. "Dow Gift Will Accelerate Composites Research." *MSU Alumni Magazine* (Spring 1992).

Minutes of the Michigan State University Board of Trustees,

1985 through 1992. MSU University Archives and Historical Collections. http://onthebanks.msu.edu/Browse/Contributor/Offices%20of%20Board%20of%20Trustees%20and%20President/Date/.

Opportunities for Renewal. The Report of the Council to Review Undergraduate Education. East Lansing: Michigan State University Office of the Provost, 1988.

Perles, George J., with Vahé Gregorian. *George Perles: The Ride of a Lifetime.* Champaign, IL: Sagamore Publishing, 1995.

Sesquicentennial Oral History Project (SOHP). MSU University Archives and Historical Collections. http://onthebanks.msu.edu/sohp/.

- Transcript of Interview with John E. Cantlon on 27 March 2000.
- Transcript of Interview with John DiBiaggio on 12 July 2000.
- Transcript of Interview with George Perles on 7 February 2001.

Smuckler, Ralph H. *A University Turns to the World: A Personal History of the Michigan State University International Story.* East Lansing: Michigan State University Press, 2003.

Underwood, Clarence, with Larry Paladino. *Greener Pastures: A Pioneer Athletics Administrator Climbs from Spartan Beginnings to the Top at Michigan State.* No publisher cited, 2005.

Chapter Five. Growth, Expansion, and Distinction

"1.4 Billion Exceeds the Campaign for MSU Goal." *Michigan State University News,* 4 October 2007. http://news.msu.edu/story/732/.

"The 1970s: IRT Helps Shape Direction of College." MSU College of Education *New Educator* (Spring 2002). http://www.educ.msu.edu/neweducator/spring02/IRT.htm.

Adams, Walter. *The Test.* New York: Macmillan, 1971.

Arthurs, Alberta. "The Humanities in the 1990s." In *Higher Learning in America, 1980–2000,* ed. Arthur Levine. Baltimore: Johns Hopkins University Press, 1993.

Bagnato, Andrew. "Michigan State Hit with Football Sanctions." *Chicago Tribune,* 17 September 1996. http://articles.chicagotribune.com/1996-09-17/sports/9609170157_1.

Bao, Bob, and Erik S. Lunde. "Spartans in Hollywood, Part II." *MSU Alumni Magazine* (Summer 2000).

Brace, Paul. *State Government and Economic Performance.* Baltimore: Johns Hopkins University Press, 1993.

The Campus Master Plan Work Team and Sasaki Associates, Inc. *Campus Master Plan Report—2020 Vision: A Community Concept for the Michigan State University Campus.* 7 December 2001. http://ipf.msu.edu/_files/pdfs/resources-campus-master-plan-2001.pdf.

Casey, Karen McKnight. E-mail communication on 23 April 2012.

Castanier, Bill. "How an MSU Professor Helped Popularize Spring Break into a National Rite of Passage." *MSU Alumni Magazine* (Summer 2011).

The Celebrity Lecture Series. http://cls.matrix.msu.edu/.

The Equity in Athletics Data Analysis Cutting Tool. http://ope.ed.gov/athletics/Index.aspx.

"Four Charged in 1999 Arson Fire at Michigan State University." *Insurance Journal,* 13 March 2008.

Geist, Gretel. E-mail communication on 22 June 2012.

Goldberger, Marvin L., Brendan A. Maher, and Pamela Ebert Flattau, eds. *Research-Doctorate Programs in the United States: Continuity and Change.* Washington, DC: National Academy Press, 1995.

Hungiville, Maurice. *From a Single Window: Michigan State University and Its Press, 1947–1997.* East Lansing: Michigan State University Press, 1998.

Jacobitz, Andy. "The Best Education: Ag School Deans Pick the Nation's Top Programs." *Farm Futures* (Mid-March 1993): 12–13.

Jones, Ken. "Celebrity Lecture Series Enjoys Major Success." *MSU Alumni Magazine* (Winter 1996).

Lunde, Erik S. "Spartans in Hollywood." *MSU Alumni Magazine* (Fall 2002).

Lunde, Erik S., and Gary Hoppenstand. "Spartans in Hollywood." *MSU Alumni Magazine* (Spring 1999).

MacCambridge, Michael, ed. *ESPN Big Ten Football Encyclopedia: The Complete History of the Conference.* New York: ESPN Books, 2007.

McConeghy, Patrick. E-mail communication on 1 March 2012.

Minutes of the Michigan State University Board of Trustees, 1992 through 2005. MSU University Archives and Historical Collections. http://onthebanks.msu.edu/Browse/Contributor/Offices%20of%20Board%20of%20Trustees%20and%20President/Date/.

"MSU Board Accepts Life Science Corridor Grant to Fund Structural Biology Center." Michigan State University Board of Trustees press release, 7 December 2001. http://trustees.msu.edu/decisions-news/2001-12/biolobygrant.html.

"MSU Board Formally Endorses MSU Promise." *MSUToday*, 10 December 1999. http://news.msu.edu/story/2053.

Multi-Racial Unity Living Experience and Intercultural Aide Program. http://mrule.msu/edu.

Perles, George J., with Vahé Gregorian. *George Perles: The Ride of a Lifetime.* Champaign, IL: Sagamore Publishing, 1995.

"Ralph Votapek: Biography." http://www.ralphvotapek.com/biography.html.

A Report to the President of Michigan State University from the Committee on the Future of the University. East Lansing: Michigan State University, 1959.

"Sam Raimi." http://www.nndb.com/people/650/000025575.

Sesquicentennial Oral History Project (SOHP). MSU University Archives and Historical Collections. http://onthebanks.msu.edu/sohp.

- Transcript of Interview with John DiBiaggio on 12 July 2000.
- Transcript of Interview with Gordon Guyer on 6 April 2000.
- Transcript of Interview with Russell Mawby on 17 May 2001.

Sheehan, Richard G. "The Professionalization of College Sports." In *Higher Education in Transition: The Challenges of the New Millennium*, ed. Joseph Losco and Brian L. Fife, 133–58. Westport, CT: Bergin and Garvey, 2000.

Underwood, Clarence, with Larry Paladino. *Greener Pastures: A Pioneer Athletics Administrator Climbs from Spartan Beginnings to the Top at Michigan State.* No publisher cited, 2005.

"The Verdehr Trio." http://www.verdehr.com/about.htm.

Wachsberger, Ken. "A Tradition Continues: The Lansing Area's Progressive Press, 1965–Present." In *Insider Histories of the Vietnam Era Underground Press, Part I.* East Lansing: Michigan

State University Press, 2011.
Word, Michelle. "Art and Art History Celebrates: 75 Years." *MSU Alumni Magazine* (Fall 2006).

Conclusion. Looking Back through the Lens of the Sesquicentennial and Looking Ahead

Bao, Bob. "Cole Gift Supports MSU's Honors College." http://www.msu.edu/unit/msuaa/magazine/s98/honors.htm.

"Boldness by Design: Strategic Positioning of Michigan State University." http://boldnessbydesign.msu.edu/Task_Forces.asp.

Galik, Mark. "Beaumont Tower: At the Crossroads of Past, Present and Future." *MSU Alumni Magazine* (Summer 1996).

Hannah, John A. *A Memoir.* East Lansing: Michigan State University Press, 1980.

"John Hannah and Land-Grant Values: Never Standing Still." MSU Office of Communications, 17 September 2004. http://news.msu.edu/story/630/.

"Michigan State Dedicates Magic Johnson Statue." 1 November 2003. http://www.msuspartans.com/sports/m-baskbl/spec-rel/110203aaa.html.

Minutes of the Michigan State University Board of Trustees, 20 September 2002. MSU University Archives and Historical Collections. http://onthebanks.msu.edu/Browse/Contributor/Offices%20of%20Board%20of%20Trustees%20and%20President/Date/.

Obituary for Wendell Westcott in *Lansing State Journal*, 2 May 2010. http://www.legacy.com/obituaries/lsj/obituary.aspx?pid=142393683.

A Report to the President of Michigan State University from the Committee on the Future of the University. East Lansing: Michigan State University, 1959.

"Restored Beaumont Bells to Break Decade of Silence." *MSU News Bulletin*, 25 April 1996. https://daggy.name/carillon/msunsa01.htm.

Thoreau, Henry David. *Walden.* Princeton, NJ: Princeton University Press, 1971.

"To the University Faculty." Cover letter by President John A. Hannah. In *A Report to the President of Michigan State University from the Committee on the Future of the University.* East Lansing: Michigan State University, 1959.

"Trustee, Spouse Commit $6 Million Gift to Honor Former MSU President." *MSUToday*, 20 September 2002. http://msutoday.msu.edu/news/2002/trustee-spouse-commit-6-million-gift-to-honor-former-msu-president/.

Wachsberger, Ken. "A Tradition Continues: The Lansing Area's Progressive Press, 1965–Present." In *Insider Histories of the Vietnam Era Underground Press, Part I.* East Lansing: Michigan State University Press, 2011.

Index

*Entries in **boldface** refer to illustrations and captions.*

E

F

G

T